# ULTIMATE MUSIC THEO
## GLORY ST. GERMAIN ARCT RMT M

### Edited by Shelagh McKibbon-U'Ren RMT UMTC

# COMPLETE RUDIMENTS

# UltimateMusicTheory.com

ISBN: 978-0-9813101-1-4

## ULTIMATE MUSIC THEORY: *The Way to Score Success!*

### The Ultimate Music Theory workbooks are for all Musicians.

The more we understand the universal language of music, the more we are capable of communicating our ideas through performing and writing music, interpreting musical compositions of others, and developing a deeper appreciation of music. It is through music education that we progress from student to musician and are able to enjoy and understand music at a more comprehensive level.

### Acknowledgements
Dedicated with love and gratitude to my husband Ray for his encouragement, and to our children Chrystal, Catherine, Ray Jr., David Joseph, Sherry Rose and our grandchildren, for their inspiration.

Published in 2011 by Gloryland Publishing
First printing - 2008.   Revised edition - 2011.
Third printing - 2018
Printed in Canada.
GlorylandPublishing.com

UltimateMusicTheory.com

Library and Archives Canada Cataloguing in Publication  St. Germain, Glory  1953-
Ultimate Music Theory Series / Glory St. Germain

### Gloryland Publishing - Ultimate Music Theory Series:

| | | |
|---|---|---|
| GP - UP1 | ISBN: 978-0-9809556-6-8 | Ultimate Prep 1 Rudiments |
| GP - UP1A | ISBN: 978-0-9809556-9-9 | Ultimate Prep 1 Rudiments Answer Book |
| GP - UP2 | ISBN: 978-0-9809556-7-5 | Ultimate Prep 2 Rudiments |
| GP - UP2A | ISBN: 978-0-9813101-0-7 | Ultimate Prep 2 Rudiments Answer Book |
| GP- UBR | ISBN: 978-0-9813101-3-8 | Ultimate Basic Rudiments |
| GP - UBRA | ISBN: 978-0-9813101-4-5 | Ultimate Basic Answer Book |
| GP - UIR | ISBN: 978-0-9813101-5-2 | Ultimate Intermediate Rudiments |
| GP - UIRA | ISBN: 978-0-9813101-6-9 | Ultimate Intermediate Answer Book |
| GP - UAR | ISBN: 978-0-9813101-7-6 | Ultimate Advanced Rudiments |
| GP - UARA | ISBN: 978-0-9813101-8-3 | Ultimate Advanced Answer Book |
| GP - UCR | ISBN: 978-0-9813101-1-4 | Ultimate Complete Rudiments |
| GP - UCRA | ISBN: 978-0-9813101-2-1 | Ultimate Complete Answer Book |

# Ultimate Music Theory Complete Rudiments
## Table of Contents

**Ultimate Music Theory - Complete Guide & Chart**

**Score:  60 - 69** Pass;  **70 - 79** Honors;  **80 - 89** First Class Honors;  **90 - 100** First Class Honors with Distinction

**Ultimate Music Theory:  *The Way to Score Success!***

# ULTIMATE MUSIC THEORY:  *The Way to Score Success!*

The focus of the **Ultimate Music Theory** Series is to simplify complex concepts and show the relativity of these concepts with practical application. These workbooks are designed to help teachers and students discover the excitement and benefits of a music theory education.

Ultimate Music Theory workbooks are based on a proven approach to the study of music theory that follows these **4 Ultimate Music Theory Learning Principles**:

♪ **Simplicity of Learning** - easy to understand instructions, examples and exercises.

♪ **Memory Joggers** - tips for all learning styles including auditory, visual and tactile.

♪ **Tie it All Together** - helping musicians understand the universal language of music.

♪ **Make it Relevant** - applying theoretical concepts to pedagogical studies.

---

The Ultimate Music Theory™ Rudiments Workbooks, Supplemental Workbooks and Exams help students prepare for successful completion of nationally recognized theory examinations including the Royal Conservatory of Music Theory Levels.

UMT Complete Rudiments Workbook plus the COMPLETE Supplemental Workbook = RCM Theory Level 8  (2016 Royal Conservatory of Music Theory Syllabus).

---

**The Ultimate Music Theory Series includes these EXCLUSIVE BONUS features**:

♪ **Ultimate Music Theory Guide & Chart** - convenient summarization to review concepts.

♪ **12 Comprehensive Review Tests** - support retention of concepts learned in previous lessons.

♫ **Note:**  Each "♫ **Note**" points out important information and handy memory tips.

♪ **80 Ultimate Music Theory Flashcards** - Vocabulary, Musical Signs, Rhythm and More! DOWNLOAD Your FREE Flashcards at UltimateMusicTheory.com FREE RESOURCES.

♫ **Note:**  The convenient and easy to use Ultimate Music Theory Answer Books match the student workbooks for quick & accurate marking.  Answer Books available for all levels.

♪ **Ultimate Music Theory FREE Resources - Instant access to Videos, Worksheets & Blog.** Become a UMT MEMBER - Get Your FREE Flashcards, Lesson Plans, Certificate & More!

UltimateMusicTheory.com

# Lesson 1      Music Notation - Clefs, Notes and Rests

**MUSIC** is written on a staff. A staff consists of **FIVE** lines and **FOUR** spaces. Notes are written on the staff to indicate the pitch (high or low) and the duration (length of sound).

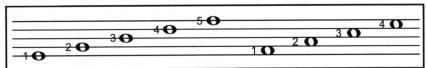

The musical alphabet consists of 7 letter names: A B C D E F G

## TREBLE CLEF and BASS CLEF

Clefs are written at the beginning of each staff.

1. Drawing the **TREBLE CLEF** or **G Clef**. Copy the following:
   a) Draw a "J" through the staff. Start above the staff and end in the space below the staff.
   b) Draw a "P" to line 4. Continue circling to the left and draw a "d" to line 1.
   c) Continue to circle up to line 3. Curl around and cross line 2. This is the "G" line.
   d) This creates a **LANDMARK** for the note "G" in the **Treble Clef**.

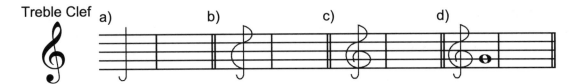

2. a) The Treble Clef **SPACE** notes are: **F A C E**. Copy and name the space notes.
   b) The Treble Clef **LINE** notes are: **E G B D F**. Copy and name the line notes.

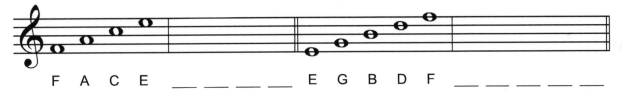

     F    A    C    E    __ __ __ __     E    G    B    D    F    __ __ __ __ __

3. Drawing the **BASS CLEF** or **F Clef**. Copy the following:
   a) Draw a black **dot** on line 4. This is the "F" line.
   b) Draw half of a heart. Curl up to line 5. End in space 1.
   c) Draw a **dot** in SPACE 4 (above the "F" line) and a **dot** in SPACE 3 (below the "F" line).
   d) This creates a **LANDMARK** for the note "F" in the **Bass Clef**.

4. a) The Bass Clef **SPACE** notes are: **A C E G**. Copy and name the space notes.
   b) The Bass Clef **LINE** notes are: **G B D F A**. Copy and name the line notes.

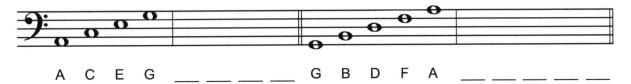

     A    C    E    G    __ __ __ __     G    B    D    F    A    __ __ __ __ __

## THE TREBLE CLEF

The **TREBLE CLEF** or **G CLEF** curls around line 2 (the "**G**" line) and indicates the location of G above Middle C. Middle C is written on its own line called a ledger line. Middle C and D are written **BELOW** the Treble Clef.

♫ **Note:** The Treble Clef written on the staff is referred to as the **Treble Staff** or **Treble Clef**.

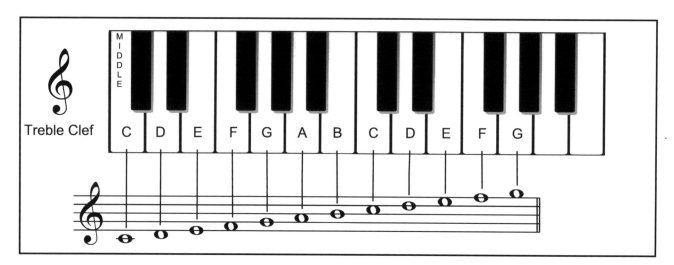

1. a) Draw a Treble Clef at the beginning of each measure.
   b) Write the notes Middle C and D below the Treble Staff.

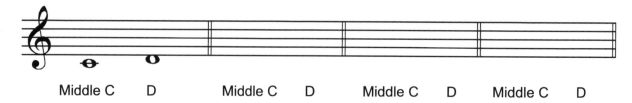

Middle C    D         Middle C    D         Middle C    D         Middle C    D

2. Name the following notes in the Treble Clef.

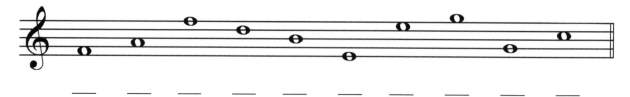

3. Write the following notes in the Treble Clef.

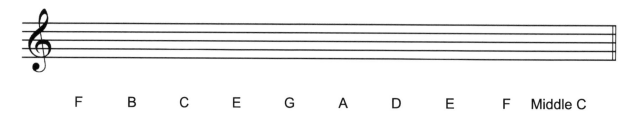

F        B        C        E        G        A        D        E        F    Middle C

6

## THE BASS CLEF

The **BASS CLEF** or **F CLEF** has 2 dots, one in the space above and one in the space below line 4 (the "**F**" line), and indicates the location of F below Middle C. Middle C and B are written **ABOVE** the Bass Clef.

♫ **Note:** The Bass Clef written on the staff is referred to as the **Bass Staff** or **Bass Clef**.

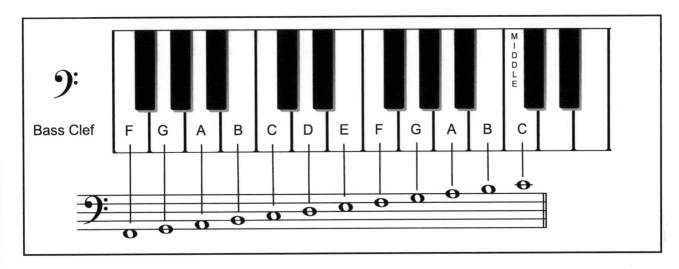

1. a) Draw a Bass Clef at the beginning of each measure.
   b) Write the notes Middle C and B above the Bass Staff.

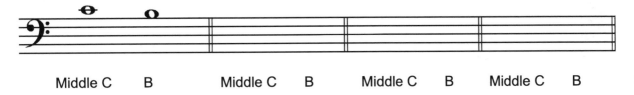

Middle C  B          Middle C  B          Middle C  B          Middle C  B

2. Name the following notes in the Bass Clef.

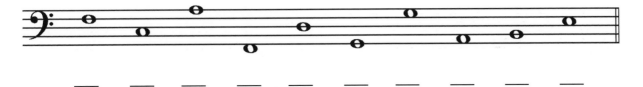

3. Write the following notes in the Bass Clef.

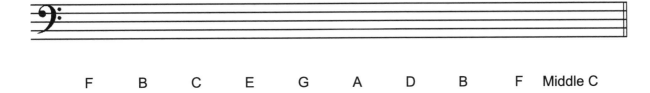

F      B      C      E      G      A      D      B      F    Middle C

7

## LANDMARK F-A-C-E and G-B-D NOTES in the TREBLE CLEF

**LANDMARK F-A-C-E** groups and **LANDMARK G-B-D** groups identify the LINES in the Treble Clef.
**Ledger Lines** are short lines used above or below the staff to extend the range of the staff.

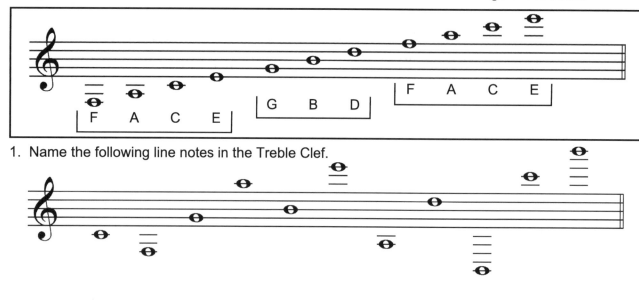

1. Name the following line notes in the Treble Clef.

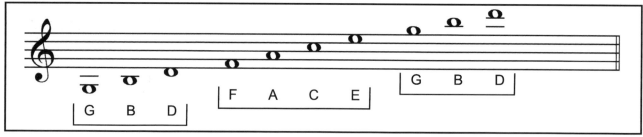

___   ___   ___   ___   ___   ___   ___   ___

**LANDMARK G-B-D** groups and **LANDMARK F-A-C-E** groups identify the SPACES in the Treble
Clef. **Ledger Lines** must be equal distance from the staff and are used as needed.

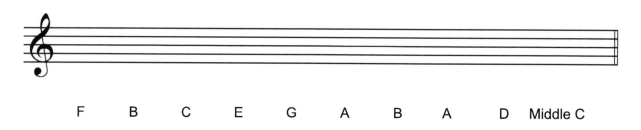

2. Name the following space notes in the Treble Clef.

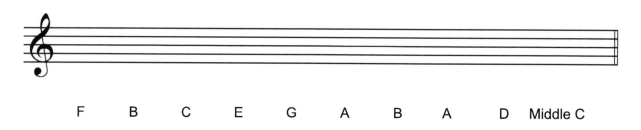

___   ___   ___   ___   ___   ___   ___   ___

3. Write the following notes in the Treble Clef. Use ledger lines above or below the staff. Use each
ledger line note only once.

F      B      C      E      G      A      B      A      D    Middle C

## LANDMARK F-A-C-E and G-B-D NOTES in the BASS CLEF

**LANDMARK F-A-C-E** groups and **LANDMARK G-B-D** groups identify the LINES in the Bass Clef.
**Ledger Lines** are short lines used above or below the staff to extend the range of the staff.

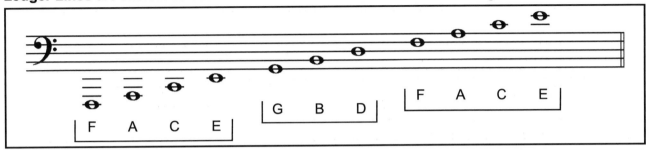

1. Name the following line notes in the Bass Clef.

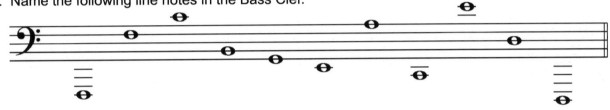

— — — — — — — — —

**LANDMARK G-B-D** groups and **LANDMARK F-A-C-E** groups identify the SPACES in the Bass Clef.
**Ledger Lines** must be equal distance from the staff and are used as needed.

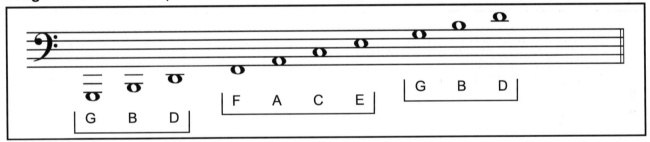

2. Name the following space notes in the Bass Clef.

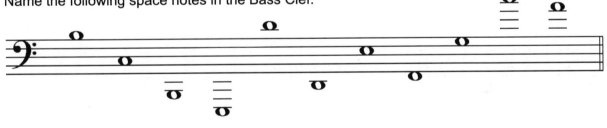

— — — — — — — — — —

3. Write the following notes in the Bass Clef.  Use ledger lines above or below the staff.  Use each
   ledger line note only once.

F      D      C      E      G      A      D      B      E   Middle C

9

## THE GRAND STAFF

The **GRAND STAFF** is made up of the Treble Clef and the Bass Clef joined together by a BRACE and a bar line. Middle C can be written in both the Treble Clef and the Bass Clef.

Notes written on the **GRAND STAFF** correspond to specific **PITCHES** on the keyboard. As notes move DOWN the Grand Staff (to the left on the keyboard), the sounds get LOWER in pitch. As notes move UP the Grand Staff (to the right on the keyboard), the sounds get HIGHER in pitch.

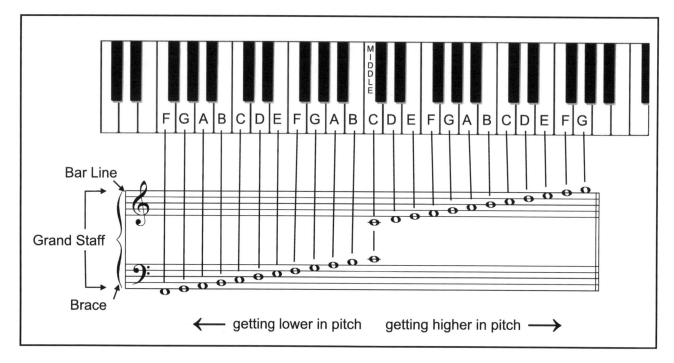

1. a) Complete the Grand Staff by adding the bar line, brace, Treble Clef and Bass Clef.
   b) Name the following notes on the Grand Staff.
   c) Draw a line from each note on the Grand Staff to the corresponding key on the keyboard (at the correct pitch).
   d) Name the key directly on the keyboard.

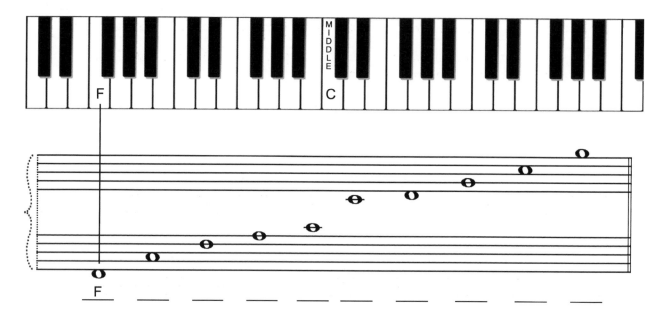

# BAR LINES, MEASURES and DYNAMICS

**BAR LINES** are lines (single thin lines) that divide the music into equal measures of time. A **MEASURE** is the space (area of music) between two bar lines. A single measure may be identified as "m." (example: m. 4). More than one measure may be identified as "mm." (example: mm. 1 - 4).

♫ **Note:** Measure numbers can be written inside a small box above the top left of each measure.

A **DOUBLE BAR LINE** (two thin bar lines together) indicates the end of a section of music.
A **DOUBLE BAR LINE** (a thin bar line and a thick bar line together) indicates the end of the piece of music. The double bar line at the end of a piece is also called a final bar line.

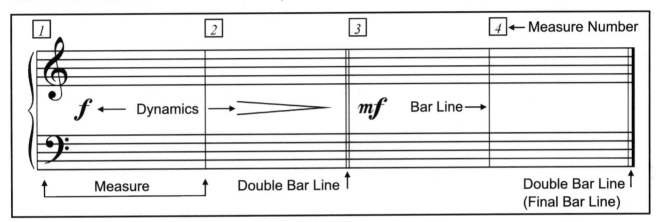

**DYNAMICS** refer to the varying degrees of loudness or softness. Dynamic markings are symbols or signs written in music to indicate different volumes of sound.

| | | |
|---|---|---|
| *pianissimo,* **pp** - very soft | *mezzo piano,* **mp** - medium (moderately) soft | *piano,* **p** - soft |
| *fortissimo,* **ff** - very loud | *mezzo forte,* **mf** - medium (moderately) loud | *forte,* **f** - loud |
| | *fortepiano,* **fp** - loud then suddenly soft | |
| | *sforzando,* **sf**, **sfz** - a sudden strong accent of a single note or chord | |
| *crescendo, cresc.* - becoming louder | | |
| *decrescendo, decresc.* or *diminuendo, dim.* - becoming softer | | |

♫ **Note:** For a single staff, dynamics are written **BELOW** the Treble Clef and **ABOVE** the Bass Clef. For the Grand Staff, dynamics are written in between the Treble Staff and Bass Staff.

1. a) Complete the Grand Staff by adding the bar line, brace, Treble Clef and Bass Clef.
   b) Number each measure in the box above the staff.
   c) Draw a double bar line (final bar line) at the end of the Grand Staff.
   d) Add the dynamic signs for "*piano*" in measure 1 and for "*crescendo*" in measure 3.

## SAME PITCH, ALTERNATE CLEF

The notes written with ledger lines **BELOW** the Treble Clef are at the **SAME PITCH** as the corresponding notes in the Bass Clef.  The notes written with ledger lines **ABOVE** the Bass Clef are at the **SAME PITCH** as the corresponding notes in the Treble Clef.

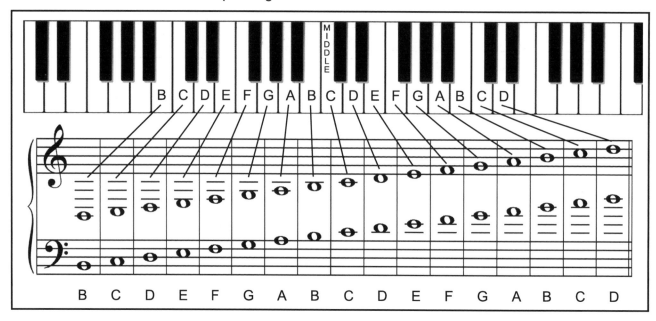

♫ **Note:** When rewriting a note at the same pitch in the alternate clef, a line note will remain a line note and a space note will remain a space note.

1. a) Rewrite the given note in each measure at the same pitch in the alternate clef.  Use ledger lines when necessary.
   b) Name the notes.

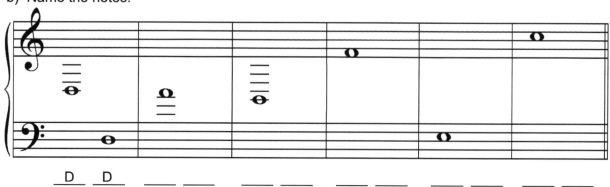

D     D     ___   ___     ___   ___     ___   ___     ___   ___

2. Rewrite the following notes at the same pitch in the alternate clef.

# C CLEFS - the ALTO CLEF and the TENOR CLEF

**C CLEF** Signs may be used to establish the placement of Middle C based upon the range of the voice or instrument. The following shows the placement of Middle C in the Treble, Bass and 5 C Clefs.

Treble    Soprano    Mezzo-Soprano    Alto    Tenor    Baritone    Bass

The **ALTO** Clef is drawn with the arrow pointing to the **THIRD** line → indicating **MIDDLE C**.

The **TENOR** Clef is drawn with the arrow pointing to the **FOURTH** line → indicating **MIDDLE C**.

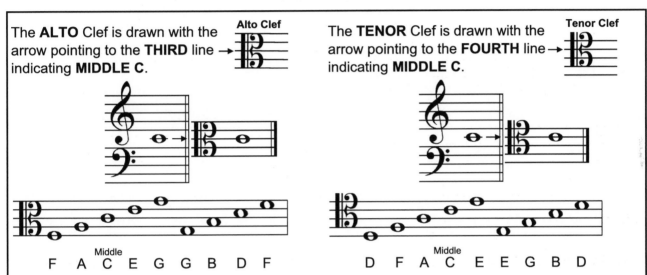

1. Draw the following clefs and Middle C on each staff.

**TREBLE CLEF**    **ALTO CLEF**    **TENOR CLEF**    **BASS CLEF**

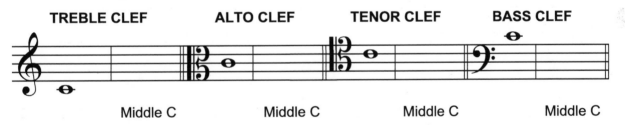

Middle C    Middle C    Middle C    Middle C

2. Name the following notes in the Alto Clef.

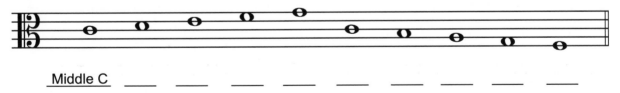

Middle C _____ _____ _____ _____ _____ _____ _____

3. Name the following notes in the Tenor Clef.

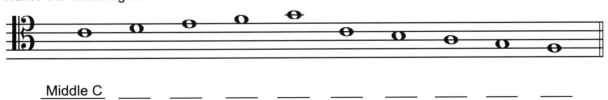

Middle C _____ _____ _____ _____ _____ _____ _____

## NOTE and REST VALUES

Each **NOTE** represents a specific time value of sound and each **REST** a specific time value of silence.

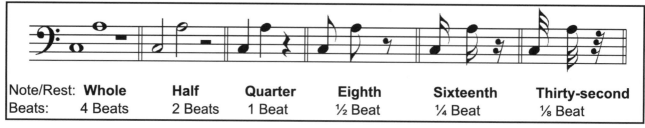

| Note/Rest: | **Whole** | **Half** | **Quarter** | **Eighth** | **Sixteenth** | **Thirty-second** |
|---|---|---|---|---|---|---|
| Beats: | 4 Beats | 2 Beats | 1 Beat | ½ Beat | ¼ Beat | ⅛ Beat |

**Stems:** When the notehead is: **ABOVE** the middle line, stem **DOWN** on the left.
**ON** the middle line, stem **DOWN** on the left or **UP** on the right.
**BELOW** the middle line, stem **UP** on the right.
A Stem is approximately one octave in length

**Flags:** For an eighth, sixteenth and thirty-second note, the FLAG goes to the RIGHT.
When writing flags, the end of the flag does not touch the notehead.

**Rests:** ⊤ hangs from line 4. ▬ sits on line 3. 𝄾 and 𝄿 start in space 3. 𝄿 starts in space 4.

1. a) Using the example above, copy the notes and rests in the Bass Clef below.
   b) Write the number of beats for each note/rest.

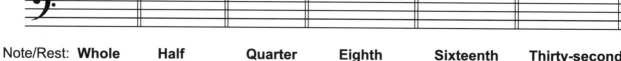

| Note/Rest: | **Whole** | **Half** | **Quarter** | **Eighth** | **Sixteenth** | **Thirty-second** |
|---|---|---|---|---|---|---|
| Beats: | ___ Beats | ___ Beats | ___ Beat | ___ Beat | ___ Beat | ___ Beat |

♫ **Note:** The note furthest away from the third line (the middle line) determines the direction of all the stems. Different combinations of note values may be beamed together.

2. Copy the following beamed notes.

Notes may be written at the **SAME** pitch in a **DIFFERENT** (or alternate) clef.

3. Rewrite the following notes at the SAME pitch in the Alto Clef, Tenor Clef and Bass Clef.

## TIE and DOTTED NOTES

**TIE** - a curved line connecting two or more notes of the **SAME PITCH**. The first note is played and held for the combined value of the tied notes. A tie can extend the note value over a bar line.

♫ **Note:** When the stems are down, the tie is written above the notes; when the stems are up, the tie is written below the notes.

1. a) Write the number of beats for each note.    b) Write the total beats for the tied notes.

a)    <u>4</u> + <u>2</u>   __ + __   __ + __   __ + __ + __   __ + __ __ + __

b)        <u>6</u>        _____   _____   _____      _____   _____

**DOTTED NOTE** - a DOT placed after a note adds "HALF THE VALUE" of the note. The dot is written to the right in the same space as the notehead of a space note and in the space above for a line note.

♫ **Note:**  ♪• dotted eighth note;  ♩• dotted quarter note;  ♩• dotted half note;  ○• dotted whole note

2. a) Write the note and the note value of the dot.   b) Write the number of beats for each dotted note.

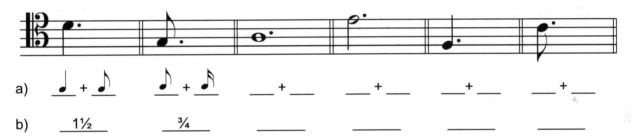

a)   <u>♩</u> + <u>♪</u>   <u>♪</u> + <u>♪</u>   __ + __   __ + __   __ + __   __ + __

b)   <u>1½</u>        <u>¾</u>        _____   _____   _____   _____

3. a) Write the number of beats for each of the following notes.    b) Name the notes in the Alto Clef.

a)    <u>3</u>   ____   ____   ____   ____   ____   ____   ____

b)    <u>B</u>   ____   ____   ____   ____   ____   ____   ____

Eighth notes and sixteenth notes can be beamed together in combinations that equal **ONE BEAT**. Eighth notes and sixteenth notes can be combined with **RESTS** to equal one beat (one quarter note).

4. Write the total number of beats in each measure.

<u>1</u>   ____   ____   ____   ____   ____   ____

## TIME SIGNATURES

A **TIME SIGNATURE** is written on the staff after the clef sign.
TWO numbers are used for a TIME SIGNATURE.

In **Simple Time**, the **TOP NUMBER** indicates how many beats are in a measure.

**2** means TWO beats per measure     1    2

**3** means THREE beats per measure    1    2    3

**4** means FOUR beats per measure    1    2    3    4

The **BOTTOM NUMBER "4"** indicates that **one quarter note** is equal to **one** beat.

A **SCOOP** ( ⌣ ) is a symbol representing one beat. Scoops are a visual aid in grouping notes and/or rests into one beat.

♩ **Note:** A whole rest equals a **whole measure of silence** in Simple Time. The top number of the Time Signature determines the number of beats given to the whole rest. A whole rest may receive 2, 3 or 4 beats.

1. a) Following the examples, add one rest below each bracket to complete the measure.
   b) Cross off the count as each beat is completed.

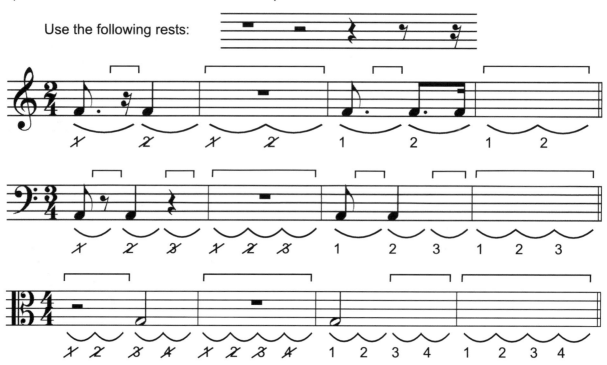

2. Complete the following.

1 whole note = _____ half notes

2 half notes = _____ quarter notes

4 quarter notes = _____ eighth notes

8 eighth notes = _____ sixteenth notes

# Lesson 1

## Review Test

**1.** Name the following notes in the **Treble Clef**.

10

---  ---  ---  ---  ---  ---  ---  ---

**2.** Name the following notes in the **Bass Clef**.

10

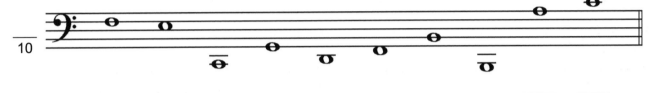

---  ---  ---  ---  ---  ---  ---  ---

**3.** Rewrite the given note in each measure at the **SAME PITCH** in the **ALTERNATE CLEF**.
Use half notes.  Name the notes.

10

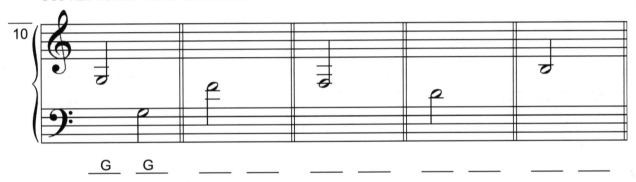

__G__  __G__  ___  ___  ___  ___  ___  ___

**4.** a) Name the following notes on the **Grand Staff**.
b) Draw a line from each note on the staff to the corresponding key on the keyboard.
c) Name the key directly on the keyboard.

10

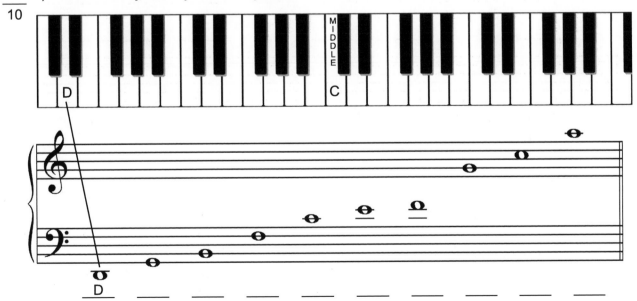

**5.** Write the name and number of beats each note or rest receives in $\frac{4}{4}$ time.

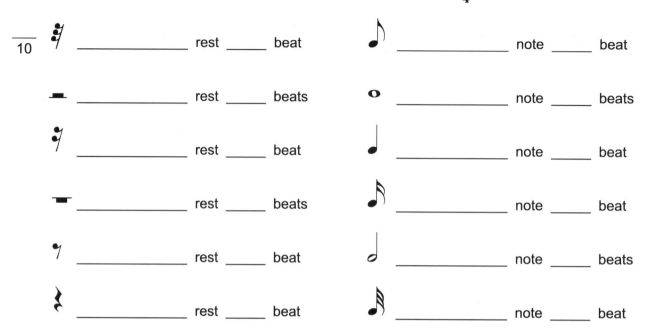

10   _____ rest ____ beat          _____ note ____ beat

_____ rest ____ beats          _____ note ____ beats

_____ rest ____ beat          _____ note ____ beat

_____ rest ____ beats          _____ note ____ beat

_____ rest ____ beat          _____ note ____ beats

_____ rest ____ beat          _____ note ____ beat

**6.** Write **ONE NOTE** that is equal to the total value of the notes in each measure.

**7.** Write **THREE NOTES** of the same value that equal the dotted note in each measure.

**8.** Write **ONE REST** below each bracket that has the same value as the note in each measure.

18

**9.** a) Rewrite the following notes at the **SAME PITCH** in the Alto Clef.  Name the notes.

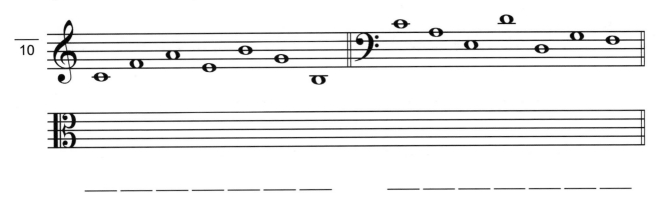

10

_____ _____ _____ _____ _____ _____        _____ _____ _____ _____ _____ _____

b) Rewrite the following notes at the **SAME PITCH** in the Tenor Clef.  Name the notes.

_____ _____ _____ _____ _____ _____        _____ _____ _____ _____ _____ _____

**10.** Match each musical term or sign with the English definition.  (Not all definitions will be used.)

| Term | | Definition |
|---|---|---|
| *tie* | _____ | a)  F Clef |
| *brace* | _____ | b)  moderately soft |
| *ledger line* | _____ | c)  up on the right or down on the left |
| *Bass Clef* | _____ | d)  adds half the value of the note |
| *Treble Clef* | _____ | e)  indicates the number of beats of silence |
| *mezzo piano, **mp*** | _____ | f)  joins the Treble Clef and Bass Clef to create the Grand Staff |
| *a dot after a note* | _____ | g)  hold for the combined value of the tied notes |
| *fortissimo, **ff*** | _____ | h)  two or more eighth notes joined together |
| *stem direction of a note on line 3* | _____ | i)  short line used for notes above or below the staff to extend the range of the staff |
| *rest* | _____ | j)  very loud |
| | | k)  G Clef |

10

19

# Lesson 2  Accidentals, Semitones, Tones and Enharmonic Equivalents

An **ACCIDENTAL** is a sign placed in front of a note that raises or lowers the pitch. An accidental placed in front of a note applies to any note that is written on that line or in that space until it is cancelled by either another accidental or by a bar line.

A **SEMITONE** (or half step) is the shortest distance in pitch between two notes and uses adjacent (closest or neighbouring) keys on the keyboard, black or white.

A **SHARP** ♯ raises a note one chromatic semitone or half step. (C to C♯)

A **FLAT** ♭ lowers a note one chromatic semitone or half step. (D to D♭)

Each black key has two names using a sharp or a flat. Example: C♯ or D♭, D♯ or E♭.

♫ **Note:** A **CHROMATIC SEMITONE** has the **SAME** letter name. Example: F to F♯ or B to B♭.

A sharp or flat is written in front (to the left) of the notehead and after (to the right) of the letter name. A sharp or flat can be a black key or a white key.

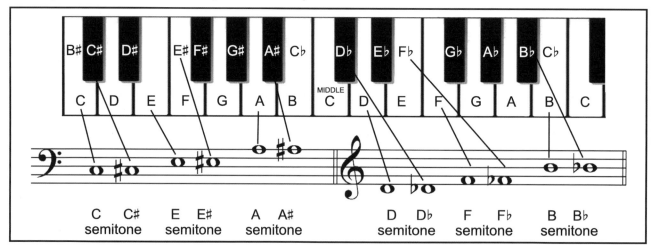

♫ **Note:** The middle of the sharp sign must be in the same space or on the same line as the note.

1. a) Raise the following notes a chromatic semitone (half step) by writing a sharp in front of each note.
   b) Name the notes.

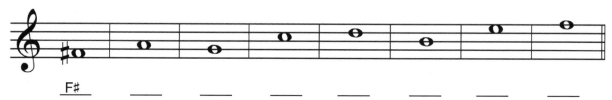

F♯ ____ ____ ____ ____ ____ ____ ____

♫ **Note:** The "half heart" of the flat sign must be in the same space or on the same line as the note.

2. a) Lower the following notes a chromatic semitone (half step) by writing a flat in front of each note.
   b) Name the notes.

G♭ ____ ____ ____ ____ ____ ____ ____

# NATURAL ♮ SIGN

A **NATURAL** ♮ sign **CANCELS** a sharp or flat.  A natural sign
raises a flat or lowers a sharp one chromatic semitone (half step).

A **NATURAL** sign is written in front of the notehead and after of the letter name.
A natural note is ALWAYS a white key.

♫ **Note:**  The **NATURAL** sign is written like the letter **L** and the number **7**.

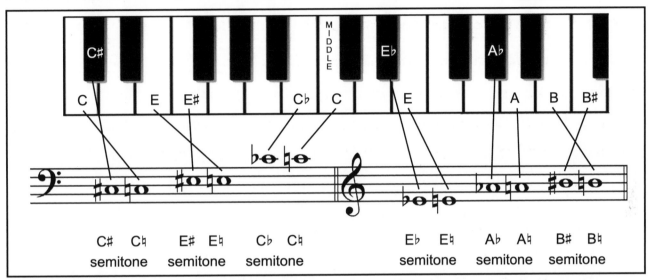

An **ACCIDENTAL** only applies to the notes on the line or in the space where it is written.  It does **NOT**
apply to notes that have the same letter name but appear in a higher or lower position on the staff.

♫ **Note:**  The middle box of the natural sign is written in the same space or on the same line
as the note.

1. a)  Draw a line from each note on the staff to the corresponding key on the keyboard.
   b)  Name the notes.

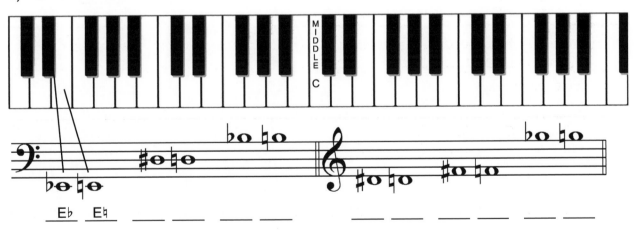

2. a)  Write a natural in front of the 2<sup>nd</sup> note in each measure.   b)  Name the notes.

# CHROMATIC SEMITONE, DIATONIC SEMITONE and ENHARMONIC EQUIVALENT

A **CHROMATIC** semitone (chromatic half step) uses the **SAME** letter name.  Example:  C to C#.

A **DIATONIC** semitone (diatonic half step) uses a **DIFFERENT** letter name.  Example:  C to D♭.

An **ENHARMONIC EQUIVALENT** is the **SAME PITCH** written with notes using different (neighbouring) letter names.  Example: C# and D♭.

♫ **Note:**  Diatonic - Different letter name;  Chromatic - Same letter name.

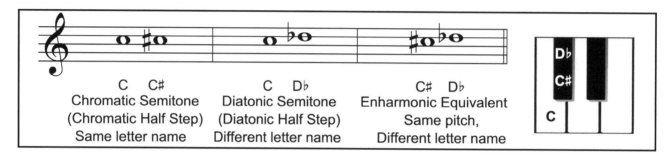

♫ **Note:**  A **CHROMATIC SEMITONE** (chromatic half step) is written as an interval of a first.

1. a)  Raise the following notes a chromatic semitone.  Use whole notes.
   b)  Draw a line from each note on the staff to the corresponding key on the keyboard.
   c)  Name the notes.

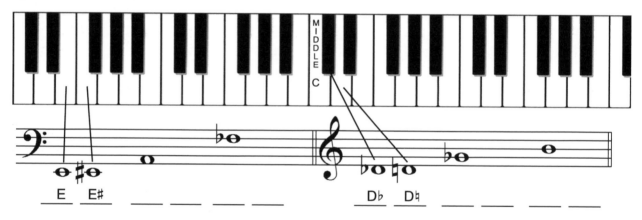

2. a)  Lower the following notes a chromatic semitone.  Use whole notes.
   b)  Draw a line from each note on the staff to the corresponding key on the keyboard.
   c)  Name the notes.

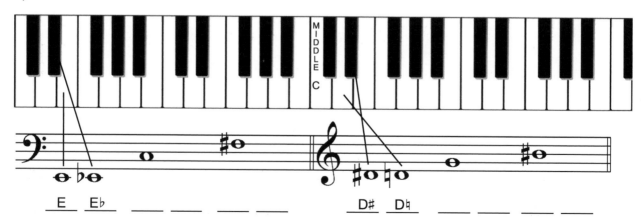

## DIATONIC SEMITONE and ENHARMONIC EQUIVALENT

♫ **Note:** A **DIATONIC SEMITONE** (diatonic half step) is written as an interval of a second.

1. a)  Raise the following notes a diatonic semitone.  Use whole notes.
   b)  Draw a line from each note on the staff to the corresponding key on the keyboard.
   c)  Name the notes.

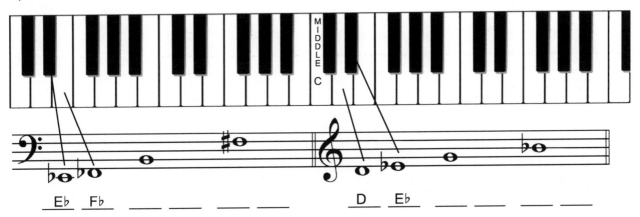

2. a)  Lower the following notes a diatonic semitone.  Use whole notes.
   b)  Draw a line from each note on the staff to the corresponding key on the keyboard.
   c)  Name the notes.

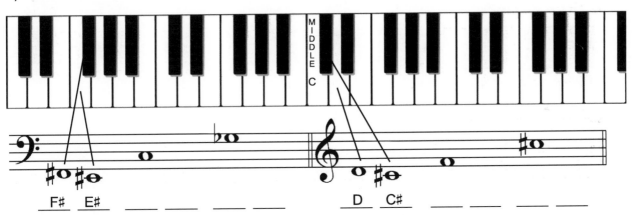

♫ **Note:** An **ENHARMONIC EQUIVALENT** is written as an interval of a second.

3. a)  Write the enharmonic equivalent for each of the following notes.  Use whole notes.
   b)  Draw a line from each note on the staff to the corresponding key on the keyboard.
   c)  Name the notes.

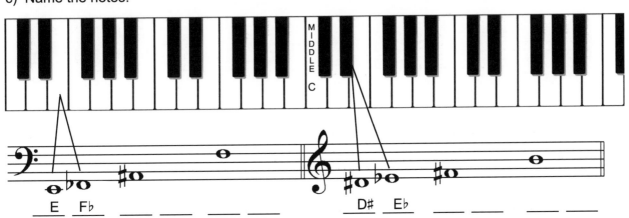

23

## WHOLE TONE (WHOLE STEP or TONE)

A **WHOLE TONE** or **WHOLE STEP** (also referred to as a **TONE**) is equal to **TWO** semitones (half steps) with one key (black or white) between them.  Example:  C to D,  C# to D#,  A♭ to B♭,  E to F#.

1.  a)  Draw a line from each note on the staff to the corresponding key on the keyboard.
    b)  Name the notes.

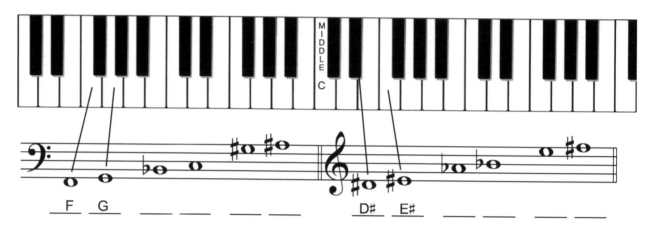

F   G   ___   ___   ___   ___       D#  E#   ___   ___   ___   ___

♫ **Note:**  A **Whole Tone** (whole step or tone) may be written as an interval of a second.

2.  a)  Raise the following notes a whole tone (whole step).  Use whole notes.
    b)  Name the notes.

G   A   ___   ___   ___   ___   ___   ___   ___   ___

3.  a)  Lower the following notes a whole tone (whole step).  Use whole notes.
    b)  Name the notes.

E♭   D♭   ___   ___   ___   ___   ___   ___

♫ **Note:**  An **Enharmonic Equivalent** is the same pitch written with notes using different letter names.

4.  Name each of the following as:  d.s. (diatonic semitone),  c.s. (chromatic semitone),
                     w.t. (whole tone)   or      e.e. (enharmonic equivalent).

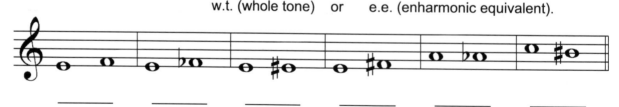

___   ___   ___   ___   ___   ___

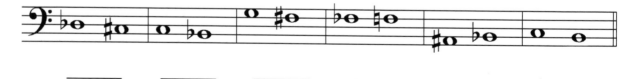

___   ___   ___   ___

# DOUBLE FLATS AND DOUBLE SHARPS

**DOUBLE FLAT** ♭♭ lowers a flat one chromatic semitone (half step) and lowers a natural note one chromatic whole tone (whole step).

**DOUBLE SHARP** ✕ raises a sharp one chromatic semitone (half step) and raises a natural note one chromatic whole tone (whole step).

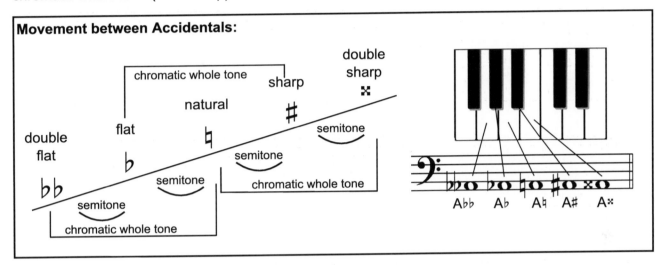

**Movement between Accidentals:**

♫ **Note:** Two semitones (half steps) equal ONE whole tone (whole step), an interval of a 1st or a 2nd.
    **CHROMATIC** (same letter name): whole step - a 1st: C - C✕   half step - a 1st: C - C♯
    **DIATONIC** (different letter name): whole step - a 2nd: C - D   half step - a 2nd: C - D♭

1. a) Raise the following notes one chromatic whole tone (whole step). Use whole notes.
   b) Name the notes.

    B♭♭    B♮    ___    ___    ___  ___    ___

2. a) Raise the following notes one diatonic whole tone (whole step). Use whole notes.
   b) Name the notes.

    C✕    D✕    ___    ___    ___  ___    ___

3. a) Lower the following notes one diatonic semitone (half step). Use whole notes.
   b) Name the notes.

    C♭♭    B♭♭    ___    ___    ___  ___    ___

## TERMS and SIGNS

| Terms and Signs | Definitions |
|---|---|
| M.D. | *mano destra*, right hand |
| M.S. | *mano sinistra*, left hand |
| $8^{va}$- - - ¬ | *ottava*, $8^{va}$, play one octave above the written pitch |
| $8^{va}$- - - ⌟ | *ottava*, $8^{va}$, play one octave below the written pitch |
| ♩_♩ | *tie:* hold for the combined value of the tied notes |
| *pedale, ped.* | pedal |
| *con pedale, con ped.,* ℘ | with pedal |
| *tre corde* | three strings; release the left (piano) pedal |
| *una corda* | one string; depress the left (piano) pedal |
| ∟＿＿＿⌟, ∟＿∧＿⌟, ℘ | pedal marking |

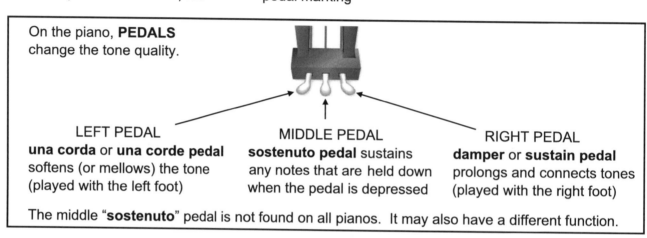

On the piano, **PEDALS** change the tone quality.

| LEFT PEDAL | MIDDLE PEDAL | RIGHT PEDAL |
|---|---|---|
| **una corda** or **una corde pedal** softens (or mellows) the tone (played with the left foot) | **sostenuto pedal** sustains any notes that are held down when the pedal is depressed | **damper** or **sustain pedal** prolongs and connects tones (played with the right foot) |

The middle "**sostenuto**" pedal is not found on all pianos. It may also have a different function.

1. Name the following pedals as: una corda, sostenuto or damper.

_____    _____    _____
        Left Pedal                     Middle Pedal                  Right Pedal

♫ **Note: OTTAVA**, or $8^{va}$, is the interval of an octave.

2. a) Draw a line from each note on the staff to the corresponding key on the keyboard.
   b) Name the key directly on the keyboard.

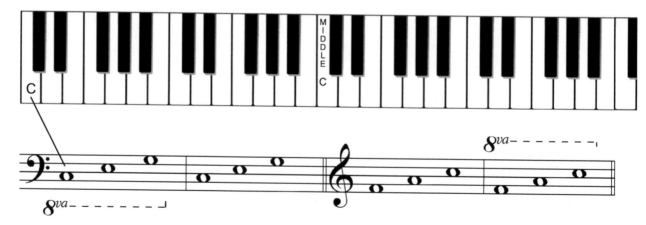

# ITALIAN TERMS

| Italian Term | Definition |
|---|---|
| arco | for stringed instruments: resume bowing after a *pizzicato* passage |
| attacca | proceed without a break |
| con sordino | with mute |
| fine | the end |
| loco | return to normal register |
| ottava, $8^{va}$ | the interval of an octave |
| pizzicato | for stringed instruments: pluck the string instead of bowing |
| primo, prima | first; the upper part of a duet |
| quindicesima alta, $15^{ma}$ | two octaves higher |
| risoluto | resolute |
| secondo, seconda | second; second or lower part of a duet |
| simile | continue in the same matter as has just been indicated |
| tacet | be silent |
| tempo | speed at which music is performed |
| tutti | a passage for the ensemble |
| volta | time (for example: *prima volta*, first time; *seconda volta*, second time) |
| volti subito, v.s. | turn the page quickly |

1. Write the term for each of the following definitions.

| _____ | _____ | _____ | _____ | _____ |
|---|---|---|---|---|
| be silent | the end | with mute | turn the page quickly | resolute |

| Italian Term | Definition |
|---|---|
| alla, all' | in the manner of |
| assai | much, very much (for example: *allegro assai*, very fast) |
| ben, bene | well (for example: *ben marcato*, well marked) |
| col, coll', colla, colle | with (for example: *coll'ottava*, with an added octave) |
| con | with |
| e, ed | and |
| ma | but (for example: *ma non troppo*, but not too much) |
| meno | less |
| molto | much, very |
| non | not |
| non troppo | not too much |
| più | more |
| poco | little |
| poco a poco | little by little |
| quasi | almost, as if |
| sempre | always, continuously |
| senza | without |
| sopra | above |
| subito | suddenly |
| troppo | too much |

2. Write the term for each of the following definitions.

| _____ | _____ | _____ | _____ | _____ |
|---|---|---|---|---|
| without | not too much | more | as if | always |

**Lesson 2**                    **Review Test**

Total Score: ____
100

1.  Name the following notes in the **Treble Clef**.

2.  a) **LOWER** the following notes one **CHROMATIC** semitone (half step).  Use whole notes.
    b) Name the notes.

Gb    Gbb    ___    ___    ___    ___

3.  a) Draw a line from each note on the staff to the corresponding key on the keyboard.
    b) Name the key directly on the keyboard.

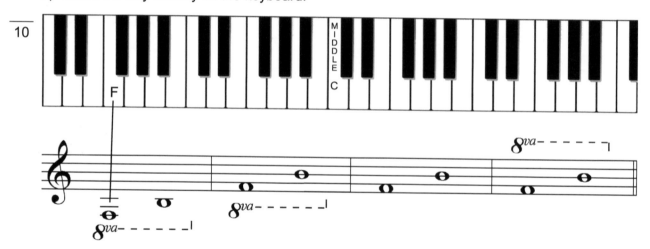

4.  a) **RAISE** the following notes one **CHROMATIC** whole tone (whole step).  Use whole notes.
    b) Name the notes.

5.  a) **LOWER** the following notes one **DIATONIC** whole tone (whole step).  Use whole notes.
    b) Name the notes.

**6.** Match each musical term or sign with the English definition.  (Not all definitions will be used.)

| Term | | Definition |
|------|---|-----------|
| con sordino | _____ | a) pedal |
| semitone | _____ | b) turn the page quickly |
| poco a poco | _____ | c) proceed without a break |
| pedale, ped. | _____ | d) cancels a sharp or a flat |
| tacet | _____ | e) three strings, release the left (piano) pedal |
| ottava, *8va* | _____ | f) a whole measure of silence |
| attacca | _____ | g) little by little |
| natural sign | _____ | h) with mute |
| tre corde | _____ | i) be silent |
| volti subito, v.s. | _____ | j) the interval of an octave |
| | | k) closest distance in pitch between 2 notes (half step) |

**7.** Rewrite the following melody at the **SAME PITCH** in the Bass Clef.  Copy the bar lines first.

10

**8.** a) Draw a line from each note on the staff to the corresponding key on the keyboard.
b) Name the notes.

10

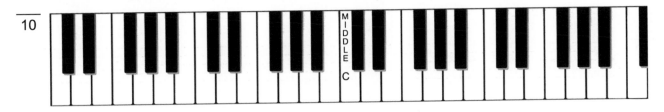

29

9. a) Add **ONE REST** below each bracket to complete the measure.
   b) Cross off the count as each beat is completed.

Use the following rests:

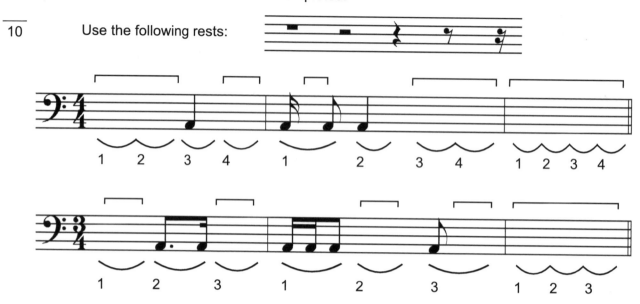

10. Analyze the following piece of music by answering the questions below.

# Sneaky

G. St. Germain

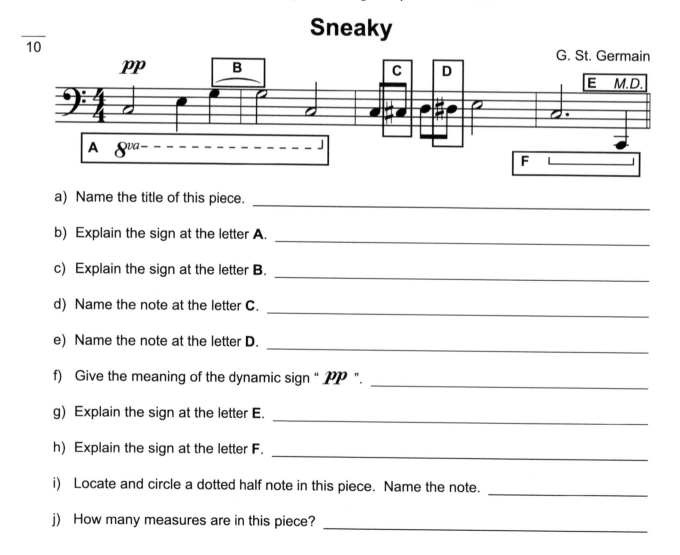

a) Name the title of this piece. _____

b) Explain the sign at the letter **A**. _____

c) Explain the sign at the letter **B**. _____

d) Name the note at the letter **C**. _____

e) Name the note at the letter **D**. _____

f) Give the meaning of the dynamic sign " **pp** ". _____

g) Explain the sign at the letter **E**. _____

h) Explain the sign at the letter **F**. _____

i) Locate and circle a dotted half note in this piece. Name the note. _____

j) How many measures are in this piece? _____

# Lesson 3     Scales and the Circle of Fifths

## MAJOR SCALES

A **MAJOR SCALE** is a series of 8 degrees (notes) in alphabetical order using a specific Major Scale Pattern of (T) **Tones** (whole tones or whole steps) and (ST) **Semitones** (half steps).
A **circumflex** " ˆ " or **caret** sign (hat) above a number ( $\hat{3}$ ) indicates the degree number of the scale.

**Major Scale Pattern**: $\hat{1}$ tone $\hat{2}$ tone $\hat{3}$ semitone $\hat{4}$ tone $\hat{5}$ tone $\hat{6}$ tone $\hat{7}$ semitone $\hat{8}$ ($\hat{1}$)

In a Major scale, semitones are between degrees (notes) $\hat{3}$ - $\hat{4}$ and degrees (notes) $\hat{7}$ - $\hat{8}$ ($\hat{1}$).
Semitones are indicated by a "semitone slur" written under the noteheads.

♫ **Note:** This pattern of tones and semitones will create a Major Scale beginning on any note.

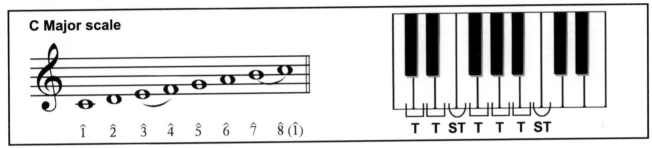

1. a) Using the example above, copy the C Major scale ascending only. Use whole notes.
   b) Number the scale degrees.
   c) Mark the semitones with a slur.

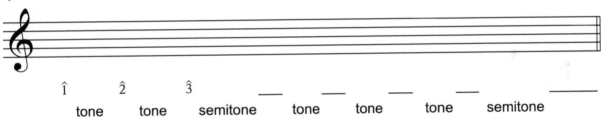

The first degree or note of the scale is called the **Tonic (I)** or **Key Note**. The Roman Numeral **"I"** is used for the Tonic. In the C Major scale, the Tonic note (I) is C.

♫ **Note:** When writing a scale **ASCENDING** (going up) and **DESCENDING** (going down), a **center bar line** may be used after the highest Tonic note.

2. a) Write the C Major scale ascending and descending. Use whole notes. Use a center bar line.
   b) Mark the semitones with a slur.
   c) Label the Tonic (I) notes.

## MAJOR SCALE PATTERN with ACCIDENTALS or a KEY SIGNATURE

When writing the **MAJOR SCALE PATTERN** beginning on notes other than C, accidentals will be required ascending and descending to keep the Major Scale Pattern of tones (whole steps) and semitones (half steps).

**Major Scale Pattern**: $\hat{1}$ tone $\hat{2}$ tone $\hat{3}$ semitone $\hat{4}$ tone $\hat{5}$ tone $\hat{6}$ tone $\hat{7}$ semitone $\hat{8}$ ($\hat{1}$)

♫ **Note:** Accidentals will be repeated in the descending scale after the center bar line.

**G Major scale** begins on the Tonic G and follows the Major Scale Pattern. G Major has 1 sharp, F♯.

1. Write the G Major scale ascending and descending. Use an accidental for the F♯.
   Use whole notes. Use a center bar line.

**F Major scale** begins on the Tonic F and follows the Major Scale Pattern. F Major has 1 flat, B♭.

2. Write the F Major scale ascending and descending. Use an accidental for the B♭.
   Use whole notes. Use a center bar line.

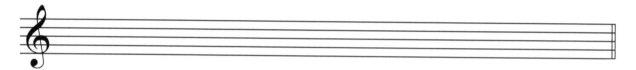

A **KEY SIGNATURE** is a group of sharps or flats that indicates the key. Instead of using accidentals, the sharps or flats from the Major Scale Patterns are placed in a specific order at the beginning of the staff, directly after the clef sign, in the Key Signature.

Key Signature:
D Major (F♯, C♯)

♫ **Note:** The **KEY** is the main tonality of the music. The Key Signature indicates whether the tonality is a Major key or its relative minor key.

When writing a **SCALE** using a **KEY SIGNATURE**, the notes begin **AFTER** the Key Signature.

**D Major scale** begins on the Tonic D and has 2 sharps, F♯ and C♯.

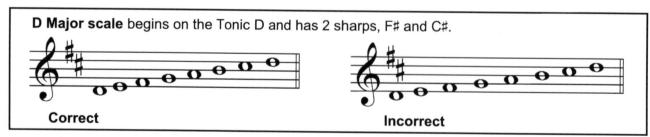

3. Write the D Major scale ascending and descending. Use a Key Signature for the F♯ and C♯.
   Use whole notes. Use a center bar line.

# CIRCLE of FIFTHS

The **CIRCLE of FIFTHS** is a map of the Major and minor Key Signatures. **MAJOR KEYS** are written around the outside of the circle using UPPER CASE letters. The numbers around the outside of the Circle of Fifths indicate how many flats or sharps are found in each key.

♫ **Note:** The distance from one key to the next key around the Circle of Fifths is **five letter names.**

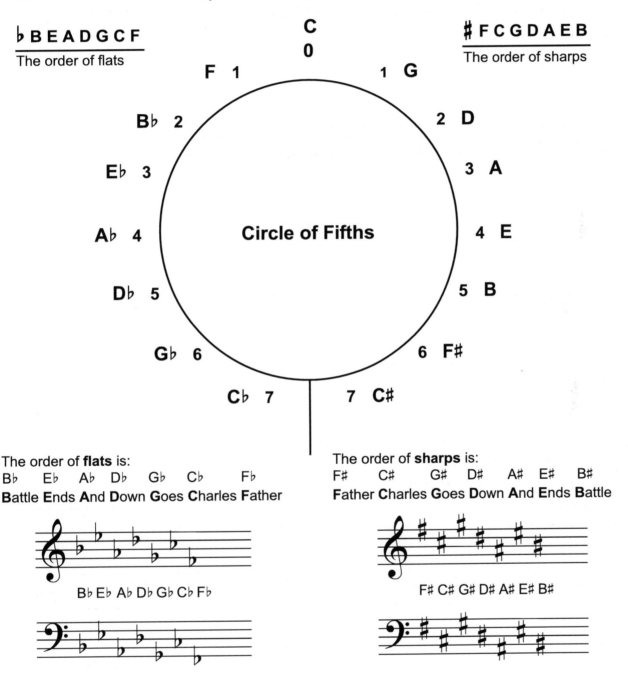

♭ **B E A D G C F**
The order of flats

**C**
**0**

♯ **F C G D A E B**
The order of sharps

F  1

1  G

B♭  2

2  D

E♭  3

3  A

A♭  4

**Circle of Fifths**

4  E

D♭  5

5  B

G♭  6

6  F♯

C♭  7

7  C♯

The order of **flats** is:
B♭   E♭   A♭   D♭   G♭   C♭      F♭
**B**attle **E**nds **A**nd **D**own **G**oes **C**harles **F**ather

The order of **sharps** is:
F♯   C♯   G♯   D♯   A♯   E♯   B♯
**F**ather **C**harles **G**oes **D**own **A**nd **E**nds **B**attle

B♭ E♭ A♭ D♭ G♭ C♭ F♭

F♯ C♯ G♯ D♯ A♯ E♯ B♯

♫ **Note:** Always write the flats and sharps in the correct order.

   1.  Write the order of flats.

   2.  Write the order of sharps.

____  ____  ____  ____  ____  ____  ____

____  ____  ____  ____  ____  ____  ____

**TRACE THE CIRCLE OF FIFTHS - MAJOR KEYS**

Major keys are written on the OUTSIDE of the Circle of Fifths.

1. Complete the Circle of Fifths:
   a) Write the order of flats on the top left.  Write the order of sharps on the top right.
   b) Start at the number "1" on the flat side with **F** (Father).  Move clockwise (to the right) **UP** a
      **FIFTH** each time.  Trace the given letters.  Use this sentence to complete the Circle of Fifths:

   Father Charles Goes Down And Ends Battle

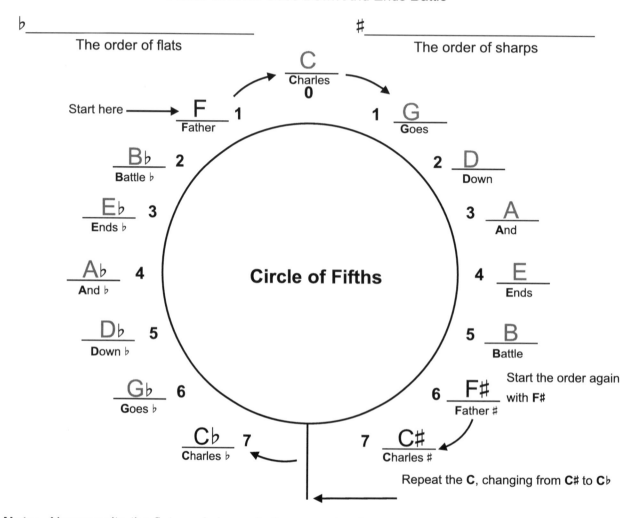

♫ **Note:** Always write the flats and sharps in the correct order.

2. a) Copy the order of flats in the Treble Clef.          b) Copy the order of sharps in the Treble Clef.

♫ **Note:** This is called the **Circle of Fifths** as the distance between each key when moving clockwise
      around the circle is **five letter names** (a fifth).

**F** G A B **C** D E F **G** A b c **D** E F G **A** b c d **E** F G A **B** c d e **F**
1  2 3 4 **5** 2 3 4 **5** 2 3 4 **5** 2 3 4 **5** 2 3 4 **5** 2 3 4 **5** 2 3 4 **5**

## WRITE THE CIRCLE OF FIFTHS - MAJOR KEYS

Major keys are written on the OUTSIDE of the Circle of Fifths.

1. Complete the Circle of Fifths:
   a) Write the order of flats on the top left. Write the order of sharps on the top right.
   b) Start at the number "1" on the flat side with **F** (Father). Move clockwise (to the right) **UP** a
      **FIFTH** each time. Use this sentence to complete the Circle of Fifths:

Father Charles Goes Down And Ends Battle

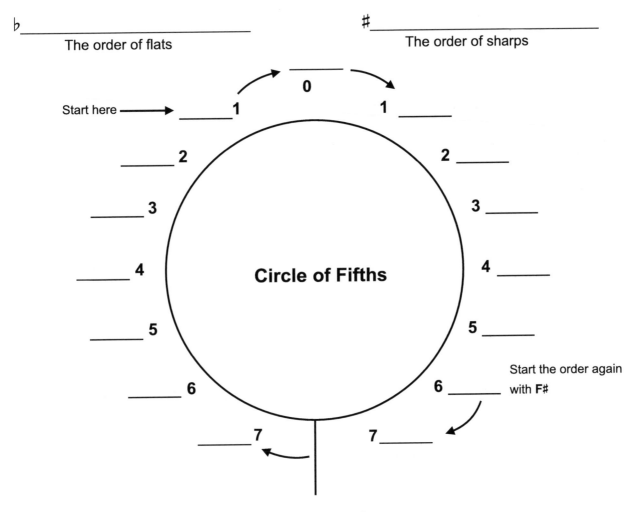

♫ **Note:** Always write the flats and sharps in the correct order.

2. a) Copy the order of flats in the Bass Clef.          b) Copy the order of sharps in the Bass Clef.

♫ **Note:** Always write **MAJOR** keys on the **OUTSIDE** of the circle **BESIDE** the numbers.
Use UPPER CASE letters for Major key names.

The sentence for the order of flats is:

**Battle Ends And Down Goes Charles Father**

The sentence for the order of sharps is:

**Father Charles Goes Down And Ends Battle**

## MAJOR KEY SIGNATURES with FLATS

To name the **MAJOR KEY with FLATS**, go to the **SECOND LAST** flat of the Key Signature. That note is the name of the Major key. Example: Key Signature is B♭ E♭ A♭: the second last flat is E♭. That names the key as E♭ Major. The exception to the rule is **F Major** which only has one flat, B♭.

♫ **Note:** The Key Signature is written at the beginning of the music after the clef.

1. Name the Major key for the following Key Signatures.

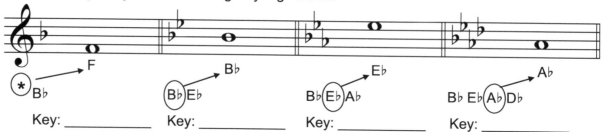

Key: _____    Key: _____    Key: _____    Key: _____

2. a) Name the following Major keys.
   b) Copy the clef (Treble or Bass), Key Signature and the Tonic note. Name the Major key.

36

## MAJOR KEY SIGNATURES with SHARPS

To name the **MAJOR KEY with SHARPS**, go to the LAST sharp of the Key Signature and go up one diatonic semitone. That note is the name of the Major key. Example: Key Signature is F# C#: last sharp is C#. From C#, go up one diatonic semitone to D. That names the key as D Major.

♫ **Note:** The Key Signature is written at the beginning of the music after the clef.

1. Name the Major key for the following Key Signatures.

Key: _____     Key: _____     Key: _____     Key: _____

2. a) Name the following Major keys.
   b) Copy the clef (Treble or Bass), Key Signature and the Tonic note. Name the Major key.

37

## MAJOR SCALES using a KEY SIGNATURE with FLATS

**MAJOR SCALES** using a **KEY SIGNATURE** can be written with OR without a center bar line. When writing a scale WITH a center bar line, the bar line is written after the highest note.

♫ **Note:** Always write scales in the **SAME WAY**, either WITH or WITHOUT a center bar line. A double bar line will be used at the end of the staff.

1. Write the following Major scales with flats, ascending and descending, using the correct Key Signature. Use whole notes.

a) B flat Major in the Treble Clef

b) E flat Major in the Treble Clef

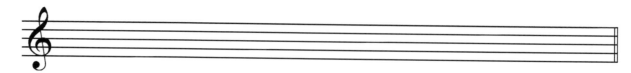

c) A flat Major in the Treble Clef

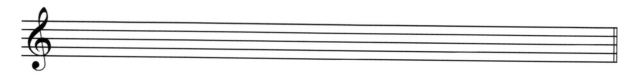

d) D flat Major in the Bass Clef

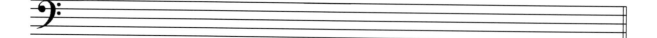

e) G flat Major in the Bass Clef

f) C flat Major in the Bass Clef

## MAJOR SCALES using a KEY SIGNATURE with SHARPS

When writing a **MAJOR SCALE** using a **KEY SIGNATURE**, with or without a center bar line, no accidentals are needed in the scale.

♫ **Note:** When writing a scale using a Key Signature, the notes begin **AFTER** the Key Signature.

1. Write the following Major scales with sharps, ascending and descending, using the correct Key Signature.  Use whole notes.

   a)  D Major in the Treble Clef

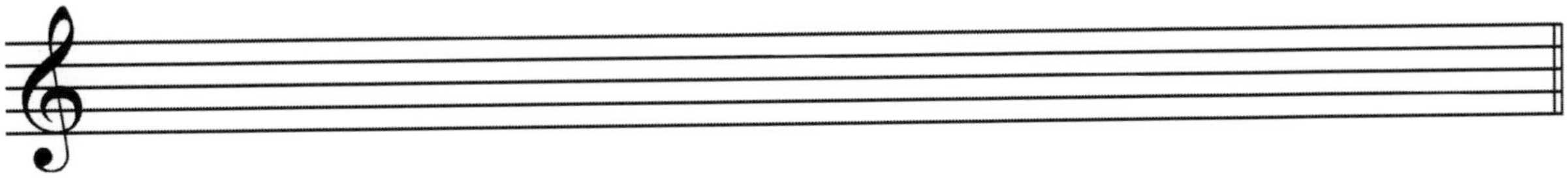

   b) A Major in the Treble Clef

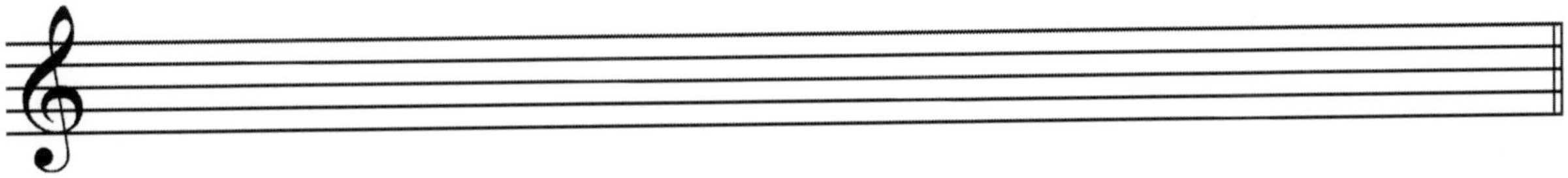

   c)  E Major in the Treble Clef

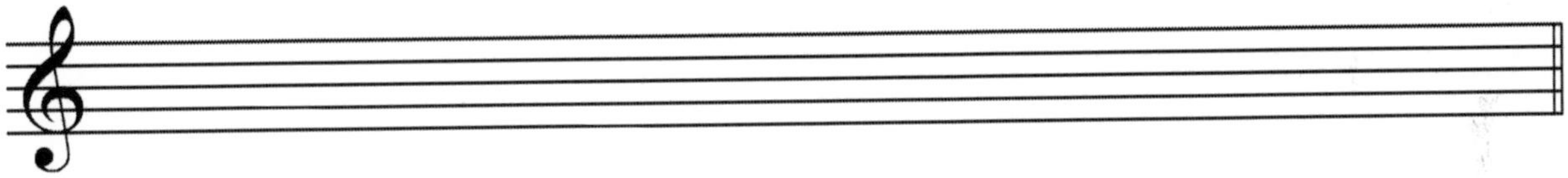

   d)  B Major in the Bass Clef

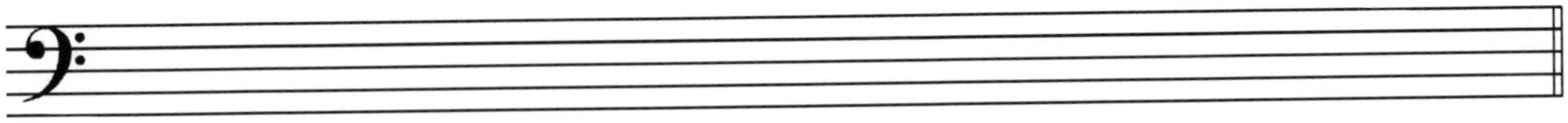

   e)  F sharp Major in the Bass Clef

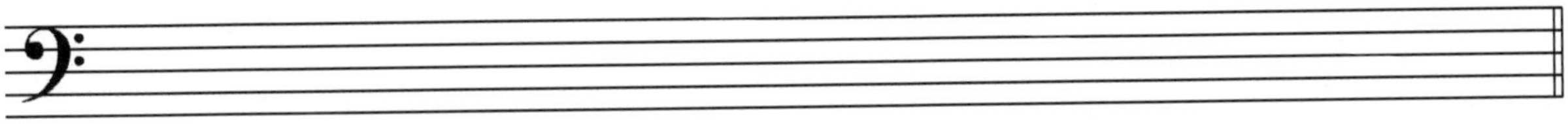

   f)  C sharp Major in the Bass Clef

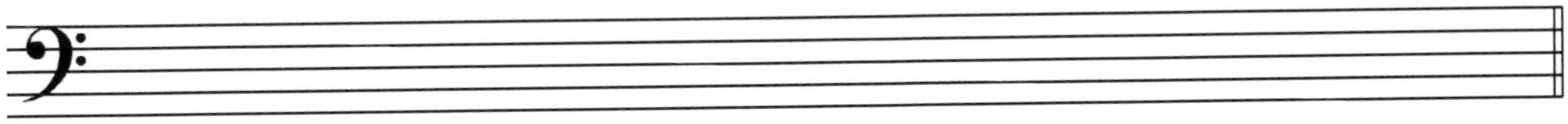

## ENHARMONIC TONIC MAJOR SCALES

**ENHARMONIC TONIC MAJOR SCALES** are scales that use the SAME pitches but are written with notes using different letter names (enharmonic equivalents).
Example:  D♭ Major scale and C♯ Major scale.

♫ **Note:**  The Circle of Fifths contains three enharmonic Major keys:
D♭ Major and C♯ Major; G♭ Major and F♯ Major; C♭ Major and B Major.

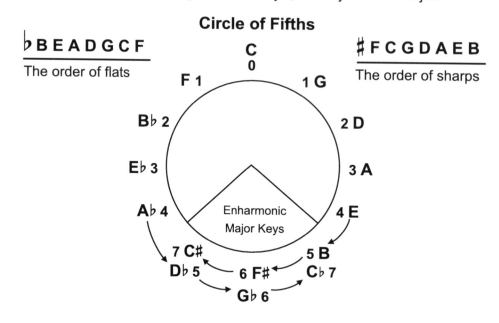

1. Name the enharmonic Tonic Major scale.  Write the enharmonic Tonic Major scale, ascending and descending, using the correct Key Signature.  Use whole notes.

a) the enharmonic Tonic Major scale of D flat Major is _____

b) the enharmonic Tonic Major scale of F sharp Major is _____

c) the enharmonic Tonic Major scale of C flat Major is _____

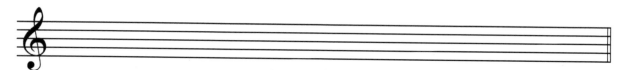

## MAJOR SCALES using ACCIDENTALS

**MAJOR SCALES** may be written using **ACCIDENTALS** or a Key Signature.  Scales may be written WITH or WITHOUT a center bar line.  Scales always end with a double bar line.

**WITH** a center bar line:  the center bar line **CANCELS** an accidental.  Accidentals must be written in the ascending AND descending scale.

**WITHOUT** a center bar line:  accidentals are written in the ascending scale only.

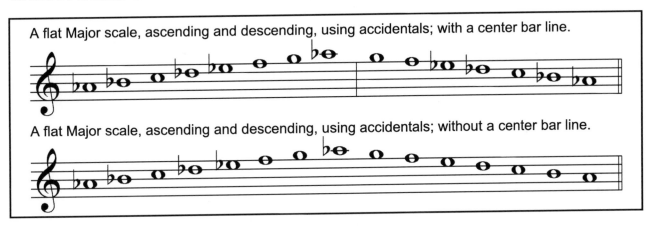

A flat Major scale, ascending and descending, using accidentals; with a center bar line.

A flat Major scale, ascending and descending, using accidentals; without a center bar line.

1.  Write the following scales, ascending and descending, using accidentals.  Use whole notes.

    a)  E Major in the Treble Clef
    b)  D flat Major in the Bass Clef
    c)  enharmonic Tonic Major of B Major in the Treble Clef
    d)  A Major in the Bass Clef
    e)  enharmonic Tonic Major of G flat Major in the Bass Clef

## CIRCLE of FIFTHS with RELATIVE MINOR KEYS

A **MAJOR** key and its **RELATIVE MINOR** key share the **SAME** Key Signature. The minor key is THREE semitones (half steps) and THREE letter names below its relative Major.

**MAJOR** keys are written on the **OUTSIDE** of the Circle of Fifths using **UPPER** case letters.
**RELATIVE MINOR** keys are written on the **INSIDE** of the Circle of Fifths using **lower** case letters.

The 1st letter of the alphabet "A" is the landmark and starting position for adding the minor keys.
 Starting with f minor on the **FLAT** side, moving clockwise (to the right), minor keys are added.

Use the minor key sentence: **father charles goes down and ends battle**

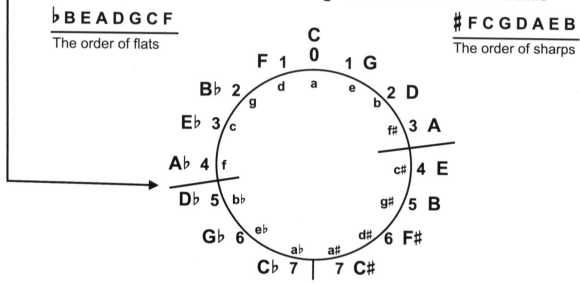

♭**B E A D G C F**
The order of flats

♯**F C G D A E B**
The order of sharps

♫ **Note:** From the Major key to its relative minor, go **DOWN** 3 semitones.
From the minor key to its relative Major, go **UP** 3 semitones.

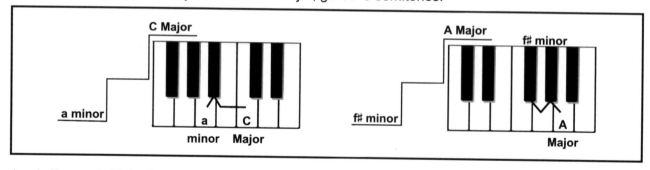

1. a) For each Major key, name its relative minor.    b) Write the Key Signature for each.

**Major -** C Major **relative minor -** a minor **Key Signature** no sharps / no flats

| Major - | relative minor | Key Signature |
|---|---|---|
| F Major | d minor | B♭ |
| B♭ Major | | |
| E♭ Major | | |
| A♭ Major | | |
| D♭ Major | | |
| G♭ Major | | |
| C♭ Major | | |

| Major - | relative minor | Key Signature |
|---|---|---|
| G Major | e minor | F♯ |
| D Major | | |
| A Major | | |
| E Major | | |
| B Major | | |
| F♯ Major | | |
| C♯ Major | | |

## WRITING THE CIRCLE of FIFTHS

When **WRITING THE CIRCLE OF FIFTHS**, use UPPER case letters for Major keys OUTSIDE the circle and lower case letters for relative minor keys INSIDE the circle.

1. Complete the Circle of Fifths:
   a) Write the order of flats on the top left and the order of sharps on the top right.
   b) Write the Major keys on the **OUTSIDE** of the circle.  Start with **F** Major and move clockwise: F, C, G, D, A, E, B.  Then repeat the order again:  F#, C#, C♭, G♭, D♭, A♭, E♭, B♭ (UPPER case).

♫ **Note:**  Use the sentence **F**ather **C**harles **G**oes **D**own **A**nd **E**nds **B**attle.

   c) Draw the landmark line under the A♭ and under the A.
   d) Write the minor keys on the **INSIDE** of the circle.  Start with **f** minor (relative of A♭ Major) and move clockwise:  f, c, g, d, a, e, b.  Then repeat the order again:  f#, c#, g#, d#, a#, a♭, e♭, b♭ (lower case).

# Circle of Fifths

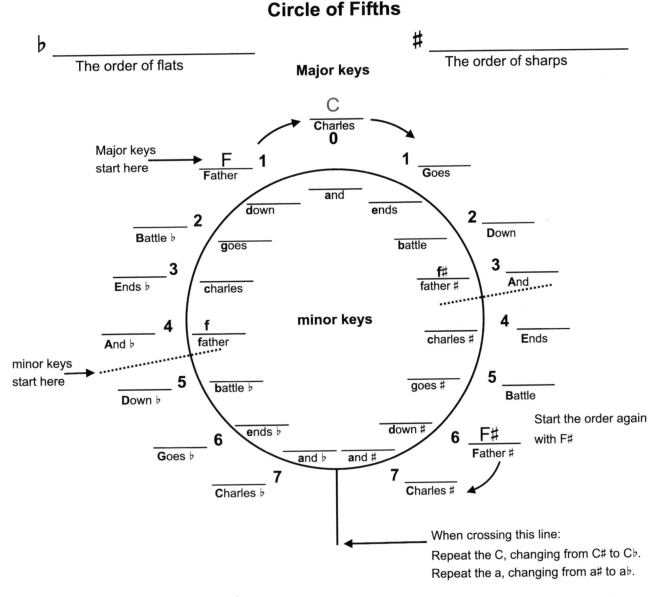

♫ **Note:**  Major keys and their relative minor keys are three semitones (three letter names) apart.

## COMPLETING the CIRCLE of FIFTHS

1. Complete the Circle of Fifths:
   a) Write the order of flats on the top left and the order of sharps on the top right.
   b) Add the numbers 0 and 1 - 7 around the outside of the circle.
   c) Write the Major keys on the outside of the circle.  Start with F Major and move clockwise.
   d) Draw the landmark lines.  Write the minor keys on the inside of the circle.  Start with f minor.

# Circle of Fifths

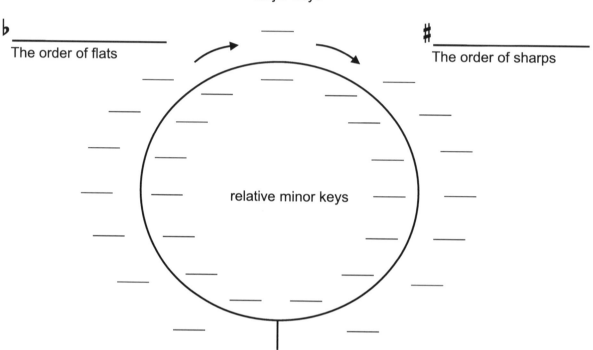

♫ **Note:** The abbreviation for Major is **Maj**; the abbreviation for minor is **min**.

2. Name the Major key and its relative minor key for each of the following Key Signatures.

Major key:  __E Maj__

minor key:  __c# min__

Major key:  _____

minor key:  _____

44

# NAMING NOTES with KEY SIGNATURES and ACCIDENTALS

An **ACCIDENTAL** placed in front of a note applies to any note that is written on that line or in that space until it is cancelled by either another accidental or by a bar line.

♫ **Note:** An **ACCIDENTAL** only applies to the notes on the line or in the space where it is written. It does **NOT** apply to notes that have the same letter name but appear in a higher or lower position on the staff.

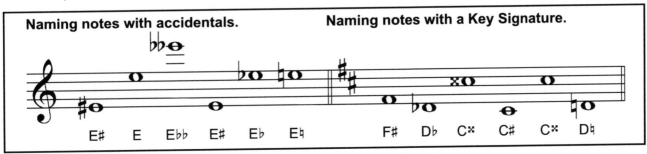

♫ **Note:** A bar line at the end of a measure cancels all accidentals in that measure.

1. Name the following notes in the Treble Clef.

G#   ___   ___   ___   ___       ___   ___   ___   ___

♫ **Note:** A Key Signature affects ALL the notes. A bar line does NOT cancel a Key Signature.

2. Name the following notes in the Bass Clef.

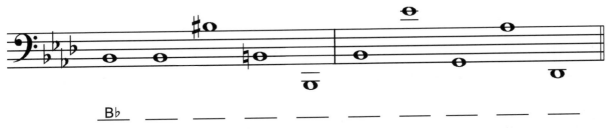

B♭   ___   ___   ___   ___   ___   ___   ___   ___

♫ **Note:** The Tonic note is the first note of the minor key. Example: C# is the Tonic note of c# minor.

3. Write the Key Signature and the Tonic note for the following minor keys. Use whole notes.

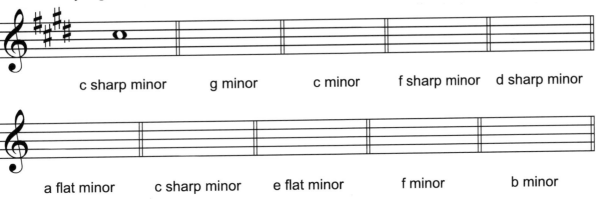

c sharp minor     g minor     c minor     f sharp minor     d sharp minor

a flat minor     c sharp minor     e flat minor     f minor     b minor

## NATURAL MINOR SCALES

A **NATURAL MINOR** scale has the **SAME** Key Signature as its relative Major.

♪ **Note:** As the word **NATURAL** indicates, **NOTHING** is added. (Like "N" in "Natural.)

Minor scales may be written using a KEY SIGNATURE or using ACCIDENTALS. The accidentals used in the minor scale are the same sharps or flats found in the Key Signature of its relative Major.

Minor scales may be written **WITH** or **WITHOUT** a center bar line.

♪ **Note:** When using a Key Signature, a natural minor scale written WITH or WITHOUT a center bar line will not require any accidentals.

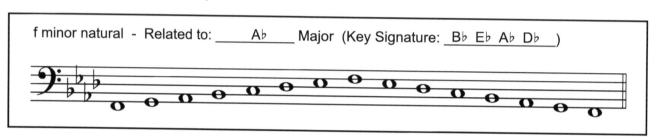

f minor natural - Related to: _____A♭_____ Major (Key Signature: _B♭ E♭ A♭ D♭_ )

♪ **Note:** Always write scales in the **SAME WAY**, either **WITH** or **WITHOUT** a center bar line.

1. a) Name the relative Major key. Name the sharps or flats in the Key Signature.
   b) Write the natural minor scale, ascending and descending. Use a Key Signature. Use whole notes.

e minor natural - Related to: _____ Major (Key Signature: _____ )

c# minor natural - Related to: _____ Major (Key Signature: _____ )

c minor natural - Related to: _____ Major (Key Signature: _____ )

## NATURAL MINOR SCALES - TONES (WHOLE STEP) and SEMITONES (HALF STEP)

**Natural Minor Scale Pattern:**

$\hat{1}$  tone  $\hat{2}$  semitone  $\hat{3}$  tone  $\hat{4}$  tone  $\hat{5}$  semitone  $\hat{6}$  tone  $\hat{7}$  tone  $\hat{8}$ ($\hat{1}$)

In a **NATURAL MINOR** scale, semitones (half steps) are between degrees (notes) $\hat{2}$ - $\hat{3}$ and $\hat{5}$ - $\hat{6}$.

♫ **Note:** When using accidentals, a natural minor scale written **WITH** a center bar line will repeat the accidentals in the descending scale.

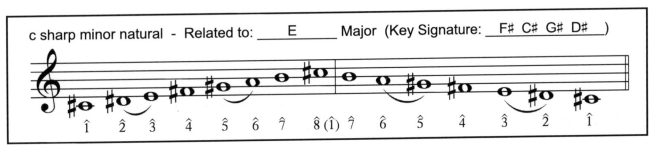

c sharp minor natural - Related to: _____ E _____ Major (Key Signature: __ F# C# G# D# __ )

♫ **Note:** When using accidentals, a natural minor scale written **WITHOUT** a center bar line will use accidentals only in the ascending scale.

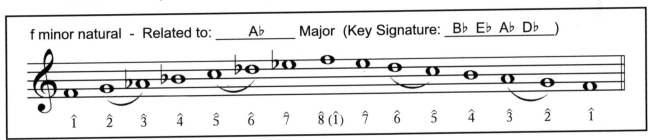

f minor natural - Related to: _____ A♭ _____ Major (Key Signature: __ B♭ E♭ A♭ D♭ __ )

♫ **Note:** "Semitone Slurs" are curved lines used to indicate the location of a semitone (half step). They do not have the same function as the slurs used in music that indicate to play smoothly. They are written under the notes and do not touch the noteheads.

1. a) Name the relative Major key. Name the sharps or flats in the Key Signature.
   b) Write the natural minor scale, ascending and descending. Use accidentals. Use whole notes.
   c) Mark the semitones (half steps) with a slur.

g minor natural - Related to: _____ Major (Key Signature: _____ )

f# minor natural - Related to: _____ Major (Key Signature: _____ )

## HARMONIC MINOR SCALES

A **HARMONIC MINOR** scale has the **SAME** Key Signature as its relative Major. In the harmonic minor scale the **7th** note is **RAISED** one chromatic semitone ascending and descending.

♫ **Note:** Find the 7 in the H.

When using a Key Signature, the raised 7th note is written with an accidental.

♫ **Note:** When using a Key Signature, a harmonic minor scale written **WITH** a center bar line will need an accidental in the ascending and descending scale.

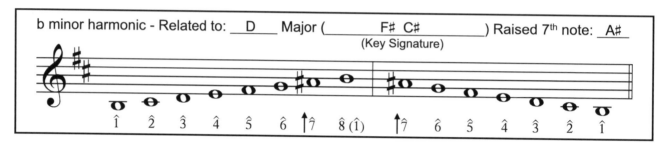

♫ **Note:** When using a Key Signature, a harmonic minor scale written **WITHOUT** a center bar line will need an accidental in the ascending scale.

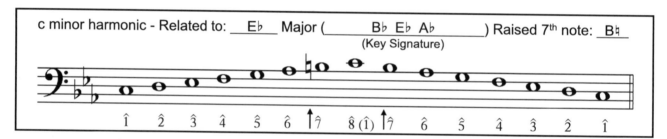

1. a) Name the relative Major key, the Key Signature and the raised 7th note of the harmonic minor.
   b) Write the harmonic minor scale, ascending and descending. Use a Key Signature and any necessary accidentals. Use whole notes.

g minor harmonic - Related to: _____ Major (_____) Raised 7th note: ____
(Key Signature)

f sharp minor harmonic - Related to: _____ Major (_____) Raised 7th note: ____
(Key Signature)

# HARMONIC MINOR SCALES - TONES (WHOLE STEPS) and SEMITONES (HALF STEPS)

**Harmonic Minor Scale Pattern:**

$\hat{1}$  tone  $\hat{2}$  semitone  $\hat{3}$  tone  $\hat{4}$  tone  $\hat{5}$  semitone  $\hat{6}$  tone + semitone  $\hat{7}$  semitone  $\hat{8}(\hat{1})$

In a **HARMONIC MINOR** scale, semitones are between degrees (notes) $\hat{2}$ - $\hat{3}$, $\hat{5}$ - $\hat{6}$ and $\hat{7}$ - $\hat{8}(\hat{1})$.

♫ **Note:** When using accidentals, a harmonic minor scale written **WITH** a center bar line will repeat the accidentals in the descending scale.

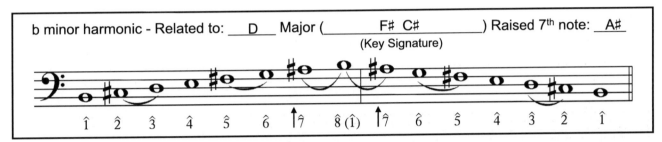

♫ **Note:** When using accidentals, a harmonic minor scale written **WITHOUT** a center bar line will only use accidentals in the ascending scale.

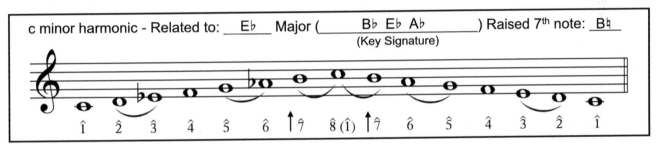

♫ **Note:** "Semitone Slurs" are written under the notes and do not touch the noteheads.

1. a) Name the relative Major key, the Key Signature and the raised 7<sup>th</sup> note of the harmonic minor.
   b) Write the harmonic minor scale, ascending and descending. Use accidentals.
      Use whole notes.
   c) Mark the semitones (half steps) with a slur.

c sharp minor harmonic - Related to: _____ Major ( _____ ) Raised 7<sup>th</sup> note: _____
(Key Signature)

d minor harmonic - Related to: _____ Major ( _____ ) Raised 7<sup>th</sup> note: _____
(Key Signature)

## MELODIC MINOR SCALE

A **MELODIC MINOR** scale has the **SAME** Key Signature as its relative Major. In the melodic minor scale, the **6th** and **7th** notes are **RAISED** one chromatic semitone **ASCENDING** and **LOWERED** one chromatic semitone **DESCENDING**. The descending melodic minor scale is the natural minor scale.

♫ **Note:** Find the 6 and 7 in the M.

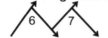

When using a Key Signature, the raised and lowered 6th and 7th notes are written with accidentals.

♫ **Note:** When using a Key Signature, a melodic minor scale written **WITH** a center bar line will use accidentals only in the ascending scale.

♫ **Note:** When using a Key Signature, a melodic minor scale written **WITHOUT** a center bar line will use accidentals in the ascending and descending scales.

1. a) Name the Key Signature, the raised 6th note and the raised 7th note of the melodic minor.
   b) Write the melodic minor scale, ascending and descending. Use a Key Signature and any necessary accidentals. Use whole notes.

c sharp minor melodic - Key Signature: _____ Raised 6th: _____ and 7th: _____

c minor melodic - Key Signature: _____ Raised 6th: _____ and 7th: _____

f minor melodic - Key Signature: _____ Raised 6th: _____ and 7th: _____

50

# MELODIC MINOR SCALES - TONES (WHOLE STEPS) and SEMITONES (HALF STEPS)

**Melodic Minor Scale Pattern:**
    **Ascending:** $\hat{1}$ tone $\hat{2}$ semitone $\hat{3}$ tone $\hat{4}$ tone $\hat{5}$ tone $\hat{6}$ tone $\hat{7}$ semitone $\hat{8}$ ($\hat{1}$)
    **Descending:** ($\hat{8}$) tone $\hat{7}$ tone $\hat{6}$ semitone $\hat{5}$ tone $\hat{4}$ tone $\hat{3}$ semitone $\hat{2}$ tone $\hat{1}$

In a **MELODIC MINOR** scale, semitones are between degrees (notes) $\hat{2}$ - $\hat{3}$ and $\hat{7}$ - $\hat{8}$ ($\hat{1}$) **ASCENDING** and between degrees (notes) $\hat{2}$ - $\hat{3}$ and $\hat{5}$ - $\hat{6}$ **DESCENDING**.

♫ **Note:** When using accidentals only, a melodic minor scale written **WITH** a center bar line will use accidentals in the ascending and descending scales.

♫ **Note:** When using accidentals, a melodic minor scale written **WITHOUT** a center bar line will use accidentals in the ascending and descending scales.

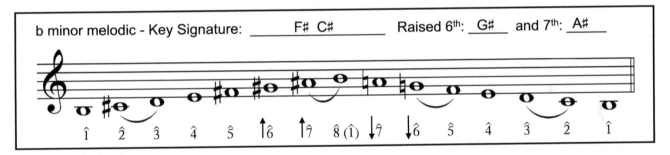

1. a) Name the Key Signature, the raised 6th note and the raised 7th note of the melodic minor.
    b) Write the melodic minor scale, ascending and descending.  Use accidentals.  Use whole notes.
    c) Mark the semitones (half steps) with a slur.


d minor melodic - Key Signature: _____ Raised 6th: _____ and 7th: _____


a minor melodic - Key Signature: _____ Raised 6th: _____ and 7th: _____

**MINOR SCALES with a DOUBLE SHARP**

There are **SIX MINOR SCALES** that contain a **DOUBLE SHARP** (𝄪). They are the harmonic and melodic minor scales of g sharp minor, a sharp minor and d sharp minor.

Harmonic minor scale: the 7th note is raised one chromatic semitone ascending and descending.

Melodic minor scale: the 6th and 7th notes are raised one chromatic semitone ascending and are lowered one chromatic semitone descending.

♫ **Note:** When a sharp is raised one chromatic semitone it becomes a **double sharp** (𝄪).

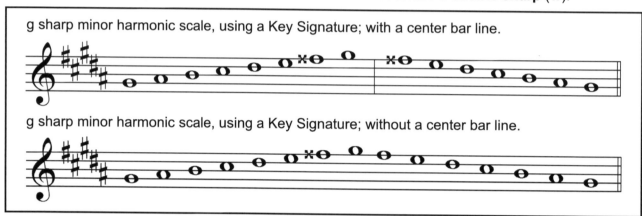

g sharp minor harmonic scale, using a Key Signature; with a center bar line.

g sharp minor harmonic scale, using a Key Signature; without a center bar line.

♫ **Note:** Scales may be written WITH or WITHOUT a center bar line. A center bar line CANCELS all accidentals but NOT the Key Signature.

1. Write the following scales, ascending and descending, using a Key Signature. Use whole notes.

    a) d sharp minor harmonic in the Treble Clef
    b) a sharp minor melodic in the Bass Clef
    c) a sharp minor harmonic in the Treble Clef
    d) g sharp minor melodic in the Bass Clef

a)

b)

c)

d)

# MINOR SCALES using ACCIDENTALS

**MINOR SCALES** may be written using **ACCIDENTALS** or a Key Signature.

**WITH** a center bar line: the center bar line **CANCELS** an accidental. Accidentals must be written in the ascending AND descending scale.

**WITHOUT** a center bar line: accidentals are written in the ascending scale; only accidentals for the lowered 6th and 7th are repeated in the descending scale.

♫ **Note:** When lowering a double sharp one chromatic semitone (half step), it becomes a **sharp**.

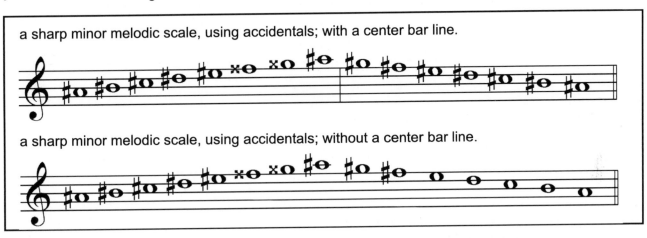

a sharp minor melodic scale, using accidentals; with a center bar line.

a sharp minor melodic scale, using accidentals; without a center bar line.

1. Write the following minor scales, ascending and descending, using accidentals.
   Use whole notes.

   a) a flat minor harmonic in the Treble Clef
   b) d sharp minor melodic in the Bass Clef
   c) g sharp minor melodic in the Treble Clef
   d) b flat minor harmonic in the Bass Clef

a)

b)

c)

d)

## TONIC MAJOR and TONIC HARMONIC MINOR SCALES

**TONIC MAJOR** and **TONIC HARMONIC MINOR SCALES** have the **SAME** Tonic (first) note. They are **NOT** related keys. They do **NOT** use the same Key Signature. The Tonic minor key will have the same Key Signature as its relative Major key.

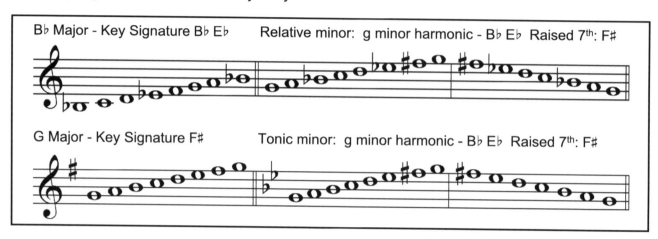

♫ **Note:** A Major scale and its relative harmonic minor scale have the SAME Key Signature.
   A Major scale and its Tonic harmonic minor scale have the SAME Tonic note.

1. Write the following scales using accidentals.  Use whole notes.
   a) Write the Major scale, ascending only.
   b) Name the Tonic minor key.  Write the Tonic harmonic minor scale, ascending and descending.

   a) F Major                    b) Tonic minor key: _____ harmonic minor

   a) D Major                    b) Tonic minor key: _____ harmonic minor

2. Write the following scales using a Key Signature.  Use whole notes.
   a) Write the Major scale, ascending only.
   b) Name the Tonic minor key.  Write the Tonic harmonic minor scale, ascending and descending.

   a) C♯ Major                   b) Tonic minor key: _____ harmonic minor

   a) A♭ Major                   b) Tonic minor key: _____ harmonic minor

# TONIC MAJOR and TONIC MELODIC MINOR SCALES

**TONIC MAJOR** and **TONIC MELODIC MINOR SCALES** have the **SAME** Tonic (first) note. They are **NOT** related keys. They do **NOT** use the same Key Signature. The Tonic minor key will have the same Key Signature as its relative Major key.

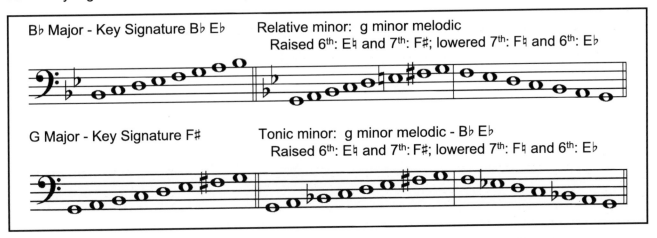

Bb Major - Key Signature Bb Eb    Relative minor: g minor melodic
Raised 6th: E♮ and 7th: F♯; lowered 7th: F♮ and 6th: Eb

G Major - Key Signature F♯    Tonic minor: g minor melodic - Bb Eb
Raised 6th: E♮ and 7th: F♯; lowered 7th: F♮ and 6th: Eb

♫ **Note:** A Major scale and its relative melodic minor scale have the SAME Key Signature.
A Major scale and its Tonic melodic minor scale have the SAME Tonic note.

1. Write the following scales using a Key Signature. Use whole notes.
   a) Write the Major scale, ascending only.
   b) Name the Tonic minor key. Write the Tonic melodic minor scale, ascending and descending.

   a) Eb Major                    b) Tonic minor key: _____ melodic minor

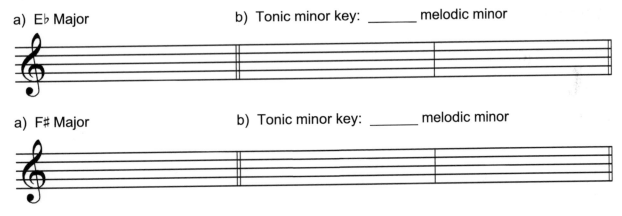

   a) F♯ Major                    b) Tonic minor key: _____ melodic minor

2. Write the following scales using accidentals. Use whole notes.
   a) Write the Major scale, ascending only.
   b) Name the Tonic minor key. Write the Tonic melodic minor scale, ascending and descending.

   a) G Major                     b) Tonic minor key: _____ melodic minor

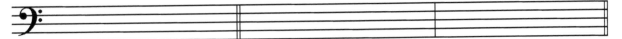

   a) B Major                     b) Tonic minor key: _____ melodic minor

# ENHARMONIC TONIC MINOR SCALES

**ENHARMONIC TONIC MINOR SCALES** are scales that use the SAME pitches but are written with notes using different letter names (enharmonic equivalents).

Example: b♭ minor scale and a♯ minor scale.

♫ **Note:** The Circle of Fifths contains three enharmonic minor keys:

b♭ minor and a♯ minor;  e♭ minor and d♯ minor;  a♭ minor and g♯ minor.

**Circle of Fifths**

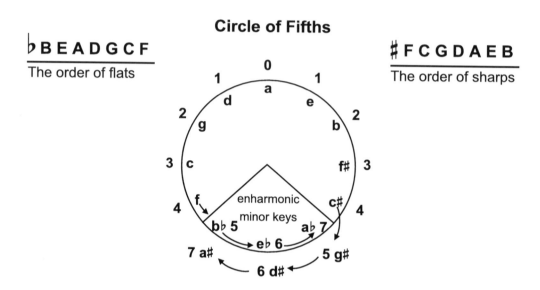

♭**BEADGCF**

The order of flats

♯**FCGDAEB**

The order of sharps

1. Name the enharmonic Tonic minor scale. Write the enharmonic Tonic minor scale, ascending and descending, using the correct Key Signature. Use whole notes.

   a) The enharmonic Tonic minor scale, melodic form, of a sharp minor is _____

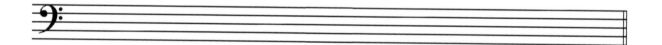

   b) The enharmonic Tonic minor scale, natural form, of e flat minor is _____

   c) The enharmonic Tonic minor scale, harmonic form, of g sharp minor is _____

# ENHARMONIC EQUIVALENTS - MAJOR or MINOR SCALES

**ENHARMONIC EQUIVALENTS** are the same pitch using different letter names.

1. Write the enharmonic equivalent names for each of the following keys directly on the keyboard.

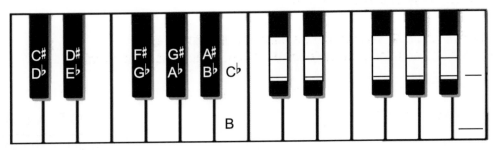

> **RELATIVE** Major and minor scales have the SAME Key Signature. They are related.
>   Example: Relative minor of C Major is a minor. Relative Major of c minor is E♭ Major.
>
> **TONIC** Major and minor scales have the SAME Tonic note. They are NOT related. Tonic Major and minor scales are also called parallel Major and minor scales.
>   Example: Tonic minor of C Major is c minor. Tonic Major of a minor is A Major.
>
> **ENHARMONIC TONIC** Major and/or minor scales BEGIN on the SAME pitch as the given key but use different letter names. They are NOT related.
>   Example: Enharmonic Major of D♭ Major is C# Major. Enharmonic minor of D♭ Major is c# minor.
>
> **ENHARMONIC RELATIVE** Major and/or minor scales BEGIN on the SAME pitch as the relative Major or minor of the given key but use different letter names. They are NOT related.
>   Example: Enharmonic relative minor of G♭ Major is d# minor.

2. For each of the following Major keys:
   a) Name the relative minor.
   b) Name the enharmonic relative minor.
   c) Name the enharmonic Tonic Major.

| Major key: | B | G♭ | C# | D♭ | F# | C♭ |
|---|---|---|---|---|---|---|
| a) Relative minor: | g# | ___ | ___ | ___ | ___ | ___ |
| b) Enharmonic relative minor: | a♭ | ___ | ___ | ___ | ___ | ___ |
| c) Enharmonic Tonic Major: | C♭ | ___ | ___ | ___ | ___ | ___ |

♫ **Note:** To determine the ENHARMONIC scale, first identify the name of the scale and then change the name to its enharmonic equivalent.

3. Name each of the following keys. Name the Key Signature of the new key.

   a) The relative minor of B Major is _____. Key Signature: _____

   b) The enharmonic relative minor of C# Major is _____. Key Signature: _____

   c) The Tonic minor of G Major is _____. Key Signature: _____

   d) The enharmonic Tonic Major of D♭ Major is _____. Key Signature: _____

   e) The enharmonic relative Major of d# minor is _____. Key Signature: _____

## KEY SIGNATURES in the ALTO CLEF and TENOR CLEF

♫ **Note:** The sharps and flats in the Key Signature for the Alto Clef are placed in the SAME directional position as in the Key Signatures for the Treble Clef and Bass Clef.

Key Signature placement in the **ALTO CLEF**

1. Write the following Key Signatures in the Alto Clef.

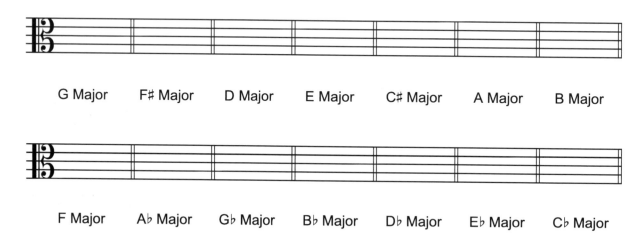

G Major    F♯ Major    D Major    E Major    C♯ Major    A Major    B Major

F Major    A♭ Major    G♭ Major    B♭ Major    D♭ Major    E♭ Major    C♭ Major

♫ **Note:** The sharps and flats in the Key Signature for the Tenor Clef are placed in the same directional position as the FLATS in the Tenor Clef, Treble Clef and Bass Clef.

Key Signature placement written in the **TENOR CLEF**

2. Write the following Key Signatures in the Tenor Clef.

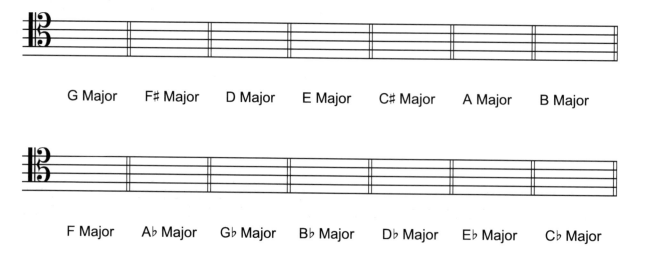

G Major    F♯ Major    D Major    E Major    C♯ Major    A Major    B Major

F Major    A♭ Major    G♭ Major    B♭ Major    D♭ Major    E♭ Major    C♭ Major

58

## WRITING SCALES in the ALTO CLEF and TENOR CLEF

When **WRITING SCALES** in the **ALTO CLEF** and **TENOR CLEF**, always place the Key Signature in the correct position on the staff.

♫ **Note:** Scales may be written WITH or WITHOUT a center bar line. A center bar line CANCELS all accidentals but NOT the Key Signature.

1.  Write the following scales, ascending and descending. Use the correct Key Signature.
    Use whole notes.

    a)  A flat Major in the Alto Clef
    b)  enharmonic relative minor, harmonic form, of C sharp Major in the Tenor Clef
    c)  f sharp minor natural in the Alto Clef
    d)  Tonic Major of e minor in the Tenor Clef
    e)  C flat Major in the Alto Clef
    f)  g sharp minor melodic in the Tenor Clef

a)

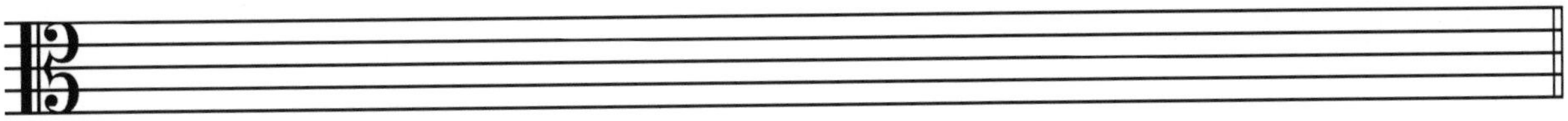

b)

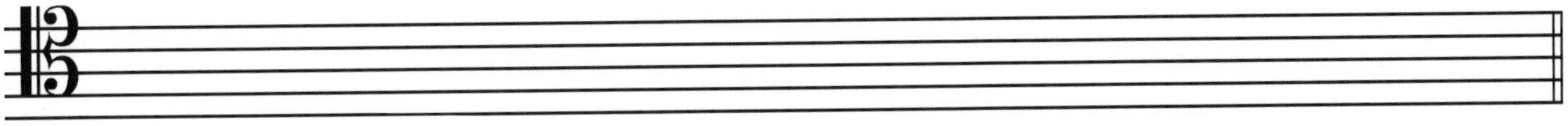

c)

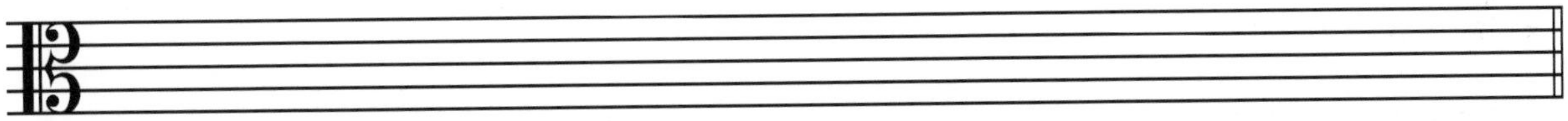

d)

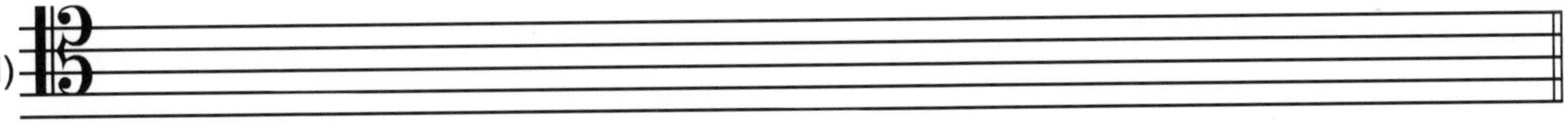

e)

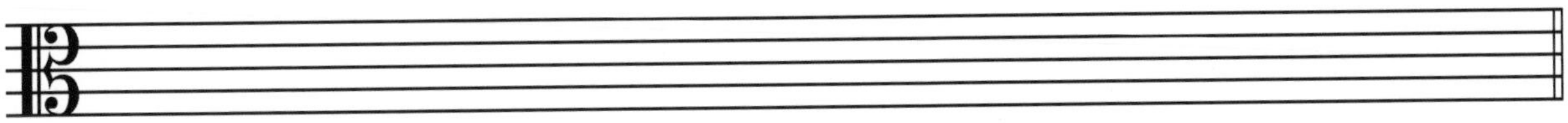

f)

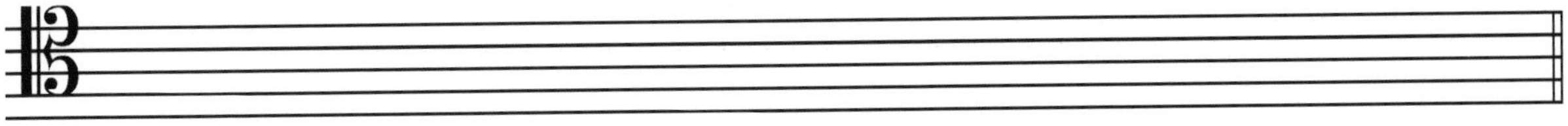

## TEMPO and CHANGES in TEMPO

**TEMPO** indicates the speed at which a piece is performed.  The tempo is written at the top left of the music above the Time Signature.  Tempo markings are usually indicated by an Italian term.

| Tempo | Definition |
|---|---|
| *adagio* | a slow tempo (slower than *andante,* but not as slow as *largo*) |
| *allegretto* | fairly fast (a little slower than *allegro*) |
| *allegro* | fast |
| *andante* | moderately slow; at a walking pace |
| *andantino* | a little faster than *andante* (moderately slow) |
| *comodo* | at a comfortable, easy tempo |
| *con moto* | with movement |
| *grave* | slow and solemn |
| *larghetto* | not as slow as *largo* (very slow) |
| *largo* | very slow |
| *lento* | slow |
| *moderato* | at a moderate tempo |
| *presto* | very fast |
| *prestissimo* | as fast as possible |
| *stringendo* | pressing, becoming faster |
| *vivace* | lively, brisk |

1.  Write the definition for each of the following tempos.

con moto: _____  grave: _____

larghetto: _____  andantino: _____

| Changes in Tempo | Definition |
|---|---|
| *accelerando, accel.* | becoming quicker |
| *allargando, allarg.* | broadening, becoming slower |
| *a tempo* | return to the original tempo |
| *calando* | becoming slower and softer |
| *fermata,* ⌢ | pause; hold the note or rest longer than its written value |
| *l'istesso tempo* | the same tempo |
| *meno mosso* | less movement, slower |
| *più mosso* | more movement, quicker |
| *rallentando, rall.* | slowing down |
| *ritardando, rit.* | slowing down gradually |
| *ritenuto, riten.* | suddenly slower, held back |
| *rubato* | with some freedom of tempo to enhance musical expression |
| *Tempo primo, Tempo I* | return to the original tempo |

2.  Write the definition for each of the following changes in tempos.

allargando: _____  ritenuto: _____

meno mosso: _____  calando: _____

# ARTICULATION TERMS and SIGNS

**ARTICULATION TERMS** and **SIGNS** indicate how a piece is performed.

| Articulation | Definition | Sign |
|---|---|---|
| marcato, marc. | marked or stressed | |
| martellato | strongly accented, hammered | |
| accent | a stressed note | |
| pesante | weighty, with emphasis | |
| legato | smooth | |
| slur | play the notes legato | |
| leggiero | light, nimble, quick | |
| staccato | detached | |
| sostenuto | sustained | |
| tenuto | held, sustained | |

♫ **Note:** An accent, slur, staccato or tenuto are written closest to the notehead and away from the stem. A staccato or tenuto may be written in the staff in order to be placed a space away from the notehead. A fermata is written above the staff.

1. Copy the music below, adding all the articulation and dynamic markings.

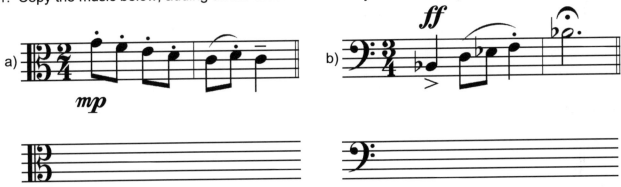

M.M. means "Maelzel's Metronome" (named after Johann Maelzel). The metronome indicates sound of regular beats and thus an exact tempo (the speed at which the music is played). The M.M. is indicated by a small note (equal to one beat) followed by the number of beats per minute, identifying the tempo. Example: M.M. ♩ = 100 - 104 indicates 100 to 104 quarter note beats per minute.

♫ **Note:** The Tempo and metronome marking (M.M.) are BOTH written above the Time Signature.

2. Analyze the following piece of music by answering the questions below.

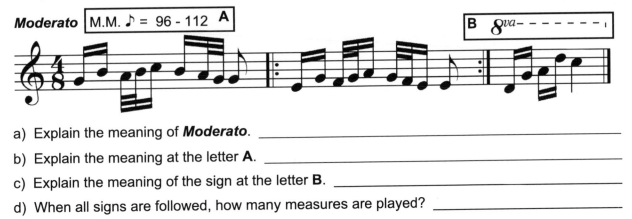

a) Explain the meaning of **Moderato**. _____

b) Explain the meaning at the letter **A**. _____

c) Explain the meaning of the sign at the letter **B**. _____

d) When all signs are followed, how many measures are played? _____

## STYLE in PERFORMANCE

| Italian Term | Definition |
|---|---|
| *ad libitum, ad lib.* | at the liberty of the performer |
| *agitato* | agitated |
| *animato* | lively, animated |
| *brillante* | brilliant |
| *cantabile* | in a singing style |
| *con brio* | with vigor, spirit |
| *con espressione* | with expression |
| *con fuoco* | with fire |
| *con grazia* | with grace |
| *dolce* | sweet, gentle |
| *dolente* | sad |
| *espressivo, espress.* | expressive, with expression |

1. Write the definition for each of the following Italian terms.

| *con grazia* | *dolente* | *con fuoco* | *dolce* | *agitato* |
|---|---|---|---|---|
| | | | | |

| Italian Term | Definition |
|---|---|
| *giocoso* | humorous, jocose |
| *grandioso* | grand, grandiose |
| *grazioso* | graceful |
| *largamente* | broadly |
| *maestoso* | majestic |
| *mesto* | sad, mournful |
| *morendo* | dying, fading away |
| *scherzando* | playful |
| *semplice* | simple |
| *sonore* | sonorous |
| *sotto voce* | soft, subdued, under the breath |
| *spiritoso* | spirited |
| *tranquillo* | quiet, tranquil |
| *vivo* | lively |

2. Write the Italian term for each of the following definitions.

| grand, grandiose | sad, mournful | lively | sonorous | playful |
|---|---|---|---|---|
| | | | | |

| humorous, jocose | dying, fading away | broadly | simple | soft, subdued |
|---|---|---|---|---|
| | | | | |

# Lesson 3      Review Test

Total Score: _____
100

**1.** Complete the Circle of Fifths with Major keys and minor keys:

10
a) Write the order of flats on the top left and the order of sharps on the top right.
b) Write the Major keys around the outside of the Circle of Fifths in the correct order.
c) Write the minor keys inside the Circle of Fifths in the correct order.

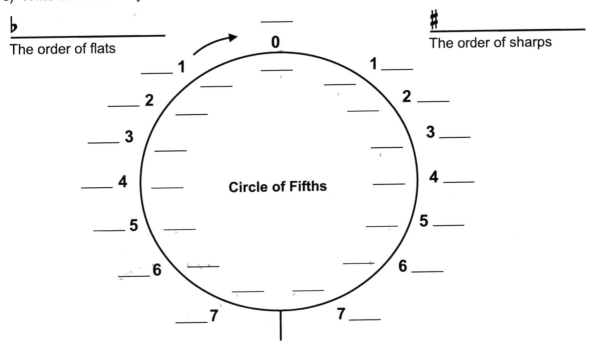

♭ _____
The order of flats

♯ _____
The order of sharps

Circle of Fifths

**2.** Write the following notes **ABOVE** the **Treble Clef**. Use ledger lines. Use dotted half notes.

10

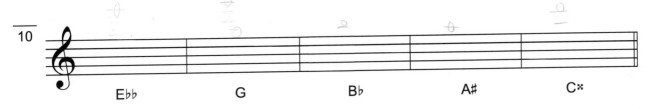

E♭♭      G      B♭      A♯      C✕

**3.** Raise the following notes a chromatic whole tone (whole step). **DO NOT** change the letter name.

10

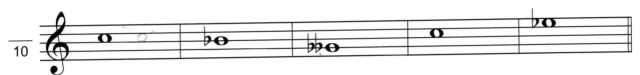

**4.** Name each of the following as: **d.s.** (diatonic semitone), **c.s.** (chromatic semitone),
**w.t.** (whole tone)    or    **e.e.** (enharmonic equivalent).

10

_____     _____     _____     _____     _____

**5.** Match each musical term or sign with the English definition.  (Not all definitions will be used.)

| | |
|---|---|
| **Term** | **Definition** |

10

| Term | | Definition |
|---|---|---|
| andantino | _____ | a) very slow |
| con pedale, ped. | _____ | b) becoming softer |
| diminuendo, dim. | _____ | c) return to the original tempo |
| a tempo | _____ | d) moderately loud |
| mezzo forte, *mf* | _____ | e) a little faster than *andante* |
| largo | _____ | f) with pedal |
| staccato, | _____ | g) right hand |
| mano destra, M.D. | _____ | h) detached |
| fine | _____ | i) without |
| pianissimo, *pp* | _____ | j) the end |
| | | k) very soft |

**6.** Write the following scales, ascending and descending, using the correct **KEY SIGNATURE**. Use whole notes.

10
a) Tonic minor, melodic form, of B flat Major in the Treble Clef
b) relative minor, harmonic form, of C sharp Major in the Bass Clef
c) enharmonic relative minor, natural form, of C flat Major in the Tenor Clef
d) enharmonic Tonic minor, melodic form, of e flat minor in the Alto Clef
e) enharmonic Tonic Major of C sharp Major in the Bass Clef

a)

b)

c)

d)

e)

**7.** Add **ONE REST** below each bracket to complete the measure. Cross off the count as each beat is completed.

Use the following rests:

**8.** Rewrite the following melody at the **SAME PITCH** in the Alto Clef.

# Alone

9.  a) Name the **MINOR KEY** for each of the following Key Signatures.
    b) Name the notes.

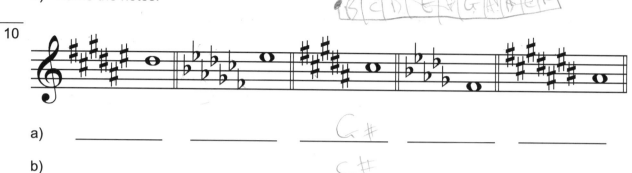

10

a) _____   _____   G#   _____   _____

b) _____   _____   C#   _____   _____


10. Analyze the following piece by answering the questions below.

10

# Lizzie the Lizard

*Giocoso*

E. Sakowsky

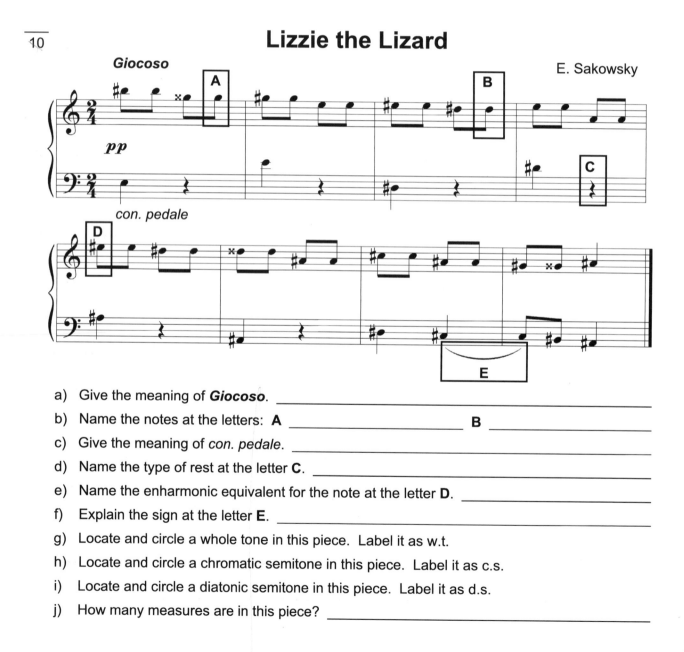

*con. pedale*

a)  Give the meaning of **Giocoso**. _____

b)  Name the notes at the letters: **A** _____  **B** _____

c)  Give the meaning of *con. pedale*. _____

d)  Name the type of rest at the letter **C**. _____

e)  Name the enharmonic equivalent for the note at the letter **D**. _____

f)  Explain the sign at the letter **E**. _____

g)  Locate and circle a whole tone in this piece.  Label it as w.t.

h)  Locate and circle a chromatic semitone in this piece.  Label it as c.s.

i)  Locate and circle a diatonic semitone in this piece.  Label it as d.s.

j)  How many measures are in this piece? _____

# Lesson 4    Technical Degree Names, Scales and Transposing

**TECHNICAL DEGREE NAMES** are used to identify the degrees of a scale.

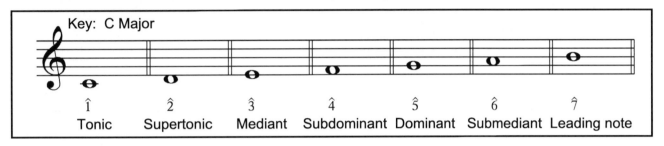

♫ **Note:** When identifying the technical degree name, start at the Tonic and count UP to determine the scale degree.

1.  Write the technical degree name for each degree of the scale.

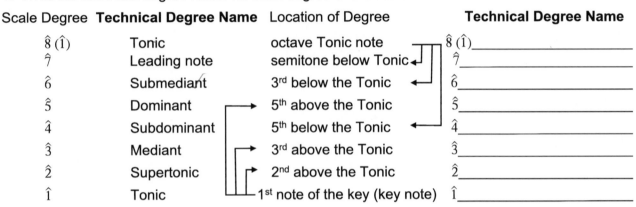

♫ **Note:** The Leading note is a semitone (half step) below the Tonic. In the natural minor scale the $\hat{7}$ degree is a whole tone (whole step) below the Tonic and is called the **SUBTONIC**.

2.  For each of the following, name the: a) Major key.    b) technical degree name for each note.

a)    ___C# Major___    _____    _____    _____    _____

b)    ___Supertonic___    _____    _____    _____    _____

3.  For each of the following, name the: a) minor key.    b) technical degree name for each note.

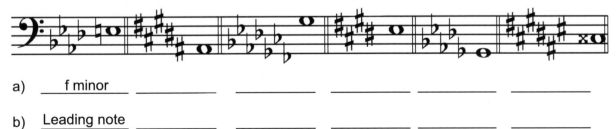

a)    ___f minor___    _____    _____    _____    _____

b)    ___Leading note___    _____    _____    _____    _____

67

**TECHNICAL DEGREES and SCALES**

**SCALES** may begin on any degree (note) of the scale. **TECHNICAL DEGREE NAMES** are used to identify each degree of a scale. Scales may be written with or without a center bar line.

1. Write the technical degree name for each degree of the scale.

| Scale Degree | **Technical Degree Name** | Location of Degree |
|---|---|---|
| $\hat{8}$ | _____ | octave Tonic note |
| $\hat{7}$ | _____ | semitone below Tonic |
| $\hat{6}$ | _____ | 3rd below the Tonic |
| $\hat{5}$ | _____ | 5th above the Tonic |
| $\hat{4}$ | _____ | 5th below the Tonic |
| $\hat{3}$ | _____ | 3rd above the Tonic |
| $\hat{2}$ | _____ | 2nd above the Tonic |
| $\hat{1}$ | _____ | 1st note of the key (Key note) |

♫ **Note:** When writing a scale, begin and end on the same technical degree. A **circumflex** " ^ " or **caret** sign (hat) above a number ( $\hat{3}$ ) indicates the degree number of the scale.

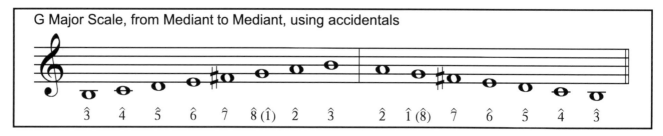

G Major Scale, from Mediant to Mediant, using accidentals

$\hat{3}$ $\hat{4}$ $\hat{5}$ $\hat{6}$ $\hat{7}$ $\hat{8}(\hat{1})$ $\hat{2}$ $\hat{3}$ $\hat{2}$ $\hat{1}(\hat{8})$ $\hat{7}$ $\hat{6}$ $\hat{5}$ $\hat{4}$ $\hat{3}$

2. Write the following scales, ascending and descending, using accidentals. Use whole notes.

a) D Major Scale, from Mediant to Mediant, in the Alto Clef

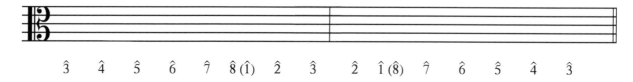

$\hat{3}$ $\hat{4}$ $\hat{5}$ $\hat{6}$ $\hat{7}$ $\hat{8}(\hat{1})$ $\hat{2}$ $\hat{3}$ $\hat{2}$ $\hat{1}(\hat{8})$ $\hat{7}$ $\hat{6}$ $\hat{5}$ $\hat{4}$ $\hat{3}$

b) B flat Major Scale, from Dominant to Dominant, in the Treble Clef

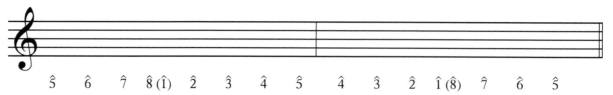

$\hat{5}$ $\hat{6}$ $\hat{7}$ $\hat{8}(\hat{1})$ $\hat{2}$ $\hat{3}$ $\hat{4}$ $\hat{5}$ $\hat{4}$ $\hat{3}$ $\hat{2}$ $\hat{1}(\hat{8})$ $\hat{7}$ $\hat{6}$ $\hat{5}$

c) E Major Scale, from Submediant to Submediant, in the Tenor Clef

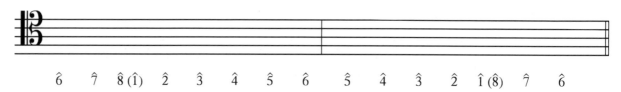

$\hat{6}$ $\hat{7}$ $\hat{8}(\hat{1})$ $\hat{2}$ $\hat{3}$ $\hat{4}$ $\hat{5}$ $\hat{6}$ $\hat{5}$ $\hat{4}$ $\hat{3}$ $\hat{2}$ $\hat{1}(\hat{8})$ $\hat{7}$ $\hat{6}$

# HARMONIC MINOR SCALES

A **HARMONIC MINOR SCALE** will use an accidental for the raised 7th note (the Leading note). When writing a harmonic minor scale starting on a scale degree other than the Tonic note, the raised 7th note ( $\uparrow\hat{7}$ ) is counted UP from the TONIC and not from the first note written for the scale.

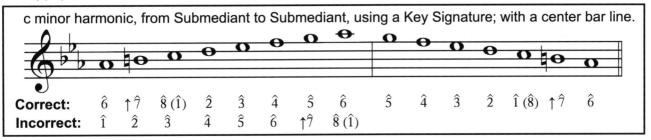

c minor harmonic, from Submediant to Submediant, using a Key Signature; with a center bar line.

| | | | | | | | | | | | | | | | |
|---|---|---|---|---|---|---|---|---|---|---|---|---|---|---|---|
| **Correct:** | $\hat{6}$ | $\uparrow\hat{7}$ | $\hat{8}\,(\hat{1})$ | $\hat{2}$ | $\hat{3}$ | $\hat{4}$ | $\hat{5}$ | $\hat{6}$ | $\hat{5}$ | $\hat{4}$ | $\hat{3}$ | $\hat{2}$ | $\hat{1}\,(8)$ | $\uparrow\hat{7}$ | $\hat{6}$ |
| **Incorrect:** | $\hat{1}$ | $\hat{2}$ | $\hat{3}$ | $\hat{4}$ | $\hat{5}$ | $\hat{6}$ | $\uparrow\hat{7}$ | $\hat{8}\,(\hat{1})$ | | | | | | | |

♫ **Note:** When writing a harmonic minor scale beginning on the LEADING NOTE, an accidental is required for the raised 7th note ( $\uparrow\hat{7}$ ) for BOTH the lower and upper Leading note.

1. Write the following harmonic minor scales, ascending and descending, using a Key Signature. Use whole notes. Write the scale degree number below each note.

   a) f sharp minor harmonic, from Leading note to Leading note, in the Treble Clef

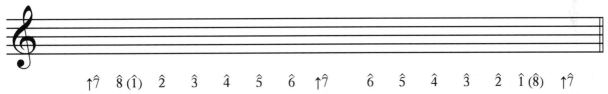

   $\uparrow\hat{7}$   $\hat{8}\,(\hat{1})$   $\hat{2}$   $\hat{3}$   $\hat{4}$   $\hat{5}$   $\hat{6}$   $\uparrow\hat{7}$   $\hat{6}$   $\hat{5}$   $\hat{4}$   $\hat{3}$   $\hat{2}$   $\hat{1}\,(8)$   $\uparrow\hat{7}$

   b) g minor harmonic, from Supertonic to Supertonic, in the Alto Clef

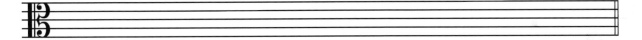

   c) a minor harmonic, from Subdominant to Subdominant, in the Tenor Clef

   d) b flat minor harmonic, from Mediant to Mediant, in the Treble Clef

♫ **Note:** The Leading note is a semitone below the Tonic. In the Natural minor scale the $\hat{7}$ degree is a whole tone below the Tonic and is called the **SUBTONIC**.

   e) d minor natural, from Subtonic to Subtonic, in the Bass Clef

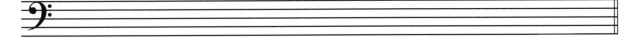

## MELODIC MINOR SCALES

When writing a **MELODIC MINOR SCALE**, the raised 6th and 7th notes are counted UP from the Tonic.

If the scale begins on the Submediant (6th degree), the raised 6th and 7th notes ( ↑6̂ ↑7̂ ) will be the first and second notes of the scale. The upper raised 6th degree is repeated - lowered at the beginning of the descending melodic minor scale. The 6th and 7th are lowered at the end of the scale.

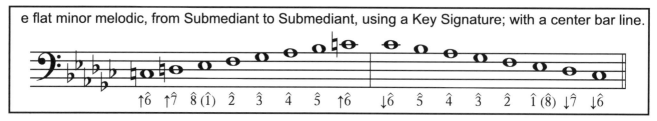
e flat minor melodic, from Submediant to Submediant, using a Key Signature; with a center bar line.

♫ **Note:** When using a center bar line, accidentals are not needed to lower the 6th and 7th notes. When NOT using a center bar line, accidentals WILL be needed in the descending scale.

1. Write the following melodic minor scales, ascending and descending, using a Key Signature. Use whole notes. Write the scale degree number below each note.

   a) c sharp minor melodic, from Submediant to Submediant, in the Alto Clef

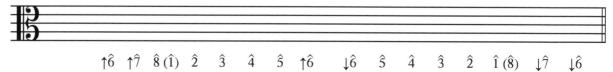

↑6̂ ↑7̂ 8̂(1̂) 2̂ 3̂ 4̂ 5̂ ↑6̂ ↓6̂ 5̂ 4̂ 3̂ 2̂ 1̂(8̂) ↓7̂ ↓6̂

   b) d minor melodic, from Submediant to Submediant, in the Treble Clef

♫ **Note:** When writing a melodic minor scale beginning on the LEADING NOTE, the raised 7th note is repeated - lowered in the descending melodic minor scale.

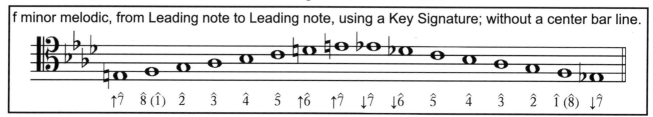
f minor melodic, from Leading note to Leading note, using a Key Signature; without a center bar line.

   c) a minor melodic, from Leading note to Leading note, in the Bass Clef

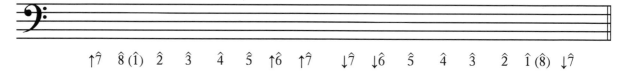

↑7̂ 8̂(1̂) 2̂ 3̂ 4̂ 5̂ ↑6̂ ↑7̂ ↓7̂ ↓6̂ 5̂ 4̂ 3̂ 2̂ 1̂(8̂) ↓7̂

   d) g sharp minor melodic, from Leading note to Leading note, in the Alto Clef

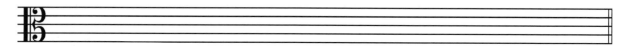

70

# MODES

A **MODE** is a '**SCALE**' primarily used in Gregorian chants. Modes originated with the ancient Greeks. A Mode has the same pattern of tones and semitones as a Major Scale. Each mode begins on a different degree of the scale.

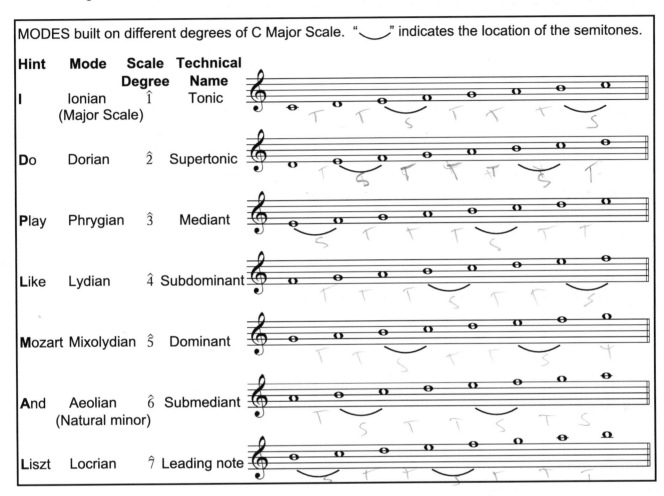

MODES built on different degrees of C Major Scale. "⌣" indicates the location of the semitones.

| Hint | Mode | Scale Degree | Technical Name |
|------|------|-------------|----------------|
| I | Ionian (Major Scale) | $\hat{1}$ | Tonic |
| Do | Dorian | $\hat{2}$ | Supertonic |
| Play | Phrygian | $\hat{3}$ | Mediant |
| Like | Lydian | $\hat{4}$ | Subdominant |
| Mozart | Mixolydian | $\hat{5}$ | Dominant |
| And | Aeolian (Natural minor) | $\hat{6}$ | Submediant |
| Liszt | Locrian | $\hat{7}$ | Leading note |

♫ **Note:** Use the "**hint**" sentence to remember the modes: **I** **D**o **P**lay **L**ike **M**ozart **A**nd **L**iszt.

1. Write the "Hint", Mode and Technical Name for each of the following scale degrees.

| Hint | Mode | Scale Degree | Technical Name |
|------|------|-------------|----------------|
| I | Ionian | $\hat{1}$ | Tonic |
| | | $\hat{2}$ | |
| | | $\hat{3}$ | |
| | | $\hat{4}$ | |
| | | $\hat{5}$ | |
| | | $\hat{6}$ | |
| | | $\hat{7}$ | |

71

## WRITING MODES

When **WRITING MODES**, use the "hint" sentence: **I** D**o** **P**lay **L**ike **M**ozart **A**nd **L**iszt. Write the letter name of the mode first, then count DOWN to determine the Tonic note of the Major Scale.

Mixolydian mode starting on E: work backwards from E, count down 5 to determine the Major scale.

Hint: **I** A **D** B **P** C# **L** D **M** E
     $\hat{1}$     $\hat{2}$     $\hat{3}$     $\hat{4}$     $\hat{5}$

E is the Dominant of A Major

( __A__ Major scale: starting on the _____Dominant_____ )

1. Write the note name of the mode. Work backwards to determine the Major key.
   Name the Major scale and the technical degree name of the first note of the scale.
   Write the following modes, ascending and descending, using accidentals. Use whole notes.

a) Dorian mode starting on E♭, hint: **I** **D** E♭
    $\hat{1}$   $\hat{2}$

( __D♭__ Major scale: starting on the _____ST_____ )

b) Phrygian mode starting on F#, hint: **I** **D** **P**
    $\hat{1}$  $\hat{2}$  $\hat{3}$

( __D#__ Major scale: starting on the _____med_____ )

c) Lydian mode starting on B, hint: **I** **D** **P** **L**
    $\hat{1}$  $\hat{2}$  $\hat{3}$  $\hat{4}$

( _____ Major scale: starting on the _____ )

d) Mixolydian mode starting on C, hint: **I** **D** **P** **L** **M** ( _____ Major scale: starting on the _____ )
    $\hat{1}$  $\hat{2}$  $\hat{3}$  $\hat{4}$  $\hat{5}$

♫ **Note:** The Aeolian mode is the natural minor scale starting on the Submediant of the Major scale.

e) Aeolian mode starting on A♭, hint: **I** **D** **P** **L** **M** **A** ( _____ Major scale: starting on the _____ )
    $\hat{1}$  $\hat{2}$  $\hat{3}$  $\hat{4}$  $\hat{5}$  $\hat{6}$

# IDENTIFYING MODES

When **IDENTIFYING MODES**, use the "hint" sentence: **I D**o **P**lay **L**ike **M**ozart **A**nd **L**iszt. Name the accidentals. Write the letter name of the Major key first, then count UP to determine the degree of the first note of the given mode.

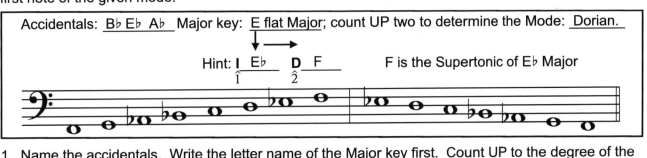

Accidentals: B♭ E♭ A♭  Major key: E flat Major; count UP two to determine the Mode: Dorian.

Hint: I  E♭  D  F   F is the Supertonic of E♭ Major
      1̂      2̂

1. Name the accidentals. Write the letter name of the Major key first. Count UP to the degree of the first note of the given mode.
   Identify the modes as: Dorian, Phrygian, Lydian, Mixolydian or Aeolian.

a) Accidentals: _____ Major key: _____ hint: I__D__P__
   Mode: _____                                   1̂   2̂   3̂

b) Accidentals: _____ Major key: _____ hint: I__D__ Mode: _____
                                                        1̂   2̂

c) Accidentals: _____ Major key: _____ hint: I__D__P__L__M__A__
   Mode: _____                                   1̂   2̂   3̂   4̂   5̂   6̂

d) Accidentals: _____ Major key: _____ hint: I__D__P__L__ Mode: _____
                                                    1̂   2̂   3̂   4̂

e) Accidentals: _____ Major key: _____ hint: I__D__P__L__M__
   Mode: _____                                   1̂   2̂   3̂   4̂   5̂

73

## MAJOR PENTATONIC, MINOR PENTATONIC and BLUES SCALES

A **PENTATONIC** scale (Penta means 5) consists of 5 notes plus the upper Tonic for a total of 6 notes.

A **Major pentatonic** scale is formed by taking a Major scale and omitting the 4th and 7th degrees.

A **minor pentatonic** scale is formed by taking the Major pentatonic scale beginning on the 6th degree.

♫ **Note:** A minor pentatonic scale is the natural minor scale, omitting the 2nd and 6th degrees.

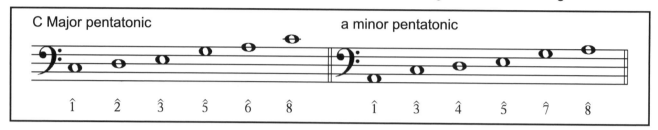

A **BLUES** scale has 7 notes and may be formed by taking a minor pentatonic scale and **ADDING** the "**blue note**". The blue note is the raised 4th or lowered 5th degree (enharmonic equivalents).

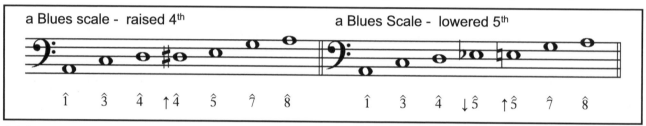

A **blues** scale may also be formed by taking a Major scale and omitting the 2nd and 6th degrees and lowering the 3rd, 5th and 7th degrees one chromatic semitone. The 5th note is repeated; first lowered one semitone, then raised one semitone. The blue note may be written as its enharmonic equivalent.

1. Identify the following scales as Major pentatonic, minor pentatonic or blues scale.

a) _____

b) _____

c) _____

d) _____

e) _____

f) _____

## OCTATONIC and WHOLE TONE SCALES

An **OCTATONIC** scale consists of 8 notes plus the upper octave note for a total of 9 notes. An octatonic scale is formed using alternating **T** (tones) and **ST** (semitones), beginning with either a tone or a diatonic semitone. Every letter name is used at least once.

♫ **Note:** Use the same letter name for the bottom and top note. Do not use an enharmonic equivalent.

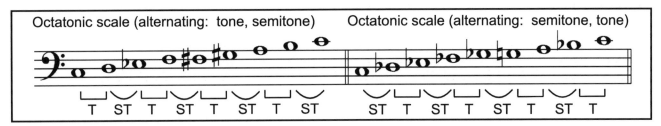

A **WHOLE TONE** scale consists of 6 consecutive whole tones. It has 6 different letter names plus the upper Tonic, for a total of 7 notes. A whole tone scale is written using sharps or flats (not both).

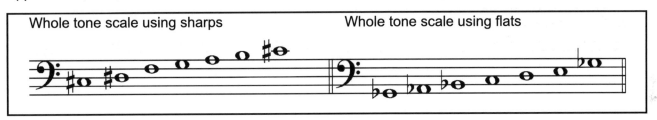

A **whole tone** scale, when using a keyboard, uses the group of two black keys or the group of three black keys. A whole tone scale omits (leaves out) one letter name. The SAME notes are used ascending and descending. Do not change the Tonic note enharmonically.

1. Write the following scales, ascending and descending, using accidentals. Use whole notes.

   a) whole tone scale starting on G

   b) whole tone scale starting on A flat

2. Identify the following scales as: Major pentatonic, minor pentatonic, blues, octatonic or whole tone.

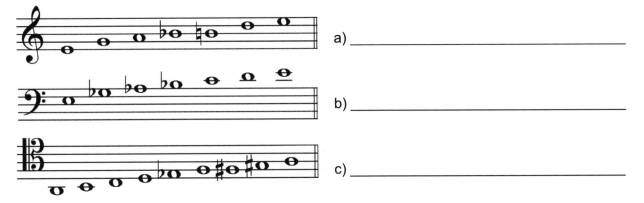

   a) _____

   b) _____

   c) _____

## HARMONIC CHROMATIC SCALES

A **CHROMATIC** scale uses all 12 semitones in the octave, for a total of 13 notes. A chromatic scale always begins and ends on the SAME Tonic note. Each letter name is used at least once, sometimes twice, but not more than twice in a row. A chromatic scale may be written using accidentals only or using a Key Signature of the Tonic note plus any necessary accidentals. A chromatic scale may be written with or without a center bar line.

There are two types of chromatic scales: **HARMONIC CHROMATIC** and **MELODIC CHROMATIC**.

A **HARMONIC CHROMATIC** scale has a set form. It uses a single Tonic, Dominant and upper Tonic note ascending, and a single Dominant and Tonic note descending. All other letter names are used twice. Double sharps or double flats may be necessary to write a letter name twice.

♫ **Note:** A bar line CANCELS an accidental. Rewrite the accidentals in the descending scale.

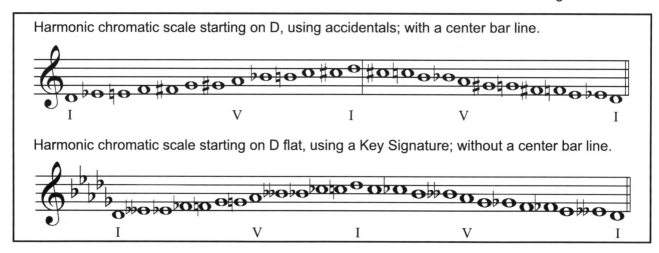

1. Write the following harmonic chromatic scales. Use whole notes.
   a) Write the notes first. Label the single Tonic (I) and Dominant (V) notes.
   b) Add accidentals to create the chromatic pattern.

   harmonic chromatic scale starting on B flat, using a Key Signature

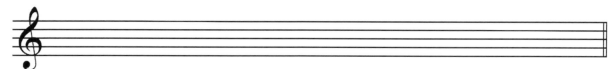

   harmonic chromatic scale starting on G sharp, using accidentals

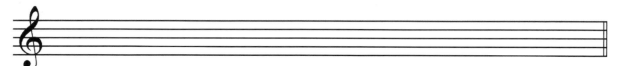

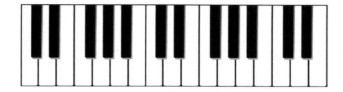

76

# MELODIC CHROMATIC SCALES

A **MELODIC CHROMATIC** scale does not have a set form.  One standard notation for writing a melodic chromatic scale is to raise the semitones on the way up (ascending) and lower them on the way down (descending).  There will be 5 single letter names and all other letter names are used twice.

♩ **Note:** If a scale begins on a flat, switch to sharps as soon as possible in the ascending scale.

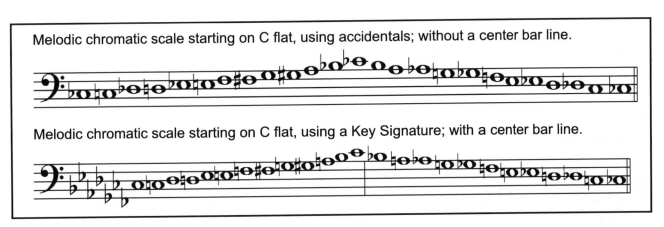

Melodic chromatic scale starting on C flat, using accidentals; without a center bar line.

Melodic chromatic scale starting on C flat, using a Key Signature; with a center bar line.

♩ **Note:** A melodic chromatic scale will not use the exact same notes ascending and descending.

A melodic chromatic scale may also be written based on the Major scale using a single note for the Mediant (III), Leading Note (VII) and upper Tonic (VIII) ascending, and Subdominant (IV) and lower Tonic (I) descending.  All other letter names will be written twice.

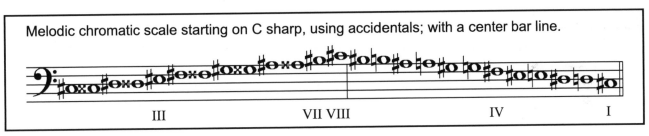

Melodic chromatic scale starting on C sharp, using accidentals; with a center bar line.

III          VII VIII          IV          I

♩ **Note:** Any standard notation that starts and ends on the same note and does not use any letter (degree) name more than twice in a row is considered correct.  Each letter name must be used at least once.

1. Write the following melodic chromatic scales.  Use any standard notation.  Use whole notes.

a) melodic chromatic scale starting on F sharp, using accidentals

b) melodic chromatic scale starting on E flat, using a Key Signature

**IDENTIFYING the KEY of a MELODY**

When **IDENTIFYING the KEY of a MELODY** use the following steps:

Step 1: Look at the **KEY SIGNATURE**. The Key Signature identifies the **Major** key or its **relative minor** key for the melody.

Key of D Major

    Key Signature:  2 sharps = D Major or b minor

Step 2: Look for **ACCIDENTALS**. A melody in a minor key WILL usually contain the raised 7$^{th}$ note of the harmonic minor scale.

Key of b minor

    Accidental:  A# = Raised 7$^{th}$ note of b minor harmonic

Step 3: Look at the **LAST NOTE**. A melody will often END on the TONIC note of the key.

Key of b minor

    Accidentals:  G# A# = Raised 6$^{th}$ and 7$^{th}$ notes of b minor melodic.  The last note is B.

♫ **Note:** A melody in a Major key will NOT usually contain the raised 6th or 7th notes of its relative minor key.

1. Name the Major key and its relative minor key for each of the following Key Signatures. Name any accidentals. Name the last note. Name the key of the melody.

Key: __F__ Major or __d__ minor    Accidentals __C#__    Last note __D__    Key of the Melody __d minor__

Key: ___ Major or ___ minor    Accidentals ___    Last note ___    Key of the Melody _____

Key: ___ Major or ___ minor    Accidentals ___    Last note ___    Key of the Melody _____

# FINAL NOTE of a MELODY

The **FINAL NOTE OF A MELODY** is not always the Tonic note.  Look at the Key Signature. Determine if the key is Major or minor by looking for accidentals (raised 7th note of the relative harmonic minor key, or the raised 6th and 7th notes of the relative melodic minor key).

♫ **Note:**  When naming the melody as a minor key, it is not necessary to identify it as harmonic or melodic.  The key is simply called minor.

1.  Name the key of each of the following melodies.

a)

Key:___a minor____

b)

Key:_____

c)

Key:_____

d)

Key:_____

e)

Key:_____

f)

Key:_____

## REPEAT SIGNS

A **REPEAT** sign is written as two **DOTS** (one in space 2 and one in space 3) in front of a double bar line (thin and thick bar lines).
A REPEAT sign indicates that the music is repeated from the beginning of the piece.
When there are **TWO** repeat signs, the music is repeated within the double bar lines.

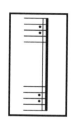

| Term | Definition |
|------|------------|
| D.C. | *da capo*, from the beginning |
| D.S. | *dal segno*, from the sign 𝄋 |
| D.C. al Fine | repeat from the beginning and end at *Fine* (the end) |
| D.S. al Fine | repeat from the sign 𝄋 and end at *Fine* (the end) |
| 𝄆 𝄇 | *repeat signs*: repeat the music within the double bars |

♩ **Note:** The sharps or flats in the Key Signature affect **ALL** the notes with the same letter name on the staff and on ledger lines .

1. For each of the following:
   a) Name the Major key.
   b) Name the notes in measures 2 and 3.
   c) Name the sharps or flats in the Key Signature.
   d) When all repeat signs are followed, how many measures are played?

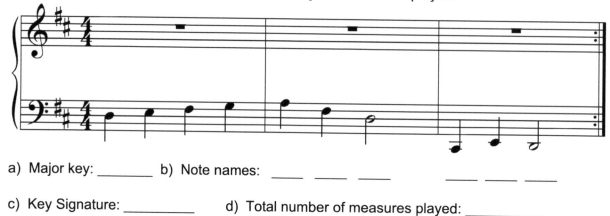

a) Major key: _____   b) Note names: ____ ____ ____    ____ ____ ____

c) Key Signature: _____    d) Total number of measures played: _____

♩ **Note:** 𝄴 Time is also known as **COMMON TIME**.  The symbol for Common Time is **C**.

a) Major key: _____   b) Note names: ____ ____ ____    ____ ____ ____

c) Key Signature: _____    d) Total number of measures played: _____

## FRENCH and GERMAN TERMS

**TERMS** are written directions given by a composer to the musician for performance of a piece of music. Terms or signs are usually written in **Italian**, but can also be written in **French**, **German** or **English**.

| French Term | Definition |
|---|---|
| *cédez* | yield; hold the tempo back |
| *léger* | light; lightly |
| *lentement* | slowly |
| *modéré* | at a moderate tempo |
| *mouvement* | tempo; motion |
| *vite* | fast |

1. Write the French term for each of the following definitions.

| tempo; motion | light; lightly | fast | slowly | a moderate tempo |
|---|---|---|---|---|

| German Term | Definition |
|---|---|
| *bewegt* | moving |
| *langsam* | slow, slowly |
| *mässig* | moderate, moderately |
| *mit Ausdruck* | with expression |
| *sehr* | very |
| *schnell* | fast |

2. Write the German term for each of the following definitions.

| with expression | very | fast | slow, slowly | moderate |
|---|---|---|---|---|

♫ **Note:** Repeat sign dots are written in space two and space three in front of a double bar line.

3. a) Write the measure number inside the square box above each measure.
   b) Rewrite the following melody at the SAME pitch in the Alto Clef.

# TRANSPOSING

**TRANSPOSING** means playing or writing music at a different pitch from the original by raising or lowering **ALL** the **NOTES** by the **SAME INTERVAL**.

♫ **Note:**   An interval is the distance in pitch between 2 notes.  An octave is an interval of an 8ᵗʰ.

A melody may be written one octave higher or one octave lower in the **same** clef or into an **alternate** clef.  The Time Signature and Key Signature of the transposed melody will remain the same as the original given melody.

♫ **Note:**   A Melody may also be rewritten at the SAME PITCH in an alternate clef.

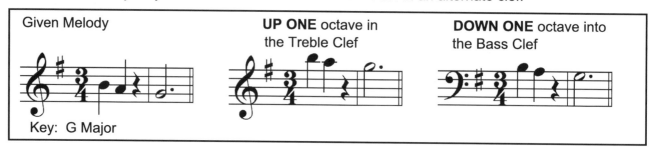

1. Transpose the melody down one octave in the Treble Clef.

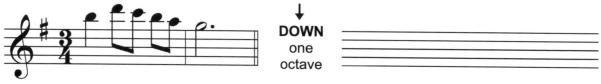

2. Transpose the melody up one octave in the Treble Clef.

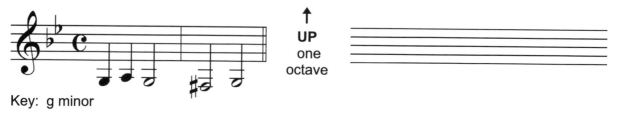

3. Transpose the melody down one octave into the Bass Clef.

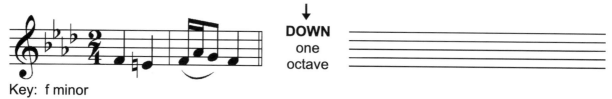

4. Rewrite the melody at the same pitch in the Bass Clef.

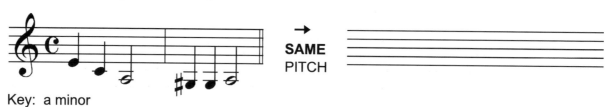

# TIPS for TRANSPOSING

**TIPS for TRANSPOSING:** Write the Clef sign, Key Signature and Time Signature. Correct the stem direction and add necessary accidentals. Write the dynamics below the Treble Staff and above the Bass Staff. Write all articulation (slurs, fermata, staccatos, etc.) in the correct position. When given, write the tempo, title and composer above the music.

♫ **Note:** When transposing up or down one octave, LINE notes become SPACE notes and SPACE notes become LINE notes. If BOTH the given melody and the transposed melody use LINE notes or SPACE notes, the melody has been transposed TWO octaves instead of ONE.

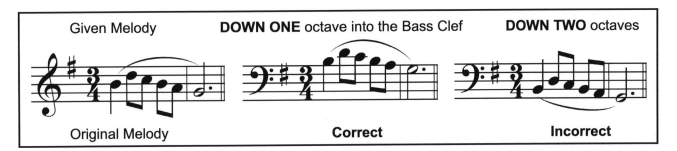

1. Transpose the melody up one octave in the Bass Clef.

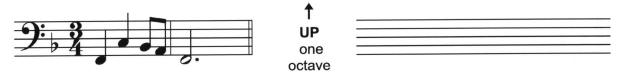

Key: F Major

2. Transpose the melody down one octave in the Bass Clef.

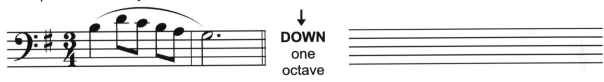

Key: G Major

3. Transpose the melody up one octave into the Treble Clef.

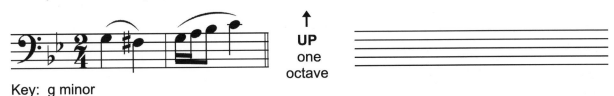

Key: g minor

4. Rewrite the melody at the same pitch in the Treble Clef.

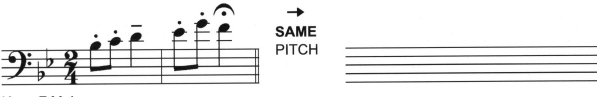

Key: F Major

# Lesson 4      Review Test

Total Score: ____
100

Write the Circle of Fifths on a blank piece of paper.  Use it as a reference when doing the review test.

**1.** Name the note below each bracket

10

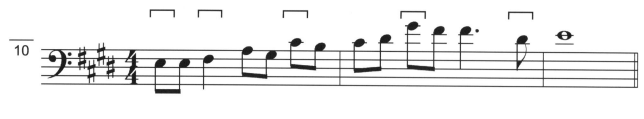

**2.** a) Name the following Major keys.
     b) Write the **TONIC** note for each Major key.  Use half notes.

10

**3.** a) Name the following minor keys.
     b) Write the **DOMINANT** note for each minor key.  Use quarter notes.

**4.** Write the following scales, ascending and descending, using **ACCIDENTALS** instead of a Key Signature.  Use whole notes.

10
     a) chromatic scale beginning on D flat (any standard notation) in the Treble Clef
     b) Lydian mode starting on A in the Bass Clef
     c) Dorian mode starting on C sharp in the Alto Clef

a)

b)

c)

**5.** a) Add **ONE REST** below each bracket to complete the measure.
   b) Cross off the count as each beat is completed.

1    2    1    2    1    2

**6.** Transpose the following melody down one octave in the **Bass Clef**.

**7.** For each of the following, name the: a) minor key.    b) technical degree name for each note.

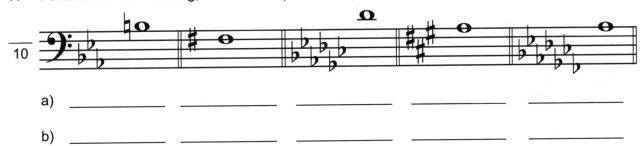

a) _____  _____  _____  _____  _____

b) _____  _____  _____  _____  _____

**8.** Match each musical term with its English definition. (Not all definitions will be used.)

| Term | | Definition |
|---|---|---|
| *quindicesima alta, 15ma* | _____ | a) stringed instruments: pluck the string instead of bowing |
| *risoluto* | _____ | b) be silent |
| *pizzicato* | _____ | c) first; the upper part of a duet |
| *arco* | _____ | d) a passage for the ensemble |
| *attacca* | _____ | e) continue in the same matter as just indicated |
| *con sordino* | _____ | f) two octaves higher |
| *primo, prima* | _____ | g) proceed without a break |
| *simile* | _____ | h) turn the page quickly |
| *tacet* | _____ | i) with mute |
| *tutti* | _____ | j) resolute |
| | | k) for stringed instruments: resume bowing after a *pizzicato* passage |

**9.** Name the following scales as whole tone, octatonic, Major pentatonic, minor pentatonic or blues.

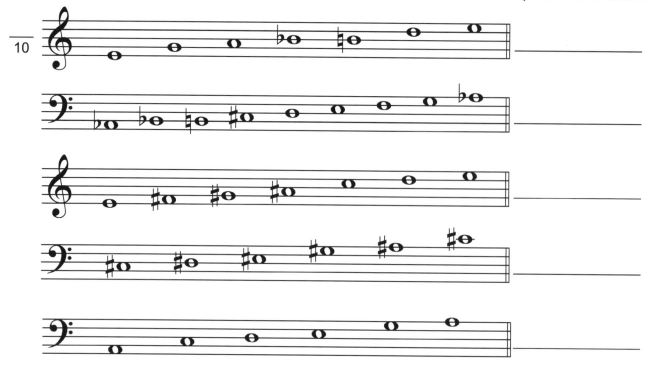

**10.** Analyze the following piece of music by answering the questions below.

# Twirling

S. McKibbon

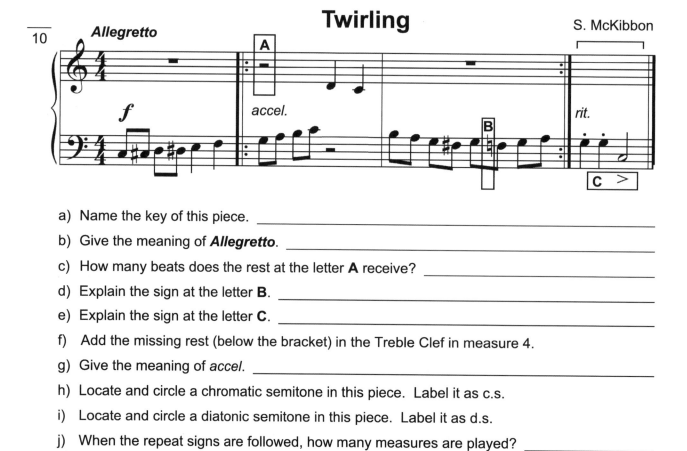

a) Name the key of this piece. _____

b) Give the meaning of **Allegretto**. _____

c) How many beats does the rest at the letter **A** receive? _____

d) Explain the sign at the letter **B**. _____

e) Explain the sign at the letter **C**. _____

f) Add the missing rest (below the bracket) in the Treble Clef in measure 4.

g) Give the meaning of *accel.* _____

h) Locate and circle a chromatic semitone in this piece.  Label it as c.s.

i) Locate and circle a diatonic semitone in this piece.  Label it as d.s.

j) When the repeat signs are followed, how many measures are played? _____

# Lesson 5     Time Signatures - Simple, Compound and Hybrid

## TIME SIGNATURES

A **TIME SIGNATURE** is written at the beginning of the music and is placed after the Key Signature. TWO numbers are used for a TIME SIGNATURE.

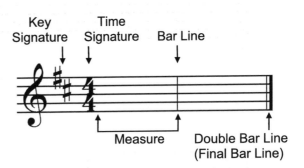

| 4 | The **TOP NUMBER** indicates how many beats in a measure. (Example: **4** - **FOUR BEATS** per measure) |
| --- | --- |
| 4 | The **BOTTOM NUMBER** indicates what kind of note equals one beat. (Example: **4** - a **QUARTER** note equals **ONE BEAT**) |

In **SIMPLE TIME** the **TOP NUMBER** is: **2**, **3** or **4**.

**2** "DUPLE"      **TWO** beats per measure

**3** "TRIPLE"      **THREE** beats per measure

**4** "QUADRUPLE"      **FOUR** beats per measure

The **BOTTOM** number indicates what kind of note equals **ONE** beat. This is called the **BASIC BEAT**.

**2**   **HALF NOTE**     =   **ONE** Basic Beat

**4**   **QUARTER NOTE**     =   **ONE** Basic Beat

**8**   **EIGHTH NOTE**     =   **ONE** Basic Beat

♫ **Note:**     **C**   is the symbol for **COMMON TIME**:   $\frac{4}{4}$ Time

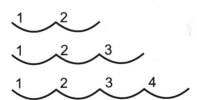   is the symbol for **CUT TIME** or **ALLA BREVE**:   $\frac{2}{2}$ Time

1. Top Number: Write the number of beats (2, 3 or 4) per measure for each Time Signature.
   Bottom Number: Draw the kind of note that equals one beat (half, quarter or eighth note).

$\frac{2}{4}$ = __2__ beats per measure
    = __♩__ note equals one beat

$\frac{3}{8}$ = ____ beats per measure
    = ____ note equals one beat

$\frac{3}{2}$ = __3__ beats per measure
    = __𝅗𝅥__ note equals one beat

**¢** = ____ beats per measure
    = ____ note equals one beat

$\frac{4}{4}$ = ____ beats per measure
    = ____ note equals one beat

$\frac{4}{2}$ = ____ beats per measure
    = ____ note equals one beat

## SIMPLE "DUPLE" TIME - TWO BASIC BEATS per MEASURE

A **GROUP** is a single note or rest, or a combination of notes or rests, that equal **ONE** BASIC BEAT.

1. a) Following the examples, scoop each beat.  Write the Basic Beat below each scoop.
   b) Add the correct Time Signature below each bracket.

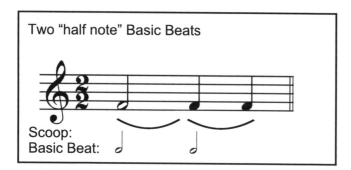

**2** two beats per measure
**2** a half note equals one beat

a)
Scoop:
Basic Beat:

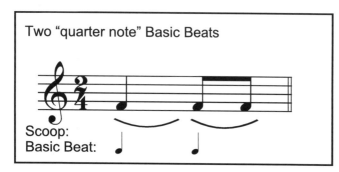

**2** two beats per measure
**4** a quarter note equals one beat

b)
Scoop:
Basic Beat:

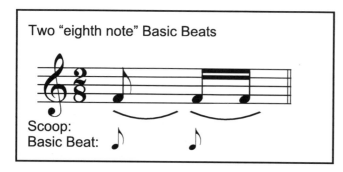

**2** two beats per measure
**8** an eighth note equals one beat

c)
Scoop:
Basic Beat:

2. a) Scoop each beat.  Write the Basic Beat below each scoop.
   b) Add bar lines.

88

## PULSE and ADDING RESTS in "DUPLE" TIME

In **"DUPLE"** Time, the **TOP** number is **2**: two beats (pulses) per measure. The **PULSE** is where the rhythmic emphasis falls in a measure. **Pulse**: **S** = **Strong**  **w** = **weak**

**Duple Pulse:**   **1 - Strong**   **2 - weak**

♫ **Note:** Use UPPER CASE **S** for Strong and lower case **w** for weak. When adding rests, complete ONE Basic Beat at a time.

1. a) Write the Basic Beat and pulse below each measure.
   b) Add rests below each bracket to complete the measure.
   c) Cross off the Basic Beat as each beat is completed.

♫ **Note:** Time Signature: The TOP number is the number of Basic Beats (equal groups) per measure. The BOTTOM number is what kind of note equals one beat (group). Look for equal groups.

2. a) Write the Basic Beat below each scoop.
   b) Add the correct Time Signature below each bracket.

Basic Beat:

## SIMPLE "TRIPLE" TIME - THREE BASIC BEATS per MEASURE

1. a) Following the examples, scoop each beat.  Write the Basic Beat below each scoop.
   b) Add the correct Time Signature below each bracket.

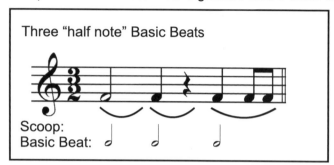

**3** three beats per measure
**2** a half note equals one beat

a)

Scoop:
Basic Beat:

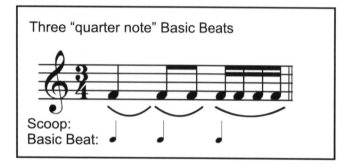

**3** three beats per measure
**4** a quarter note equals one beat

b)

Scoop:
Basic Beat:

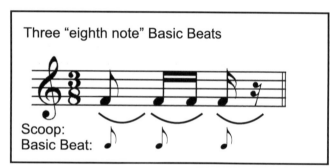

**3** three beats per measure
**8** an eighth note equals one beat

c)

Scoop:
Basic Beat:

♫ **Note:**  In $\frac{3}{2}$ time, a **whole rest** receives 3 beats of silence and is used for a whole measure.

In $\frac{3}{2}$ time, a **whole rest** receives 2 beats of silence for beats 1 and 2 (Strong - weak) when a half note value is on beat 3.

2. a) Scoop each beat.  Write the Basic Beat below each scoop.
   b) Add bar lines.

90

## PULSE and ADDING RESTS in "TRIPLE" TIME

In **"TRIPLE"** Time, the **TOP** number is **3**: three beats (pulses) per measure. The **PULSE** is where the rhythmic emphasis falls in a measure. **Pulse:   S = Strong    w = weak**

Triple Pulse:        1 - Strong     2 - weak    3 - weak

When adding **MORE THAN ONE REST** to complete ONE Basic Beat, build outward (forward or backward) from the given note. Add rests to each breakdown (part) of a beat to equal the time value of one Basic Beat.

1. a) Following the examples:  write the breakdown, Basic Beat and pulse below each measure.
   b) Add rests below each bracket to complete the measure.
   c) Cross off the Basic Beat as each beat is completed.

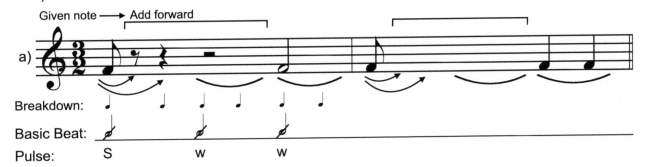

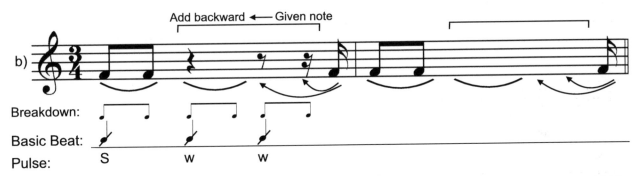

♫ **Note:**  When eighth notes or sixteenth notes are **BEAMED together**, they belong to the **SAME** group.  When they are **NOT beamed together**, they belong to **DIFFERENT** groups.

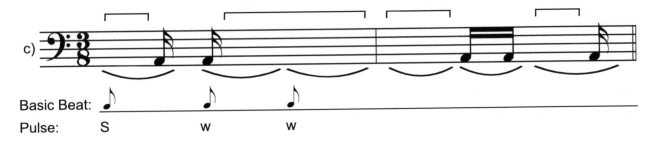

2. a) Write the Basic Beat below each scoop.
   b) Add the correct Time Signature below each bracket.

Basic Beat:

## SIMPLE "QUADRUPLE" TIME - FOUR BASIC BEATS per MEASURE

1. a) Following the examples, scoop each beat.  Write the Basic Beat below each scoop.
   b) Add the correct Time Signature below each bracket.

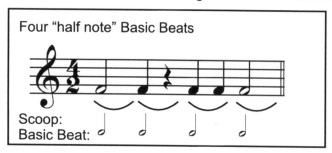

**4** four beats per measure
**2** a half note equals one beat

a)

Scoop:
Basic Beat:

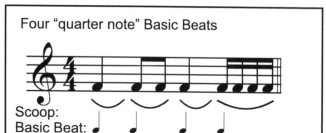

**4** four beats per measure
**4** a quarter note equals one beat

b)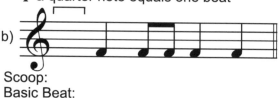

Scoop:
Basic Beat:

♫ **Note:**  **C** is the symbol for $\frac{4}{4}$ time, also called Common Time.

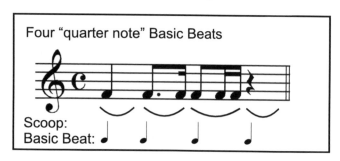

**C** = **4** four beats per measure
= **4** a quarter note equals one beat

c)

Scoop:
Basic Beat:

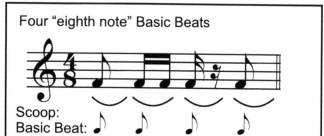

**4** four beats per measure
**8** an eighth note equals one beat

d)

Scoop:
Basic Beat:

♫ **Note:**  In $\frac{4}{2}$ time, the **BREVE** (double whole note: ‖o‖ ) or **BREVE REST** (double whole rest: ▬ )
   is equal to 4 beats (4 half notes).  The **WHOLE** rest is equal to 2 beats (2 half notes).

2. a) Scoop each beat.  Write the Basic Beat below each scoop.
   b) Add bar lines.

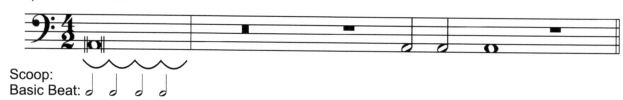

Scoop:
Basic Beat:

92

# PULSE and ADDING RESTS in "QUADRUPLE" TIME

In **"QUADRUPLE"** Time, the **TOP** number is **4**: four beats (pulses) per measure. The **PULSE** is where the rhythmic emphasis falls in a measure. **Pulse:  S = Strong    w = weak    M = Medium**

**Quadruple Pulse:  1 - Strong    2 - weak    3 - Medium    4 - weak**

---

**REST RULES:**
A Strong joins a weak into one rest (**S + w**).  A Medium joins a weak into one rest (**M + w**).
A weak can not be joined to a Medium or a weak.  It must use 2 separate rests (**w ~ M** and **w ~ w**).

---

The **plus (+)** sign indicates to **join** the Strong + weak (**S + w**) and the Medium + weak (**M + w**) pulses.

The **tilde (~)** sign (pronounced TILL-day) indicates to **NOT** join the weak ~ Medium  (**w ~ M**) pulses or the weak ~ weak (**w ~ w**) pulses.

♫ **Note:**  A whole rest fills a whole measure with silence and combines all pulses into ONE rest.
A Strong pulse is then combined with ALL the pulses into ONE whole rest.

1. a)  Add rests below each bracket to complete the measure.  The "+" sign indicates to join pulses and the "~" sign indicates to separate (not join) pulses.
   b)  Cross off the Basic Beat as each beat is completed.

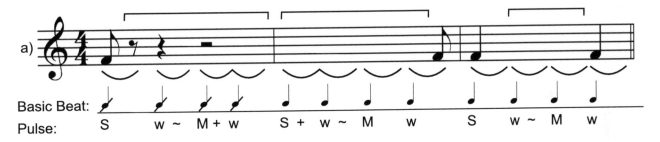

2. a)  Write the Basic Beat below each scoop.
   b)  Add the correct Time Signature below each bracket.

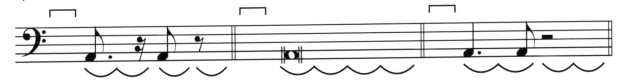

Basic Beat:

## WHOLE RESTS and BAR LINES

A **WHOLE REST** fills an entire measure of silence in **ANY** time signature.
The **TOP NUMBER** indicates the number of beats given to the **WHOLE** rest.

♫ **Note:** The exception to the rule is $\frac{4}{2}$ time in which a BREVE REST ( ▬ ) fills the whole measure.

1. Write the number of beats given to the rest in each measure.

2. a) Scoop each beat. Write the Basic Beat below each scoop.
   b) Add bar lines.

a)

Scoop:
Basic Beat:

b)

Scoop:
Basic Beat:

c)

Scoop:
Basic Beat:

d)

Scoop:
Basic Beat:

e)
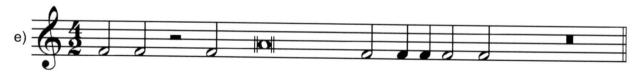

Scoop:
Basic Beat:

94

# COMBINING TWO BASIC BEATS using RESTS

When **COMBINING TWO BASIC BEATS** using rests:

A Strong pulse (beat) joins a weak pulse (beat) into one rest (**S + w**).
A Medium pulse (beat) joins a weak pulse (beat) into one rest (**M + w**).
A weak can NOT be joined to a Medium or a weak.  It must use 2 separate rests (**w ~ M** and **w ~ w**).

♫ **Note:**  A **WEAK** beat can **NOT** hold on to another beat.
        A weak beat (pulse) always stands alone.  w  ~  M  or  w  ~  w

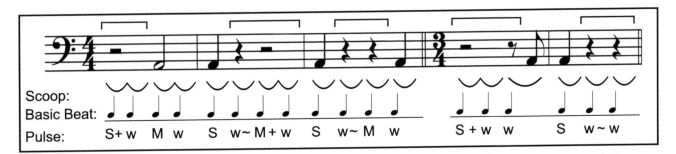

1. a)  Scoop each beat.  Add the "**+**" sign when joining pulses (S + w or M + w) and the "**~**" sign
       when not joining the pulses (w ~ M or w ~ w).
   b)  Add rests below each bracket to complete the measure.
   c)  Cross off the Basic Beat as each beat is completed.

95

# TRIPLET and the ANACRUSIS

A **TRIPLET** is indicated by the number "**3**" written above or below a group of three notes. A triplet is a group of three notes played in the time of two notes of the same note value.

1. Copy the chart below.

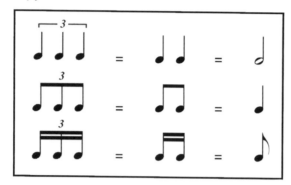 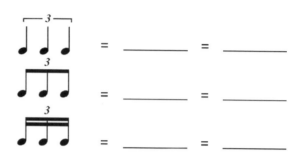

An **ANACRUSIS, PICK-UP** or **UPBEAT** is a note or group of notes in the FIRST incomplete measure at the beginning of the music. The LAST (final) measure at the end of the music will also be an incomplete measure. Together they equal one COMPLETE measure.

♫ **Note:** When numbering the measures, the first COMPLETE measure (not the anacrusis) is counted as measure number one. [1]

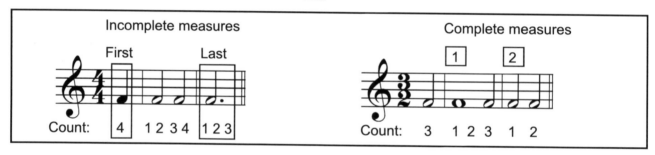

2. a) Add bar lines to complete the following rhythms.
   b) Write the counts under each measure.

a)

Count:       3

b)

Count:       4

c)

Count:       2

96

## ADDING TIME SIGNATURES and INCOMPLETE MEASURES

When **ADDING** a **TIME SIGNATURE**, the first measure may be an **INCOMPLETE MEASURE** (anacrusis or upbeat). Begin at the SECOND MEASURE to find the total number of beats.

♫ **Note:** If the first measure is an anacrusis, the beats in the first and last measures combined will equal one complete measure. The **LAST** measure will begin with the **Strong** pulse.

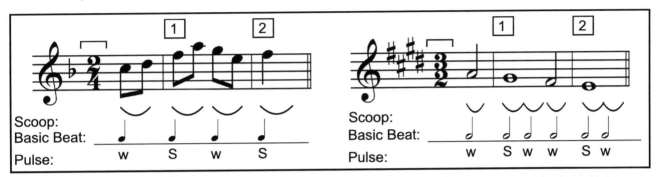

1. a) Beginning at the first complete measure, scoop each beat. Write the Basic Beat and pulse below each scoop.
   b) Add the correct Time Signature below each bracket.
   c) Write the measure numbers in the square box at the beginning of each measure.

## COMPLETING A BASIC BEAT with MORE THAN ONE REST

When adding **MORE THAN ONE REST** to complete **ONE BASIC BEAT**, start with the **GIVEN NOTE** and add the equal rest value to complete the beat.

1. a) Scoop each beat.
   b) Add rests below each bracket. Start with the given note and move forwards or backwards to complete one beat at a time.
   c) Cross off the Basic Beat as each is completed.

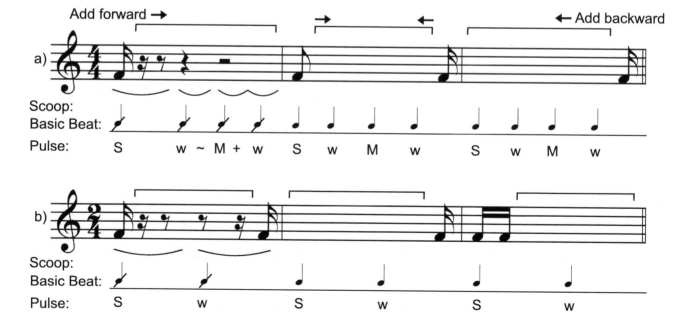

## ADDING RESTS

Before **ADDING RESTS**, determine if the Basic Beat is an eighth note, quarter note or half note.

♫ **Note:** The bottom number of the Time Signature determines the value of the Basic Beat.

1. a) Write the Basic Beat and the pulse below each measure.
   b) Add rests below each bracket to complete the measure.
   c) Cross off the Basic Beat as each beat is completed.

## ADDING BAR LINES

When **ADDING BAR LINES**, look for equal groups of the Basic Beat. Determine how many Basic Beats are in a measure. The first measure may be an anacrusis (incomplete measure).

♩ **Note:** A whole rest indicates silence for a whole measure in every Time Signature except for $\frac{4}{2}$. In $\frac{4}{2}$, a **BREVE REST** (◼) is used to indicate a whole measure of silence.

1. a) Add bar lines.    b) Write the Basic Beat and the pulse below each measure.

Basic Beat: _____

Pulse: _____

Basic Beat: _____

Pulse: _____

Basic Beat: _____

Pulse: _____

Basic Beat: _____

Pulse: _____

Basic Beat: _____

Pulse: _____

## ADDING TIME SIGNATURES

When **ADDING TIME SIGNATURES**, look for equal groups.  Determine how many Basic Beats are in a measure.

1.  Add the correct Time Signature below each bracket to complete the following rhythms.

2.  Identify if the rests under the brackets are CORRECT or INCORRECT.

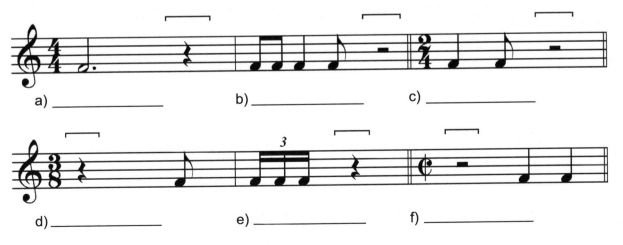

a) _____

b) _____

c) _____

d) _____

e) _____

f) _____

## SIMPLE TIME and COMPOUND TIME

In **SIMPLE TIME** the top number is **2**, **3** or **4**.  In **COMPOUND TIME** the top number is **6**, **9** or **12**.

♫ **Note:** Compound Time is always in groups of 3.  Three pulses equal one DOTTED pulse.
Three Basic Beats equal one DOTTED Compound Basic Beat.

| SIMPLE TIME | COMPOUND TIME (groups of 3) |
|---|---|
| Pulse: S = Strong   w = weak   M = Medium | Compound Dotted Pulse:<br>S• = Sww    w• = Mww    M• = Mww |
| Top Number:  Number of beats per measure | Top Number:  Number of beats per measure |
| **2**   S   w | **6**   Sww  Mww<br>S•   w• |
| **3**   S   w   w | **9**   Sww  Mww  Mww<br>S•   w•   w• |
| **4**   S   w   M   w | **12**   Sww  Mww  Mww  Mww<br>S•   w•   M•   w• |
| Bottom Number:  Basic Beat = 1 count<br>Bottom      Basic | Bottom Number:  Basic Beat = 1 count<br>Bottom      Basic   (group of 3)   = Compound<br>Number    Beat |
| **2**       𝅗𝅥 | |
| **4**       ♩ | **4**    ♩  ( ♩♩♩ )  = 𝅗𝅥• |
| **8**       ♪ | **8**    ♪  ( ♪♪♪ )  = 𝅘𝅥𝅮• |
| **16**      𝅘𝅥𝅯 | **16**   𝅘𝅥𝅮  ( 𝅘𝅥𝅯𝅘𝅥𝅯𝅘𝅥𝅯 )  = ♪• |
| Simple Time:<br>Basic Beat = one note (**NO DOT**) | Compound Time:  (group of 3)<br>Compound B.B. (Basic Beat) = one **DOTTED** note |

1.  Write one DOTTED pulse equal to each group of three pulses in $\frac{12}{8}$ time.  (S• w• or M•)

$\frac{12}{8}$    Pulse:    Sww      Mww      Mww      Mww

Compound Pulse:    S•_____    _____    _____    _____

2.  Write one DOTTED note (Compound B.B.) equal to each group of 3 Basic Beats.

Basic Beat: ♩♩♩          Basic Beat: ♪♪♪          Basic Beat: 𝅘𝅥𝅯𝅘𝅥𝅯𝅘𝅥𝅯

Compound B. B.: 𝅗𝅥•     Compound B. B.: _____        Compound B. B.: _____

# COMPOUND TIME:  DOTTED REST

A **DOTTED REST** is ONLY used in **COMPOUND TIME** and is used for complete GROUPS of three

1. Write one dotted rest below the bracket that has the same value as the dotted note in the measure.

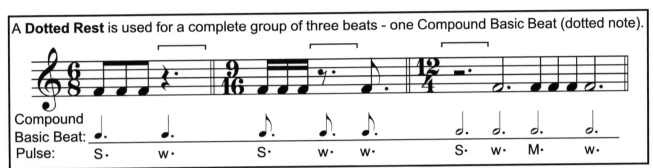

2. a) Add one dotted rest below each bracket to complete the measure.
   b) Cross off the Compound Basic Beat as each beat is completed.

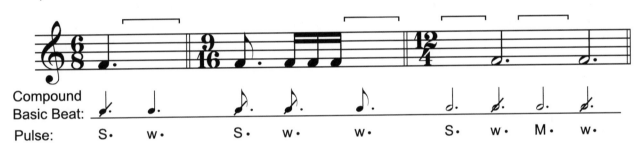

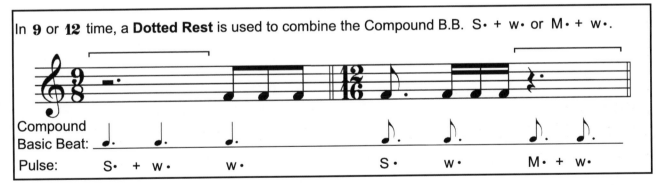

3. a) Add one dotted rest below each bracket to complete the measure.
   b) Cross off the Compound Basic Beat as each beat is completed.

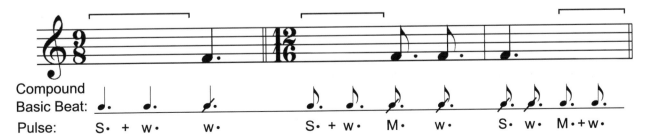

**SIMPLE "DUPLE" TIME and COMPOUND "DUPLE" TIME (TWO EQUAL GROUPS)**

In Simple Time each group will equal one Basic Beat. (one note - no dot)
In Compound Time each group will equal one Compound Basic Beat. (one DOTTED note)

1. a. Scoop the equal groups. Write the Basic Beat and (when necessary) write the Compound Basic Beat below each measure.
   b. Add the correct Time Signature below each bracket.

## COMPOUND "DUPLE" TIME (TWO GROUPS of THREE)

In $\frac{6}{4}$ time, there are 6 ♩ notes in each measure.  This is the Basic Beat.  These 6 ♩ notes are divided into 2 groups of 3 ♩♩♩ notes, and equal 2 ♩. notes.  This is the Compound Basic Beat.  2 x 3 = 6.

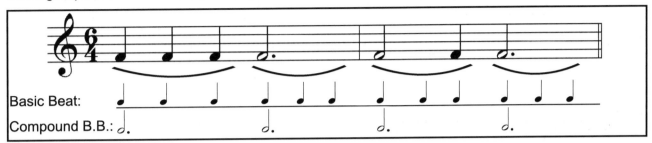

$\frac{6}{8}$ = 6 ♪ notes (Basic Beat); 2 groups of 3 ♪♪♪ notes = 2 ♩. notes  (Compound B.B.)

$\frac{6}{16}$ = 6 ♬ notes (Basic Beat); 2 groups of 3 ♬♬♬ notes = 2 ♪. notes  (Compound B.B.)

1. a) Scoop the equal groups.  Write the Basic Beat and Compound B.B. below each measure.
   b) Add the correct Time Signature below each bracket.

Basic Beat: _____

Compound B.B.: _____

Basic Beat: _____

Compound B.B.: _____

Basic Beat: _____

Compound B.B.: _____

Basic Beat: _____

Compound B.B.: _____

# SIMPLE "TRIPLE" TIME and COMPOUND "TRIPLE" TIME (THREE EQUAL GROUPS)

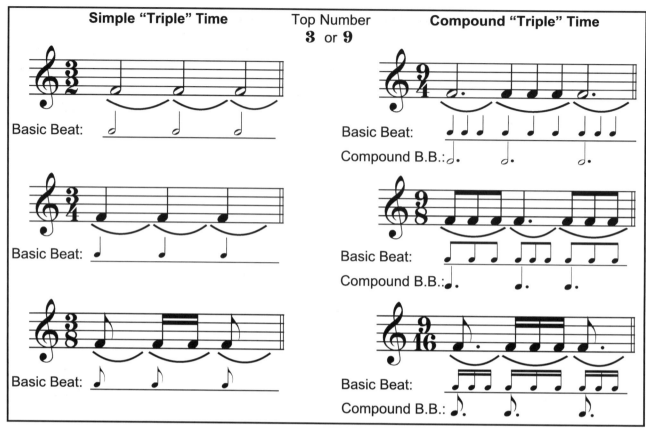

1. a. Scoop the equal groups. Write the Basic Beat and (when necessary) write the Compound Basic Beat below each measure.
   b. Add the correct Time Signature below each bracket.

a)

Basic Beat: _____

b)

Basic Beat: _____

Compound B.B.: _____

c)

Basic Beat: _____

d)

Basic Beat: _____

Compound B.B.: _____

e)

Basic Beat: _____

f)

Basic Beat: _____

Compound B.B.: _____

## COMPOUND "TRIPLE" TIME (THREE GROUPS of THREE)

In $\frac{9}{4}$ time, there are 9 ♩ notes in each measure. This is the Basic Beat. These 9 ♩ notes are divided

into 3 groups of 3 ♩♩♩ notes, and equal 3 ♩. notes. This is the Compound Basic Beat. 3 x 3 = 9.

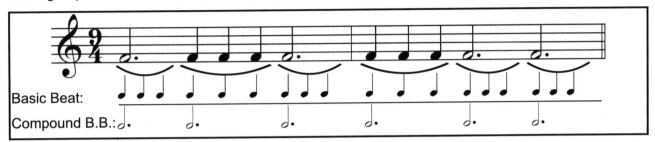

$\frac{9}{8}$ = 9 ♪ notes (Basic Beat); 3 groups of 3 ♫♪ notes = 3 ♩. notes (Compound B.B.)

$\frac{9}{16}$ = 9 ♪ notes (Basic Beat); 3 groups of 3 ♫♪ notes = 3 ♪. notes (Compound B.B.)

1. a) Scoop the equal groups. Write the Basic Beat and Compound B.B. below each measure.
   b) Add the correct Time Signature below each bracket.

Basic Beat: _____

Compound B.B.: _____

Basic Beat: _____

Compound B.B.: _____

Basic Beat: _____

Compound B.B.: _____

Basic Beat: _____

Compound B.B.: _____

## SIMPLE "QUADRUPLE" TIME and COMPOUND "QUADRUPLE" TIME (FOUR EQUAL GROUPS)

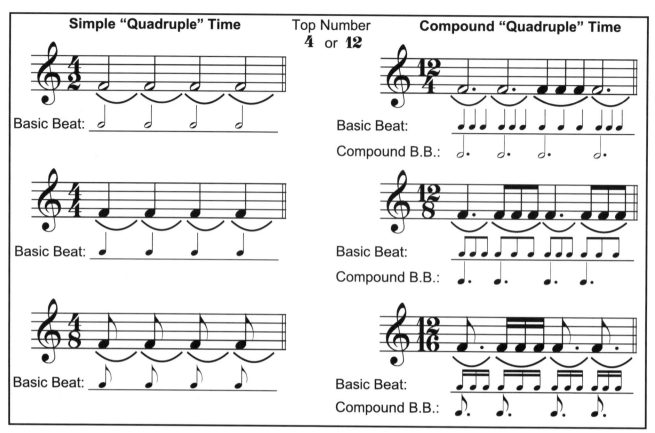

1. a) Scoop the equal groups.  Write the Basic Beat and (when necessary) write the Compound
   Basic below each measure.
   b) Add the correct Time Signature below each bracket.

a)

Basic Beat: _____

b)

Basic Beat: _____

Compound B.B.: _____

c)

Basic Beat: _____

d)

Basic Beat: _____

Compound B.B.: _____

e)

Basic Beat: _____

f)

Basic Beat: _____

Compound B.B.: _____

# COMPOUND "QUADRUPLE" TIME (FOUR GROUPS of THREE)

In $\frac{12}{4}$ time, there are 12 ♩ notes in each measure. This is the Basic Beat. These 12 ♩ notes are divided into 4 groups of 3 ♩♩♩ notes, and equal 4 ♩. notes. This is the Compound B.B. 4 x 3 = 12.

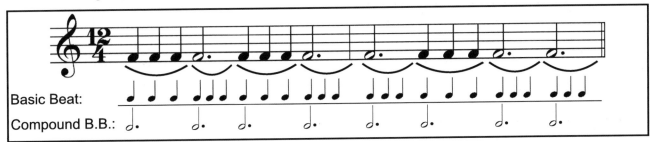

$\frac{12}{8}$ = 12 ♪ notes (Basic Beat); 4 groups of 3 ♪♪♪ notes = 4 ♩. notes (Compound B.B.)

$\frac{12}{16}$ = 12 ♬ notes (Basic Beat); 4 groups of 3 ♬♬♬ notes = 4 ♪. notes (Compound B.B.)

1. a) Scoop the equal groups. Write the Basic Beat and Compound B.B. below each measure.
   b) Add the correct Time Signature below each bracket.

a)

Basic Beat: _____

Compound B.B.: _____

b)

Basic Beat: _____

Compound B.B.: _____

c)

Basic Beat: _____

Compound B.B.: _____

d)

Basic Beat: _____

Compound B.B.: _____

109

## COMBINING BASIC BEATS and COMPOUND BASIC BEATS USING RESTS

| When **COMBINING BASIC BEATS** using **RESTS**: | |
|---|---|
| A Strong pulse joins a weak pulse or two weak pulses into one rest. | S + w   or   S + w + w |
| A Medium pulse joins a weak pulse or two weak pulses into one rest. | M + w   or   M + w + w |
| A weak pulse can NOT be joined to a Medium or a weak pulse. | w ~ M   or   w ~ w |

♫ **Note:  Plus (+)** sign: **join** the S + w (+ w) and M + w (+ w)
          **Tilde (~)** sign: do **NOT** join the w ~ M or w ~ w

1. a) Write the Basic Beat and pulse AND the Compound Basic Beat and pulse below each measure.
   b) Add rests below each bracket to complete the measure.
   c) Cross off the Basic Beat and the Compound B.B. as each beat is completed.

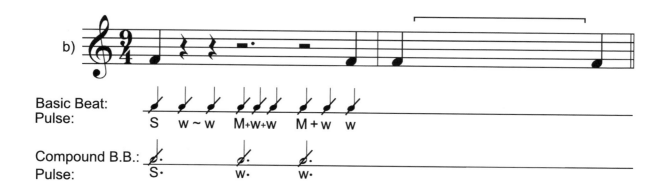

## ADDING RESTS in COMPOUND TIME

| When combining **COMPOUND BASIC BEATS** using **RESTS**: | |
|---|---|
| A Strong dotted pulse joins a weak dotted pulse into one rest. | S·+ w· |
| A Medium dotted pulse joins a weak dotted pulse into one rest. | M· + w· |
| A weak dotted pulse can NOT be joined to a Medium or a weak pulse. | w· ~ M· or w· ~ w· |

♫ **Note:** Plus (+) sign: **join** the **S·+w·** and **M·+w·**  Tilde (~) sign: do **NOT** join the **w·~M·** or **w·~w·**

1. Add rests below each bracket to complete the measure. Cross off the Basic Beat and the Compound Basic Beat as each beat is completed.

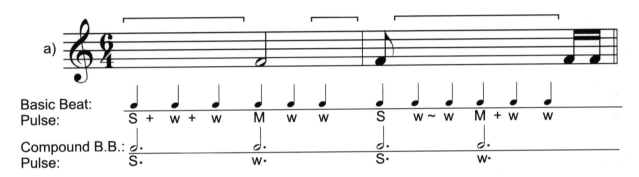

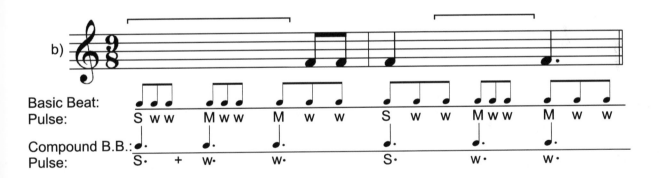

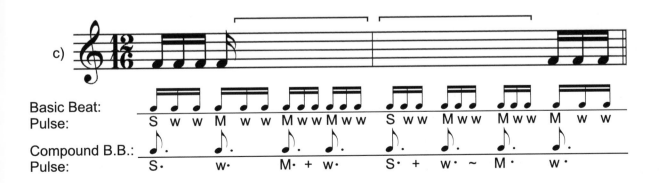

## DOTTED WHOLE REST in COMPOUND TIME

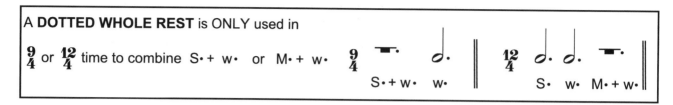

A **DOTTED WHOLE REST** is ONLY used in
$\frac{9}{4}$ or $\frac{12}{4}$ time to combine S• + w•  or  M• + w•

♫ **Note:** A **REST** for a **STRONG** beat or **MEDIUM** beat is combined with a **weak** beat. A rest for a **weak** beat stands alone. The dot after a dotted rest always goes in space three.

1.  a) Add rests below each bracket to complete the measure.
    b) Cross off the Basic Beat and the Compound Basic Beat as each beat is completed.

## WHOLE REST in COMPOUND TIME

A **WHOLE REST** fills any measure with silence in Compound Time.

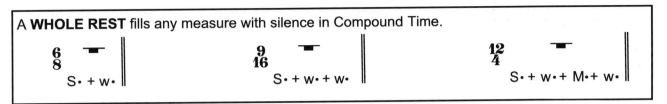

♫ **Note:** A **WHOLE REST** combines a **STRONG** beat with all the other beats. The top number of the Compound Time Signature indicates the number of beats the whole rest receives.

1. a) Add rests below each bracket to complete the measure.
   b) Cross off the Basic Beat and the Compound Basic Beat as each beat is completed.

113

## IRREGULAR GROUPS in SIMPLE TIME and COMPOUND TIME

An **IRREGULAR GROUP** in Simple Time or Compound Time is identified by a small number above or below a group of notes. The number indicates how many notes are in the group. An irregular group is played in the time of a regular group of the SAME note value.

♫ **Note:** Simple Time regular groups are 2 or 4. Compound Time regular groups are 3 or 6.
An irregular group is equal to one regular group (usually one beat).

---

**Irregular Groups in Simple Time**
A Quintuplet (group of 5), a Sextuplet (group of 6) and a Septuplet (group of 7) are played in the time of 4 notes of the same value.

 or  or

---

1. a) Write the number of regular notes that equal each irregular group in Simple Time.
   b) Write the regular group of notes that equal each irregular group of notes in Simple Time.

**Quintuplet**
a) 5 notes played in the time of = _____ notes     b)  = _____

**Sextuplet**
a) 6 notes played in the time of = _____ notes     b) = _____

**Septuplet**
a) 7 notes played in the time of = _____ notes     b)  = _____

♫ **Note:** An irregular group is usually equal to one beat but can be half a beat or two beats in value.

2. Complete the count below each Basic Beat.

Basic Beat:
Count:      1      2 3 4

---

**Irregular Groups in Compound Time**
A Duplet (group of 2) and a Quadruplet (group of 4) are played in the time of 3 notes of the same value.

---

3. a) Write the number of regular notes that equal each irregular group in Compound Time.
   b) Write the regular group of notes that equal each irregular group of notes in Compound Time.

**Duplet**
a) 2 notes played in the time of = _____ notes     b) = _____

**Quadruplet**
a) 4 notes played in the time of = _____ notes     b) = _____

# IRREGULAR GROUPS with DIFFERENT REGULAR GROUPS

**Irregular Groups in Compound Time**

A Quintuplet (group of 5) and a Septuplet (group of 7) are played in the time of 3 or 6 notes of the same value based on the Time Signature and the value of the other notes or rests in the measure.

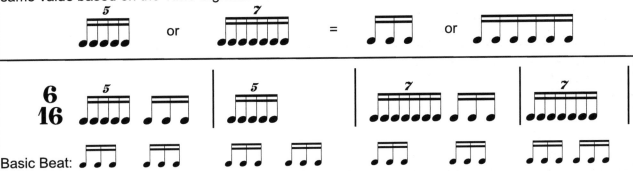

1. a) Write the number of regular notes that equal each irregular group in Compound Time.
   b) Write the regular group of notes that equal each irregular group of notes in Compound Time.

**Quintuplet**
a) 5 notes played in the time of = _____ notes        b) $\overset{5}{\boxed{\text{♪♪♪♪♪}}}$ = _____

OR

**Quintuplet**
a) 5 notes played in the time of = _____ notes        b) $\overset{5}{\boxed{\text{♪♪♪♪♪}}}$ = _____

**Septuplet**
a) 7 notes played in the time of = _____ notes        b) $\overset{7}{\boxed{\text{♪♪♪♪♪♪♪}}}$ = _____

OR

**Septuplet**
a) 7 notes played in the time of = _____ notes        b) $\overset{7}{\boxed{\text{♪♪♪♪♪♪♪}}}$ = _____

2. Add the correct Time Signature below each bracket.

115

## DOUBLE DOTTED NOTES

A **DOUBLE DOTTED NOTE** has 2 dots. The first dot equals half the value of the note. The second dot equals half the value of the first dot.

1. Write the note value of the dotted note and the note value of each dot.

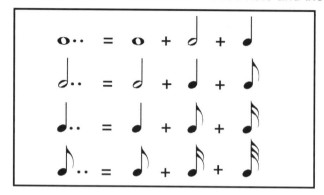

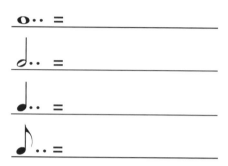

2. Add bar lines to complete the following rhythms.

a)

b) 

c) 

3. Add the correct Time Signature below each bracket.

a)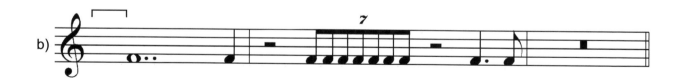

b) 

c)

# ADDING RESTS, BAR LINES and TIME SIGNATURES

1.  a)  Write the Basic Beat and the pulse below each measure.
    b)  Add rests below each bracket to complete the measure.
    c)  Cross off the Basic Beat as each beat is completed.

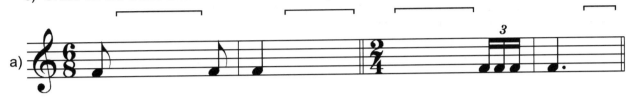

Basic Beat: _____
Pulse:

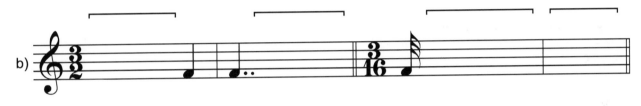

Basic Beat: _____
Pulse:

2.  Add bar lines to complete the following rhythms.

3.  Add the correct Time Signature below each bracket.

## HYBRID TIME - HYBRID DUPLE TIME

**HYBRID TIME** (Mixed Meter) is a combination of Simple Time (Basic Beat is one undotted note) and Compound Time (Compound Basic Beat is one dotted note). Hybrid meter can be in duple, triple or quadruple time. The **TOP** number is **5, 7, 9, 10** or **11**. The **BOTTOM** number is **2, 4, 8** or **16**.

### HYBRID DUPLE TIME

| In Hybrid **DUPLE** Time the **TOP** number is always **5**. The 5 pulses are grouped as follows: | | | | | |
|---|---|---|---|---|---|
| **TWO** Groups of: | 3 2 | **OR** | 2 3 | | |
| Pulse: | S w w  M w | **OR** | S w  M w w | | |
| Hybrid Pulse: | S·    w | **OR** | S    w· | | |

♫ **Note:** Use the same pattern of 3-2 or 2-3 to complete each rhythm.

1. a) Following the examples, write the Basic Beat, pulse and Hybrid pulse under each measure.
   b) Add bar lines to complete the following rhythms.

a)

Basic Beat: 

Pulse:   S  w  w  M  w

Hybrid Pulse: S· (o·)   w (o)

b)

Basic Beat: 

Pulse:   S  w  M  w  w

Hybrid Pulse: S (♩)   w· (♩·)

c)

Basic Beat: 

Pulse:   S  w  w  M  w

Hybrid Pulse: S· (♩·)   w (♩)

d)

Basic Beat: 

Pulse:   S  w  M  w  w

Hybrid Pulse: S (♪)   w· (♪·)

118

## HYBRID TRIPLE TIME

In **HYBRID TRIPLE TIME**, when **7** is the top number in the Time Signature, the 7 Basic Beats will combine into one dotted and two undotted Hybrid Pulses.

♫ **Note:** A dotted note will be used for one dotted Hybrid pulse.

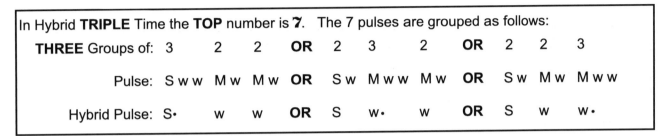

| In Hybrid **TRIPLE** Time the **TOP** number is **7**. The 7 pulses are grouped as follows: | | | | | | | | | | | |
|---|---|---|---|---|---|---|---|---|---|---|---|
| **THREE** Groups of: | 3 | 2 | 2 | **OR** | 2 | 3 | 2 | **OR** | 2 | 2 | 3 |
| Pulse: | S w w | M w | M w | **OR** | S w | M w w | M w | **OR** | S w | M w | M w w |
| Hybrid Pulse: | S• | w | w | **OR** | S | w• | w | **OR** | S | w | w• |

♫ **Note:** Use the same pattern of 3-2-2 or 2-3-2 or 2-2-3 to complete each rhythm.

1. a) Following the examples, write in the Basic Beat, pulse and Hybrid pulse under each measure.
   b) Add bar lines to complete the following rhythms.

## HYBRID QUADRUPLE TIME

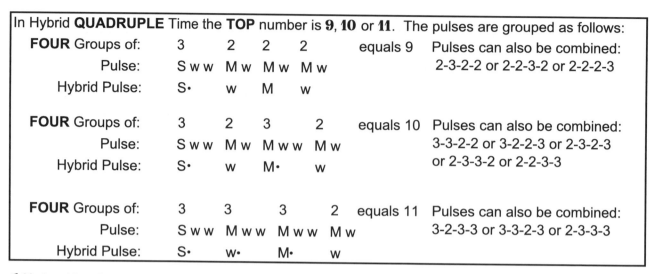

| | | | | | | |
|---|---|---|---|---|---|---|
| In Hybrid **QUADRUPLE** Time the **TOP** number is **9**, **10** or **11**. The pulses are grouped as follows: |

**FOUR** Groups of:     3    2    2    2     equals 9    Pulses can also be combined:
Pulse:     S w w   M w   M w   M w     2-3-2-2 or 2-2-3-2 or 2-2-2-3
Hybrid Pulse:   S•     w    M    w

**FOUR** Groups of:     3    2    3    2     equals 10   Pulses can also be combined:
Pulse:     S w w   M w   M w w   M w     3-3-2-2 or 3-2-2-3 or 2-3-2-3
Hybrid Pulse:   S•     w    M•    w     or 2-3-3-2 or 2-2-3-3

**FOUR** Groups of:     3    3    3    2     equals 11   Pulses can also be combined:
Pulse:     S w w   M w w   M w w   M w     3-2-3-3 or 3-3-2-3 or 2-3-3-3
Hybrid Pulse:   S•    w•    M•    w

♫ **Note:** Use the same pattern of 2's and 3's to complete each rhythm.

1. a) Following the examples, write in the Basic Beat, pulse and Hybrid pulse under each measure.
   b) Add bar lines to complete the following rhythms.

## TIME SIGNATURES and RESTS in HYBRID TIME

When adding **TIME SIGNATURES** in Hybrid Time, look for groups and determine the Basic Beat.

♩ **Note:** Notes held for a full measure must be written as tied notes.

1. a) Write the Basic Beat and Hybrid Beat (dotted note or undotted note) below each measure.
   b) Add the correct Time Signature below the bracket for each of the following rhythms.

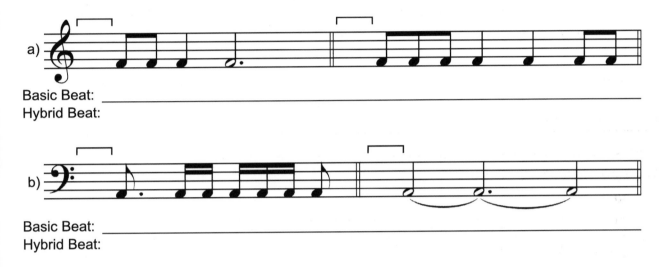

Basic Beat: _____

Hybrid Beat: _____

Basic Beat: _____

Hybrid Beat: _____

When adding **RESTS** to Hybrid Time, determine the pattern of Strong and weak beats. A dotted rest is only used when completing a group of three pulses: one Compound Basic Beat = one dotted rest.

♩ **Note:** Rests are combined for: **S + w** or **M + w** or **S· + w·** or **M· + w·**
   A **dotted** pulse **CANNOT** be combined with an **undotted** pulse.
   **S· ~ w** or **M· ~ w** or **S ~ w·** or **M ~ w·**

2. a) Add rests below each bracket to complete the following measures.
   b) Cross off the Basic Beat as each beat is completed.

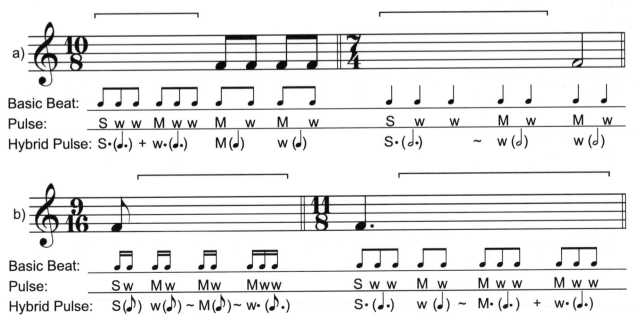

121

## WHOLE REST and DOTTED WHOLE REST in HYBRID TIME

A **WHOLE REST** fills ANY measure in Hybrid Time. An exception to the rule is Hybrid "**2**" time when a whole rest may fill a whole measure with silence OR it may receive 2 beats (**S + w** or **M + w**).

A **DOTTED WHOLE REST** is equal to 3 half notes and is used when completing a group of three half note Basic Beats. A dotted whole rest receives 3 beats (**S + w + w** or **M + w + w**).

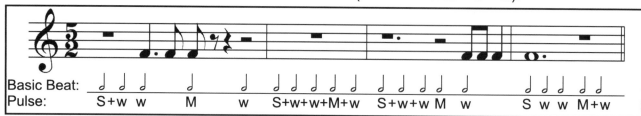

♫ **Note:** Notes that are beamed together belong to the SAME Basic Beat.

1. a) Write the Basic Beat, pulse and Hybrid pulse below each measure.
   b) Add rests below each bracket to complete the measure.
   c) Cross off the Basic Beat as each beat is completed.

122

# Lesson 5 — Review Test

Total Score: _____

100

Write the Circle of Fifths on a blank piece of paper.  Use it as a reference when doing the review test.

1. a) Write the **ENHARMONIC EQUIVALENT** for each of the following notes.  Use whole notes.
   b) Name **BOTH** notes.

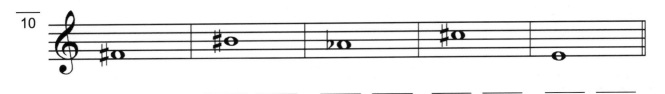

10

_____  _____  _____  _____  _____

2. Rewrite the given melody at the **SAME PITCH** in the Tenor Clef.

10

3. Write the following notes in the Bass Clef, using the correct **KEY SIGNATURE** for each.
   Use dotted half notes.

10 a) the **LEADING NOTE** of f sharp minor harmonic
   b) the **MEDIANT** of c minor harmonic
   c) the **SUBDOMINANT** of A Major
   d) the **SUPERTONIC** of D flat Major
   e) the **SUBMEDIANT** of e minor harmonic

a)          b)          c)          d)          e)

4. Name each of the following as: **d.s.** (diatonic semitone), **c.s.** (chromatic semitone),
   **w.t.** (whole tone)   or   **e.e.** (enharmonic equivalent).

10

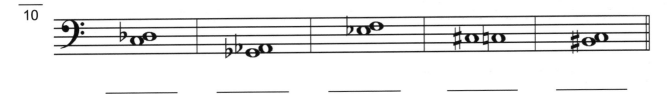

**5.** Name the following scales as Major, harmonic minor, melodic minor, natural minor, chromatic, whole tone, octatonic, blues, Major pentatonic or minor pentatonic.

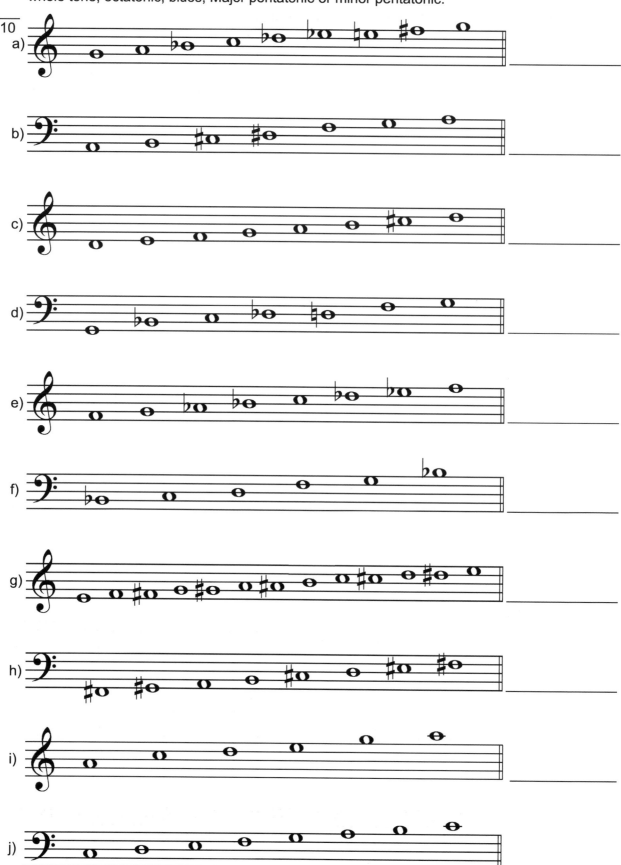

a) _____

b) _____

c) _____

d) _____

e) _____

f) _____

g) _____

h) _____

i) _____

j) _____

124

**6.** a) Write the Basic Beat and the pulse below each measure.
b) Add rests below each bracket to complete the measure.
c) Cross off the Basic Beat as each beat is completed.

Basic Beat: _____

Pulse:

Basic Beat: _____

Pulse:

**7.** Add bar lines to the following rhythms.

**8.** Add the correct **TIME SIGNATURE** below each bracket for the following rhythms.

125

**9.** Match each musical term with its English definition.  (Not all definitions will be used.)

**Term**

**10**

poco a poco — 

allargando — 

sforzando, *sf*, *sfz* — 

leggiero — 

più mosso — 

animato — 

grazioso — 

stringendo — 

mano destra — 

staccato — 

**Definition**

a) broadening, becoming slower

b) more movement, quicker

c) pressing, becoming faster

d) little by little

e) right hand

f) graceful

g) light, nimble, quick

h) detached

i) lively, animated

j) left hand

k) a sudden strong accent of a single note or chord

**10.** Analyze the following piece of music by answering the questions below.

# No More Pizza!

**10**

**Allegro**

G. St. Germain

a) Name the title of this piece. _____

b) Name the key of this piece. _____

c) Name the flats in the Key Signature. _____

d) Explain the sign at the letter **A**. _____

e) Explain the sign at the letter **B**. _____

f) Name the note at letter **C**. _____

g) Name the note at letter **D**. _____

h) Give the meaning of *diminuendo* (*dim*). _____

i) Give the meaning of *rallentando* (*rall.*). _____

j) When observing the repeat sign, how many measures of music are played? _____

# Lesson 6     Intervals - Simple, Compound and Inversions

## HARMONIC and MELODIC INTERVALS

An **INTERVAL** is the distance in pitch between TWO notes. Numbers (1, 2, 3, etc.) are used to identify the size of the interval. To identify the interval, count each line and each space from the lower note to the higher note. The lower note is always counted as 1.

Example: C - D is an interval of a SECOND (2), C - E is an interval of a THIRD (3).

## HARMONIC INTERVALS

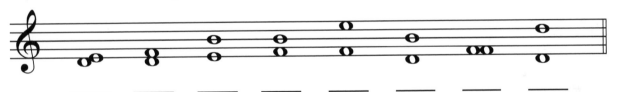

A **HARMONIC** interval is written one note **ABOVE** the other, both played at the same time (together). **H** is for Harmony.

♫ **Note:** A harmonic interval of a first (1) and a second (2) cannot be written one note on top of the other. They are written side-by-side (touching each other).

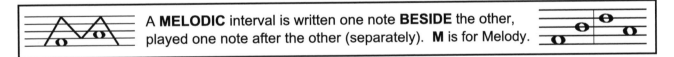

Interval:   1      2      3      4      5      6      7      8

1. Name each of the following harmonic intervals.

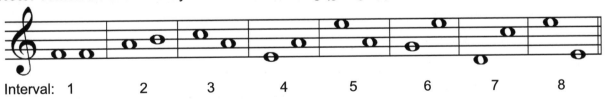

## MELODIC INTERVALS

A **MELODIC** interval is written one note **BESIDE** the other, played one note after the other (separately). **M** is for Melody.

♫ **Note:** A melodic interval may be written ascending (going up) or descending (going down).

Interval: 1      2      3      4      5      6      7      8

2. Name each of the following melodic intervals.

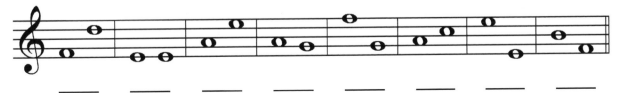

## PERFECT and MAJOR INTERVALS

**PERFECT INTERVALS** are 1, 4, 5 and 8.
The abbreviation for Perfect is "**Per**".

**MAJOR INTERVALS** are 2, 3, 6 and 7.
The abbreviation for Major is "**Maj**".

The **LOWER** note of the interval is the **TONIC** of the Major key.  If D is the lower note, intervals are written based on the notes of the D Major scale.

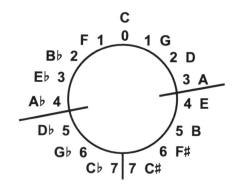

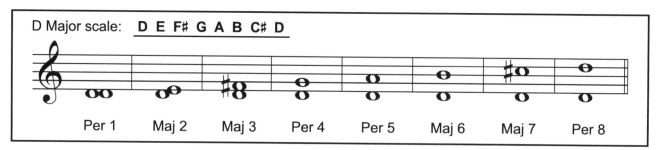

♫ **Note:**  The LOWER note names the Major key.

1.  Write melodic intervals above each given note D (Key of D Major).  Use accidentals.
    Use whole notes.

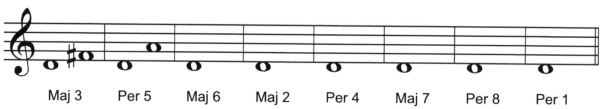

E Major scale:  **E F♯ G♯ A B C♯ D♯ E**

2.  Write harmonic intervals above each given note E (Key of E Major).  Use accidentals.
    Use whole notes.

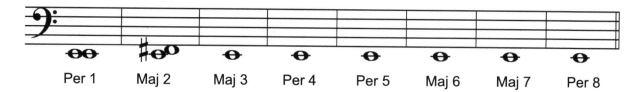

3.  Write melodic intervals above each given note E (Key of E Major).  Use accidentals.
    Use whole notes.

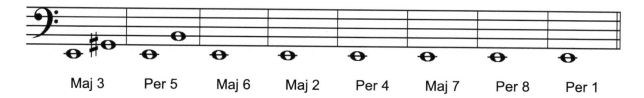

128

# HARMONIC and MELODIC INTERVALS

For **HARMONIC** intervals of a 1, 2, 3, 4, 5 and 6: when **BOTH** notes have accidentals, the accidental is written closest to the higher note and further away from the lower note.

For **HARMONIC** intervals of a 7 and 8: when **BOTH** notes have accidentals, the accidentals are written lined up vertically (above each other).

♫ **Note:** When writing a harmonic interval, and there is no room for correct placement of accidentals, it is acceptable to place the accidental further away from the upper note.

A flat Major scale: Ab Bb C Db Eb F G Ab

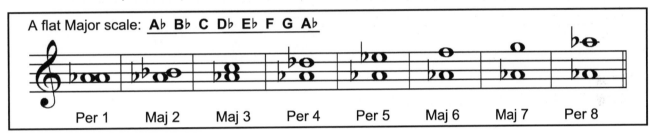

1. Write harmonic intervals above each given note Ab. Use accidentals. Use whole notes.

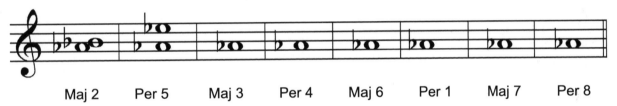

Maj 2      Per 5      Maj 3      Per 4      Maj 6      Per 1      Maj 7      Per 8

♫ **Note:** The LOWER note names the Major key.

2. Write the note names of the G Major scale. Name the melodic intervals.

G Major scale: _____

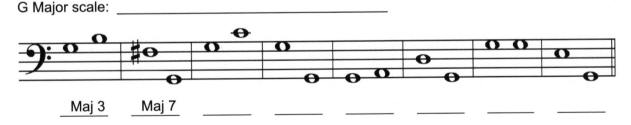

__Maj 3__   __Maj 7__   ____   ____   ____   ____   ____   ____

3. Write the note names of the B flat Major scale. Name the harmonic intervals.

B flat Major scale: _____

__Maj 3__   ____   ____   ____   ____   ____   ____   ____

129

## IDENTIFYING and WRITING HARMONIC INTERVALS

1. Complete the Circle of Fifths:
   a) Write the order of flats and sharps.
   b) Write the Major keys on the outside of the circle.

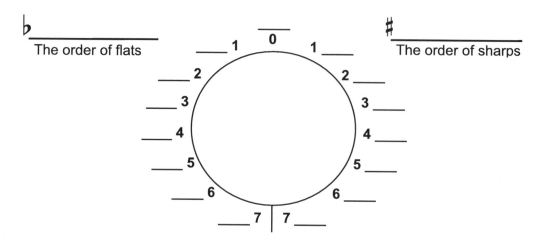

b _____
The order of flats

# _____
The order of sharps

♫ **Note:** The LOWER note names the Major key. Use the Circle of Fifths to identify the sharps or flats in the Key Signature for each Major key.

2. Name the following harmonic intervals.

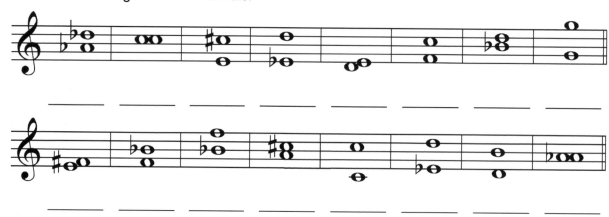

3. Write harmonic intervals above the given notes. Use accidentals. Use whole notes.

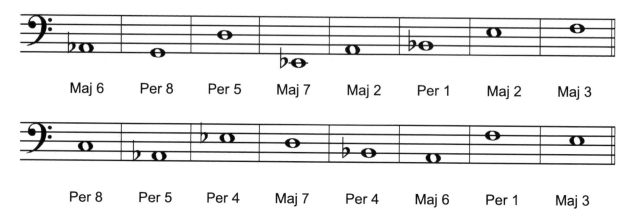

| Maj 6 | Per 8 | Per 5 | Maj 7 | Maj 2 | Per 1 | Maj 2 | Maj 3 |

| Per 8 | Per 5 | Per 4 | Maj 7 | Per 4 | Maj 6 | Per 1 | Maj 3 |

## MAJOR and MINOR INTERVALS

A **MINOR** interval is **ONE** chromatic semitone (half step) **SMALLER** than a Major interval.
Only the intervals **2**, **3**, **6** and **7** can become minor.  The abbreviation for minor is "**min**".

♫ **Note:**  The intervals of 1, 4, 5 and 8 are **PERFECT**.  The interval of a Perfect 1 is also known as a
**Perfect Unison**.  The interval of a Perfect 8 is also known as a **Perfect Octave** (8ve).

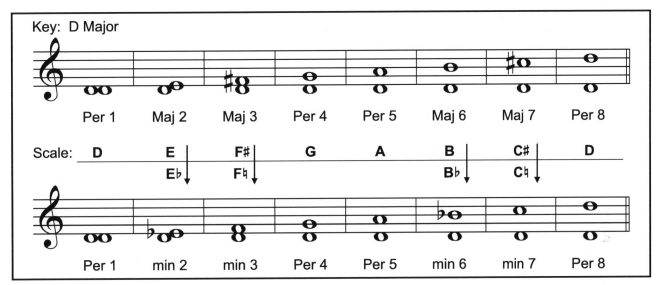

1. a)  Write the note names of the A Major scale.
   b)  Write the harmonic intervals above the given notes.

A Major scale: _____

Per 1    Maj 2    Maj 3    Per 4    Per 5    Maj 6    Maj 7    Per 8

Per 1    min 2    min 3    Per 4    Per 5    min 6    min 7    Per 8

♫ **Note:**  A Major 2, 3, 6 and 7 becomes minor by lowering the top note one chromatic semitone.

2. a)  Change the following Major intervals into minor intervals by lowering the top note one chromatic
      semitone (chromatic half step).
   b)  Name the intervals.

Maj 3   min 3   Maj 6   min 6   ____ ____ ____ ____ ____ ____ ____ ____

## IDENTIFYING and WRITING MELODIC INTERVALS

1. Complete the Circle of Fifths:

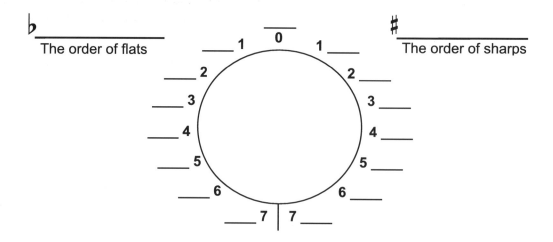

♩ **Note:** The LOWER note names the Major key. Use the Circle of Fifths to identify the sharps or flats in the Key Signature for each Major key. A minor interval is one chromatic semitone (chromatic half step) smaller than a Major interval.

2. Name the following melodic intervals.

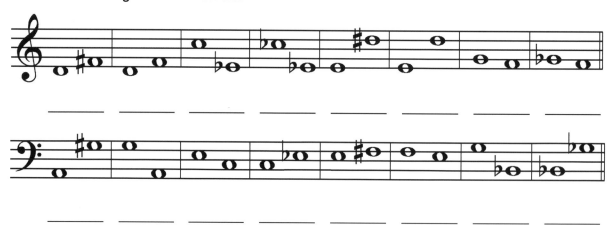

3. Write melodic intervals above the given notes. Use accidentals. Use whole notes.

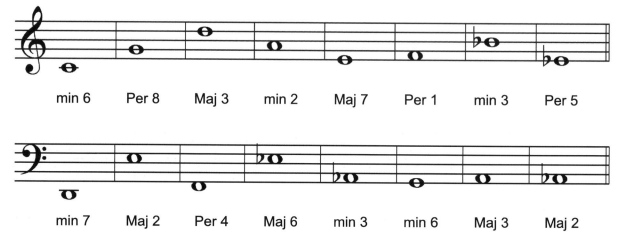

## NAMING INTERVALS with a KEY SIGNATURE

When **NAMING INTERVALS** with a **KEY SIGNATURE**, count the distance between the two notes to determine the interval number (1, 2, 3, etc.). Observe the Key Signature and any accidentals in the measure that may affect the given notes. The **LOWER** note of the interval determines the **Major key** used to name the interval.

♫ **Note:** The Key Signature of the melody will affect ALL the notes on the staff (and on ledger lines).

1. Following the examples, name the intervals by completing the following:

Key Signature:  _F♯  C♯_

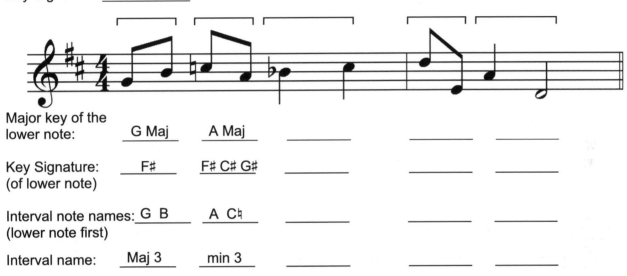

| Major key of the lower note: | G Maj | A Maj | | | |
|---|---|---|---|---|---|
| Key Signature: (of lower note) | F♯ | F♯ C♯ G♯ | | | |
| Interval note names: (lower note first) | G  B | A  C♮ | | | |
| Interval name: | Maj 3 | min 3 | | | |

♫ **Note:** Each interval is based upon the Major Key Signature of the lower note.

2. a) Name the sharps or flats in the Key Signature.
   b) Name the melodic intervals below each bracket.

a) Key Signature: _____

b) Intervals: _____ _____ _____ _____ _____ _____

a) Key Signature: _____

b) Intervals: _____ _____ _____ _____ _____ _____

133

## PERFECT, MAJOR and MINOR INTERVALS

1. Write the following harmonic intervals above each of the given notes.  Use whole notes.

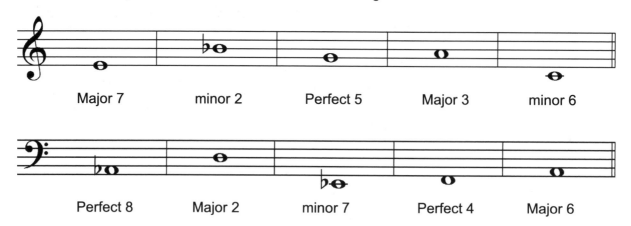

Major 7        minor 2        Perfect 5        Major 3        minor 6

Perfect 8        Major 2        minor 7        Perfect 4        Major 6

2. a) Name the following harmonic intervals.

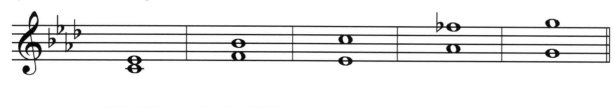

_____        _____        _____        _____        _____

b) Name the following melodic intervals.

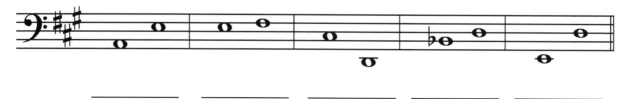

_____        _____        _____        _____        _____

3. a) Write the following harmonic intervals above each of the given notes.  Use whole notes.

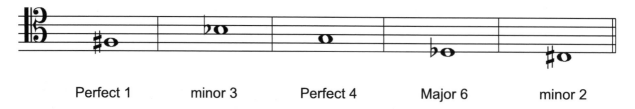

Perfect 1        minor 3        Perfect 4        Major 6        minor 2

b) Write the following melodic intervals above each of the given notes.  Use whole notes.

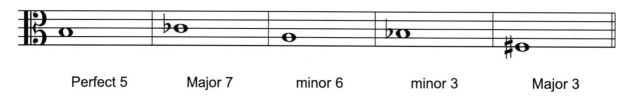

Perfect 5        Major 7        minor 6        minor 3        Major 3

## AUGMENTED and DIMINISHED INTERVALS

### AUGMENTED INTERVAL

An **Augmented interval** is one semitone
**LARGER** than a Perfect or Major interval.

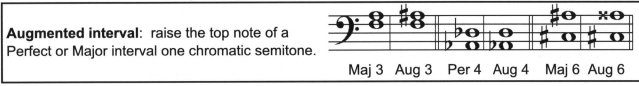

♫ **Note:** To change a Perfect or Major interval into an AUGMENTED interval: raise the top note one
chromatic semitone (half step), or lower the bottom note one chromatic semitone (half step).

**Augmented interval**: raise the top note of a
Perfect or Major interval one chromatic semitone.

Maj 3   Aug 3   Per 4   Aug 4   Maj 6   Aug 6

♫ **Note:** Abbreviations:  Major = **Maj**; Perfect = **Per**; Augmented = **Aug**.

1. a) Change these Perfect or Major intervals into Augmented intervals by raising the top note one
chromatic semitone (half step).  Use whole notes.

   b) Name the intervals.

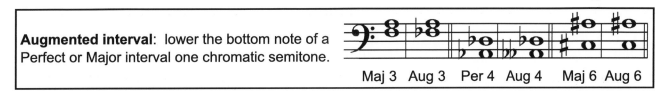

**Augmented interval**: lower the bottom note of a
Perfect or Major interval one chromatic semitone.

Maj 3   Aug 3   Per 4   Aug 4   Maj 6   Aug 6

2. a) Change these Perfect or Major intervals into Augmented intervals by lowering the bottom note
one chromatic semitone (half step).  Use whole notes.

   b) Name the intervals.

## DIMINISHED INTERVAL

A **diminished interval** is one semitone
**SMALLER** than a Perfect or minor interval.
A Perfect 1 (unison) cannot become diminished.

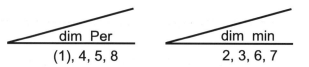

dim Per      dim min

(1), 4, 5, 8      2, 3, 6, 7

♪ **Note:** To change a Perfect or minor interval into a DIMINISHED interval: lower the top note one
chromatic semitone (half step), or raise the bottom note one chromatic semitone (half step).

**Diminished interval**: lower the top note of a
Perfect or minor interval one chromatic semitone.

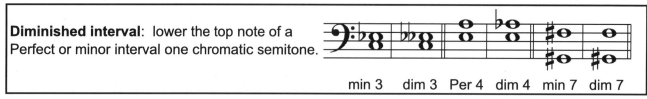

min 3    dim 3    Per 4    dim 4    min 7    dim 7

♪ **Note:** Abbreviations: Perfect = **Per**; minor = **min**; diminished = **dim**.

1. a) Change these Perfect or minor intervals into diminished intervals by lowering the top note one
   chromatic semitone (half step). Use whole notes.
   b) Name the intervals.

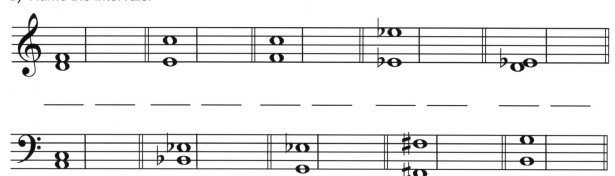

**Diminished interval**: raise the bottom note of a
Perfect or minor interval one chromatic semitone.

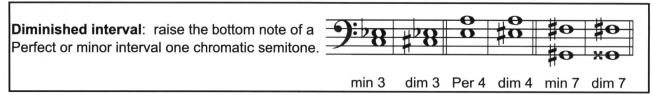

min 3    dim 3    Per 4    dim 4    min 7    dim 7

2. a) Change these Perfect or minor intervals into diminished intervals by raising the bottom note
   one chromatic semitone (half step). Use whole notes.
   b) Name the intervals.

136

# DIMINISHED INTERVAL to AUGMENTED INTERVAL

## DIMINISHED (semitone larger➡) PERFECT (semitone larger➡) AUGMENTED

A Perfect interval - one chromatic semitone LARGER becomes Augmented.
A Perfect interval - one chromatic semitone SMALLER becomes diminished.

dim Per Aug

1, 4, 5, 8

♫ **Note:** An interval of a Perfect 1 (unison) may become Augmented but NOT diminished.

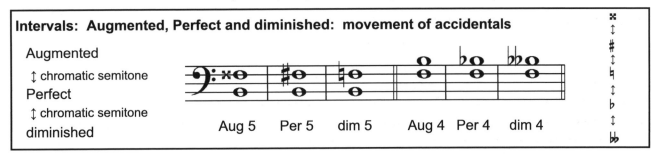

**Intervals: Augmented, Perfect and diminished: movement of accidentals**

Augmented
↕ chromatic semitone
Perfect
↕ chromatic semitone
diminished

Aug 5  Per 5  dim 5    Aug 4  Per 4  dim 4

1. Change the following Perfect intervals into Augmented intervals and then into diminished intervals by changing the top note one chromatic semitone (half step). Use whole notes.

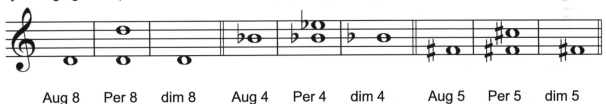

Aug 8  Per 8  dim 8    Aug 4  Per 4  dim 4    Aug 5  Per 5  dim 5

## DIMINISHED (semitone larger➡) MINOR (semitone larger➡) MAJOR (semitone larger➡) AUGMENTED

A Major interval - one chromatic semitone LARGER becomes Augmented.
A Major interval - one chromatic semitone SMALLER becomes minor.
A Major interval - two chromatic semitones SMALLER becomes diminished.

dim min Maj Aug

2, 3, 6, 7

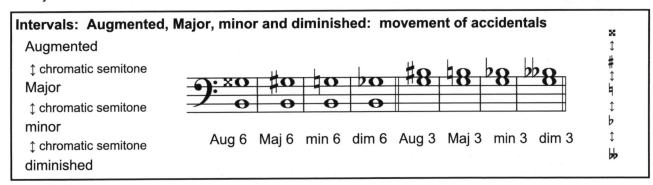

**Intervals: Augmented, Major, minor and diminished: movement of accidentals**

Augmented
↕ chromatic semitone
Major
↕ chromatic semitone
minor
↕ chromatic semitone
diminished

Aug 6  Maj 6  min 6  dim 6    Aug 3  Maj 3  min 3  dim 3

2. Change the following Major intervals into Augmented intervals, and then into minor intervals and diminished intervals by changing the top note one chromatic semitone. Use whole notes.

Aug 6  Maj 6  min 6  dim 6    Aug 7  Maj 7  min 7  dim 7    Aug 3  Maj 3  min 3  dim 3

## HARMONIC and MELODIC INTERVALS BELOW a GIVEN NOTE

> **INTERVALS:** The type/quality of an interval changes when moving a chromatic semitone (half step).
>
> Intervals 2, 3, 6, 7    **Diminished** ⌣semitone⌣ **minor** ⌣semitone⌣ **Major** ⌣semitone⌣ **Augmented**
>               dim                 min             Maj             Aug
>
>       Intervals 1, 4, 5, 8    **Diminished** ⌣semitone⌣ **Perfect** ⌣semitone⌣ **Augmented**
>                      dim                 Per             Aug

### Intervals BELOW a Given Note

To write an interval **BELOW** a given note, follow these steps:

Step 1: Count down to determine the note that is the interval number below the given note. Write that note without an accidental.

Step 2: Determine the type/quality of the interval (Augmented, Perfect, Major, minor or diminished) based upon the Major Key Signature of the bottom note.

Step 3: Using accidentals (double sharp, sharp, flat or double flat), move one chromatic semitone (half step) at a time to adjust the bottom note until the correct interval is formed.

♫ **Note:** Do NOT change the given note. Determine the Major or Perfect interval below the given note first. Raise or lower the bottom note to form the correct interval. The bottom note may be a double flat or a double sharp.

> **Harmonic interval** - Augmented 3 **BELOW** the given note D.
>
> Down a 3rd from D is B. Key of B Major (F♯ C♯ G♯ D♯ A♯).
> The interval of B to D is a min 3. (B to D♯ = Maj 3; B to D = min 3)
> **Lower** the bottom note B to B♭. The interval of B♭ to D is a Maj 3.
> **Lower** the bottom note B♭ to B♭♭. The interval of B♭♭ to D is an Augmented 3.

1. Write the following harmonic intervals below the given notes.

    Aug 2            Aug 4            Maj 6            Per 5            Aug 7            min 3

> **Melodic interval** - diminished 3 **BELOW** the given note E.
>
> Down a 3rd from E is C. Key of C Major (no ♯s or ♭s).
> The interval of C to E is a Maj 3.
> **Raise** the bottom note C to C♯. C♯ to E is a min 3.
> **Raise** the bottom note C♯ to C𝄪. The interval of C𝄪 to E is a diminished 3.

2. Write the following melodic intervals below the given notes.

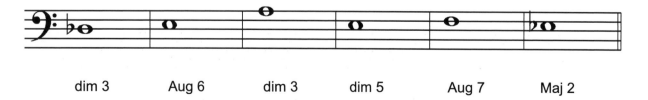

    dim 3            Aug 6            dim 3            dim 5            Aug 7            Maj 2

## INTERVALS - DIMINISHED, MINOR, MAJOR, PERFECT and AUGMENTED

**Major** or **Perfect** intervals are identified by the Major key of the BOTTOM note.

**Augmented**, **minor** and **diminished** intervals are raised or lowered in pitch based on the Key Signature of the Major key.

Use the Circle of Fifths as a reference.

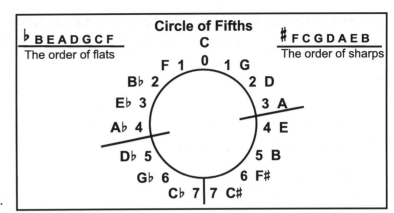

1. Name the following melodic intervals.

_____  _____  _____  _____  _____

If the bottom note is NOT a Major key on the Circle of Fifths, change the accidental to a Major key. Determine the interval based on the Major key. Ex: F♭♭ becomes F Major.

Move the lower note, one semitone at a time, back to the original pitch to determine the given interval.

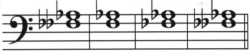

| F♭♭ to A♭ | F - A♭ | F♭ - A♭ | F♭♭ - A♭ |
|-----------|--------|---------|----------|
| Key: F Major | min 3 | Maj 3 | Aug 3 |

♫ **Note:** When both notes move up or down the same distance, the interval name remains the same.
    Example: Perfect 4: D to G, D♯ to G♯, D♭ to G♭, D𝄪 to G𝄪, D♭♭ to G♭♭.

2. Name the following melodic intervals.

_____  _____  _____  _____  _____

♫ **Note:** When writing a harmonic second below a given note, the lower note is written to the left.

3. Write the following harmonic intervals BELOW the given note.

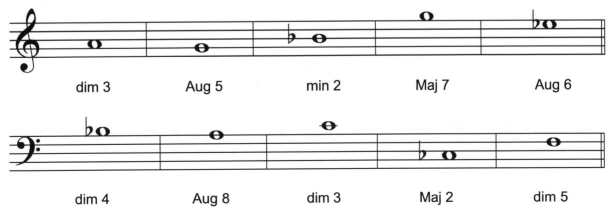

| dim 3 | Aug 5 | min 2 | Maj 7 | Aug 6 |

| dim 4 | Aug 8 | dim 3 | Maj 2 | dim 5 |

## SIMPLE INTERVALS

A **SIMPLE INTERVAL** is NO LARGER than a Perfect octave. When writing intervals below a given note, always determine the Major or Perfect interval first. The bottom note determines the Major key.

♫ **Note:** Harmonic interval is written one note ABOVE the other, played together (at the same time). Melodic interval is written one note BESIDE the other, played one note after the other.

1. Write the following harmonic intervals below the given notes. Do not change the given note.

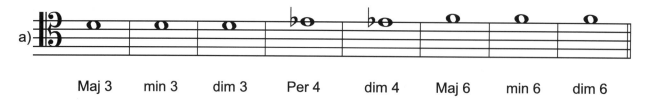

|  Maj 3 | min 3 | dim 3 | Per 4 | dim 4 | Maj 6 | min 6 | dim 6 |

♫ **Note:** When writing a harmonic second below a given note, the lower note is written to the left. When there is **no room** for correct placement, it may be written to the right of the given note.

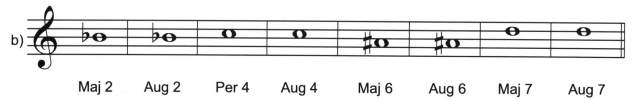

|  Maj 2 | Aug 2 | Per 4 | Aug 4 | Maj 6 | Aug 6 | Maj 7 | Aug 7 |

2. Write the following melodic intervals below the given notes. Do not change the given note.

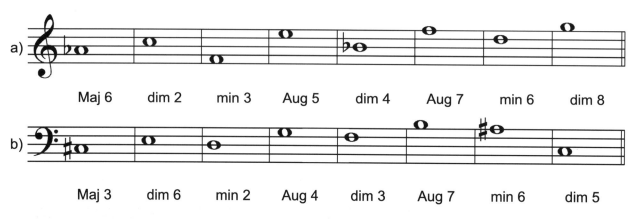

|  Maj 6 | dim 2 | min 3 | Aug 5 | dim 4 | Aug 7 | min 6 | dim 8 |

|  Maj 3 | dim 6 | min 2 | Aug 4 | dim 3 | Aug 7 | min 6 | dim 5 |

3. Name the following melodic intervals.

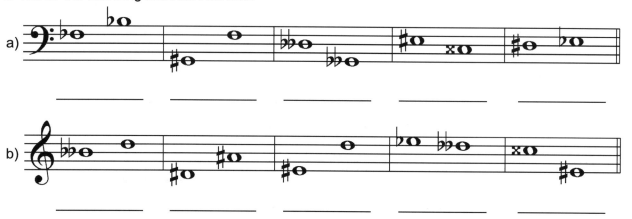

## TRITONE and INTERVALS using a KEY SIGNATURE

A **TRITONE** is an interval of three tones (whole tones).
A tritone divides an octave in half exactly.

There are 6 whole tones in a Perfect octave.

♫ **Note:** A tritone may be written as an
Augmented 4 or a diminished 5.

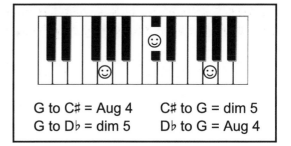

G to C# = Aug 4      C# to G = dim 5
G to D♭ = dim 5      D♭ to G = Aug 4

1.  Name the intervals by completing the following:

Key Signature: _____

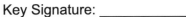

Major key of the
lower note:       _____ _____        _____ _____        _____

Key Signature:    _____ _____        _____ _____        _____
(of lower note)

Interval note names: _____ _____      _____ _____        _____
(lower note first)

Interval name:    _____ _____        _____ _____        _____

♫ **Note:** Each interval is based upon the Major Key Signature of the lower note.

2.  a)  Name the sharps or flats in the Key Signature.
    b)  Name the melodic intervals below each bracket.

a)  Key Signature: _____

b)  Intervals:    _____    _____    _____    _____    _____

a)  Key Signature: _____

b)  Intervals:    _____    _____    _____    _____

## SIMPLE INTERVALS and INVERSIONS

An **INVERSION** of a **SIMPLE INTERVAL** occurs when the interval is turned upside down.  A Simple interval and its inversion always equal 9.  Example:  A Major 3 becomes a minor 6 (3 + 6 = 9).

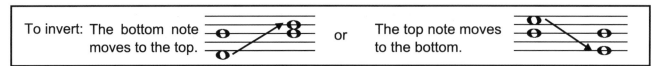

When inverting intervals:

| MAJOR | becomes | MINOR |
|---|---|---|
| MINOR | becomes | MAJOR |
| AUGMENTED | becomes | DIMINISHED |
| DIMINISHED | becomes | AUGMENTED |
| PERFECT | stays | PERFECT |

The combined number of the **HARMONIC** interval and its inversion **ALWAYS** equals **NINE**.

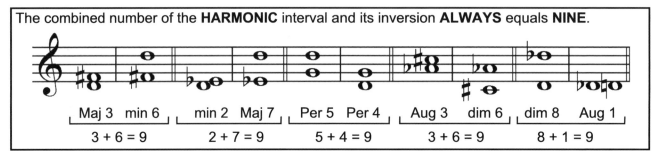

| Maj 3  min 6 | min 2  Maj 7 | Per 5  Per 4 | Aug 3  dim 6 | dim 8  Aug 1 |
|---|---|---|---|---|
| 3 + 6 = 9 | 2 + 7 = 9 | 5 + 4 = 9 | 3 + 6 = 9 | 8 + 1 = 9 |

1.  Name the following intervals and their inversions.

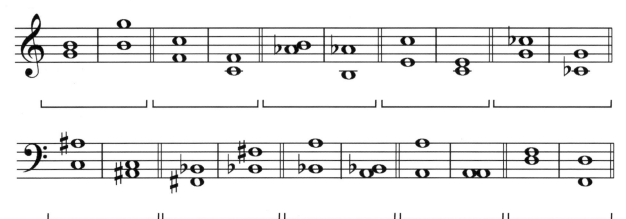

2.  a)  Name the following harmonic intervals.
    b)  Invert each interval in the same clef.  Name the inversions.

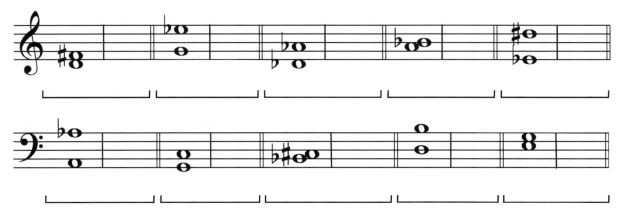

## MELODIC INTERVAL INVERSIONS and INVERSIONS into a DIFFERENT CLEF

**Harmonic interval** - one note above the other.  **Melodic interval** - one note beside the other.  When a melodic interval is inverted, either note may be written first.  The interval remains the same.

♫ **Note:**  The quality of an interval is determined by the Major key of the lower note.

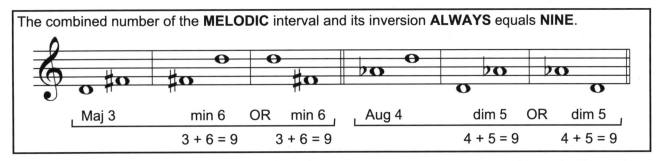

The combined number of the **MELODIC** interval and its inversion **ALWAYS** equals **NINE**.

| Maj 3 | min 6 | OR | min 6 | Aug 4 | dim 5 | OR | dim 5 |
|-------|-------|----|-------|-------|-------|----|-------|
|       | 3 + 6 = 9 | | 3 + 6 = 9 |   | 4 + 5 = 9 | | 4 + 5 = 9 |

1. a) Name the following melodic intervals.
   b) Invert each interval in the same clef.  Name the inversions.

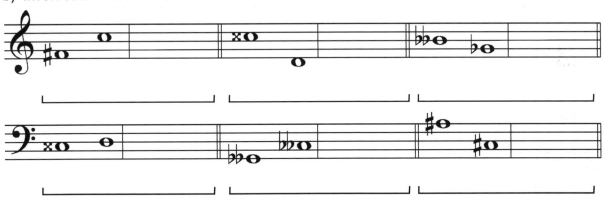

Harmonic or melodic intervals may be inverted into a **DIFFERENT** clef.  An inversion of an interval is turning it upside down.  The combined number of the interval and its inversion always equals nine.

♫ **Note:**  When inverting into a different clef, notes use the same letter names.  However, neither of the inverted notes needs to stay at the same pitch as the given interval.

2. a) Following the example, name the following intervals.
   b) Invert each interval in the Bass Clef below.  Name the inversions.

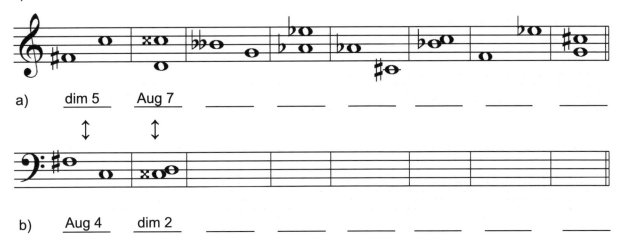

a)    dim 5     Aug 7     _____     _____     _____     _____

b)    Aug 4     dim 2     _____     _____     _____     _____

## COMPOUND INTERVALS

A **COMPOUND INTERVAL** is LARGER than a Perfect octave. Identify a Compound interval as a Simple interval first by lowering the top note one octave or by raising the bottom note one octave.

♫ **Note:** The type/quality of a Simple interval is the **SAME** as the type/quality of a Compound interval (Perfect, Major, minor, Augmented or diminished).

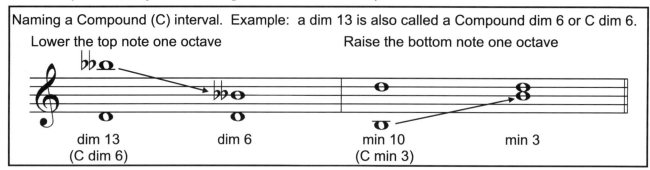

Naming a Compound (C) interval. Example: a dim 13 is also called a Compound dim 6 or C dim 6.

Lower the top note one octave          Raise the bottom note one octave

dim 13          dim 6          min 10          min 3
(C dim 6)                      (C min 3)

♫ **Note:** Name the Simple interval FIRST, then the Compound interval. They have the SAME quality. The Simple interval number **PLUS** "7" equals the Compound interval number.

1. Change the following Compound intervals into Simple intervals by lowering the top note one octave. Name the Simple interval first, then name the Compound interval.

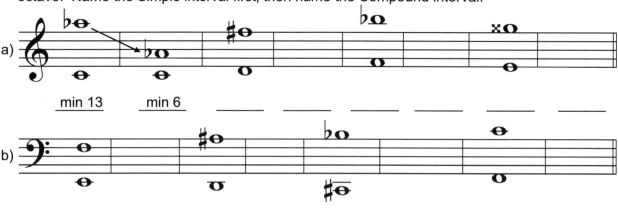

min 13          min 6

♫ **Note:** The Compound interval number **MINUS** "7" equals the Simple interval number.

2. Change the following Compound intervals into Simple intervals by raising the bottom note one octave. Name the Simple interval first, then name the Compound interval.

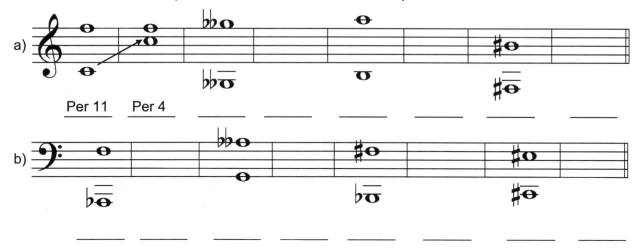

Per 11          Per 4

## COMPOUND INTERVALS and INVERSIONS

An **INVERSION** of a **COMPOUND INTERVAL** becomes a Simple interval. A Compound interval and its inversion always equal 16. Example: A Major 10 inverts to a minor 6 (10 + 6 = 16).

♫ **Note:** Inverting a Compound interval may be done by:
   a) lowering the top note TWO octaves.
   b) raising the bottom note TWO octaves.
   c) lowering the top note one octave AND raising the bottom note one octave.

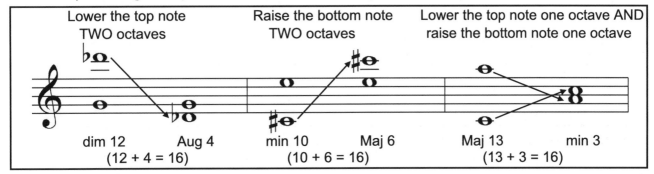

| Lower the top note TWO octaves | Raise the bottom note TWO octaves | Lower the top note one octave AND raise the bottom note one octave |
|---|---|---|
| dim 12      Aug 4 | min 10      Maj 6 | Maj 13      min 3 |
| (12 + 4 = 16) | (10 + 6 = 16) | (13 + 3 = 16) |

♫ **Note:** A Compound interval has the same quality as the Simple interval plus 7 (dim 4 + 7 = dim 11).

1. a) Rewrite the following Compound intervals as Simple intervals [in the square brackets].
      Name the Compound interval.
   b) Invert the Compound interval. (Use any method for inverting.) Name the inversion.

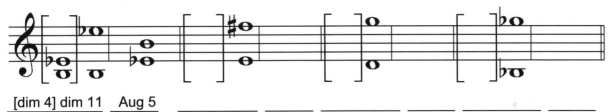

[dim 4] dim 11    Aug 5    _____  _____  _____  _____  _____

♫ **Note:** An **Augmented 8** is a Compound interval (larger than a Perfect octave). When inverted, the Aug 8 becomes a dim 8, a Simple interval (smaller than a Perfect octave).

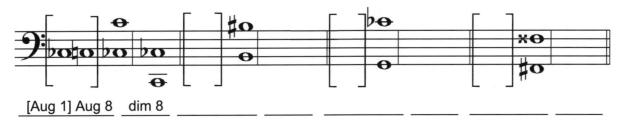

[Aug 1] Aug 8    dim 8    _____  _____  _____  _____  _____

A **Perfect 1** (unison) is the smallest possible interval. If EITHER note of a Perfect 1 (unison) is raised or lowered a chromatic semitone, it becomes an Aug 1.

♫ **Note:** An interval is always named based upon the lower note, therefore an interval of a first (unison) can NOT be diminished. It can only be Perfect or Augmented.

2. Name the following intervals.

Aug 1    _____  _____  _____  _____  _____  _____  _____

# ENHARMONIC EQUIVALENTS

An **ENHARMONIC EQUIVALENT** is the SAME PITCH written with a different note name. (A♭ - G♯)
All intervals have enharmonic equivalents. They have the same pitch or sound but are written using different note names. The upper note, lower note or both notes may be changed enharmonically.

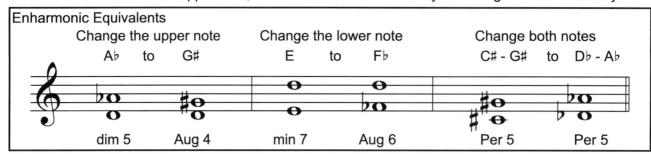

♫ **Note:** A dim 5 and an Aug 4 are enharmonic equivalent intervals called a TRITONE. A tritone consists of three whole tones (whole steps).

1. a) Name the following tritones.
   b) Write the enharmonic equivalent tritone. Name the new tritone.

       dim 5     Aug 4      _____     _____     _____     _____

2. a) Name the following intervals.
   b) Change the upper notes enharmonically and rename the intervals.

      _____     _____     _____     _____

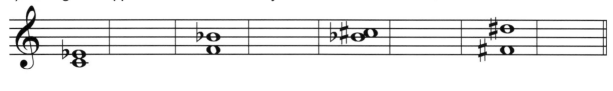

      _____     _____     _____     _____

3. a) Name the following intervals.
   b) Change the lower notes enharmonically and rename the intervals.

      _____     _____     _____     _____

      _____     _____     _____     _____

# Lesson 6      Review Test

Total Score: ____
100

Write the Circle of Fifths on a blank piece of paper.  Use it as a reference when doing the review test.

**1.**    a) Write the following melodic intervals **BELOW** the given notes.  Use whole notes.

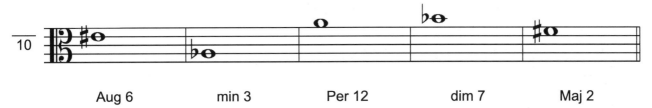

       Aug 6        min 3        Per 12        dim 7        Maj 2

   b) Invert the above intervals in the Bass Clef.  Use whole notes.  Name the inversions.

_____    _____    _____    _____    _____

**2.**    a) Write the following harmonic intervals **ABOVE** the given notes.
       b) Change the upper notes enharmonically and rename the intervals.  Use whole notes.

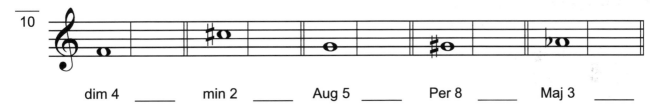

     dim 4 _____    min 2 _____    Aug 5 _____    Per 8 _____    Maj 3 _____

**3.**    Name the following intervals.

_____    _____    _____    _____    _____

**4.**    Name each of the following as:  **d.s.** (diatonic semitone),  **c.s.** (chromatic semitone),
                    **w.t.** (whole tone)  or  **e.e.** (enharmonic equivalent).

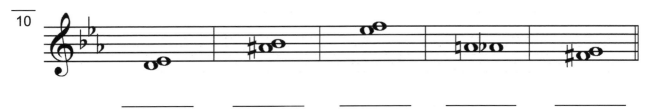

_____    _____    _____    _____    _____

5.  a)  Name the **MINOR** key for each of the following Key Signatures.
    b)  Give the **TECHNICAL DEGREE NAME** for each note (Tonic, Supertonic, etc.).

    a)  _____   _____     _____     _____     _____

    b)  _____   _____     _____     _____     _____

6.  a)  Write the Basic Beat and the pulse below each measure.
    b)  Add rests below each bracket to complete the measure.
    c)  Cross off the Basic Beat as each beat is completed.

Basic Beat: _____

Pulse:

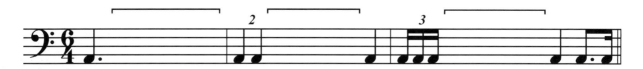

Basic Beat: _____

Pulse:

Basic Beat: _____

Pulse:

7.  Transpose the following melody **DOWN** one octave into the **Bass Clef**.

**8.** Write the following scales, ascending and descending, in the clefs indicated.  Use accidentals. Use whole notes.

a)  enharmonic Tonic minor, melodic form, of B flat Major

b)  whole tone scale starting on G

c)  e flat minor melodic from Leading note to Leading note

d)  Aeolian mode starting on on f sharp

e)  chromatic scale starting on A flat

10

a)

b)

c)

d)

e)

f) Name the following scales as octatonic, Major pentatonic, minor pentatonic or blues.

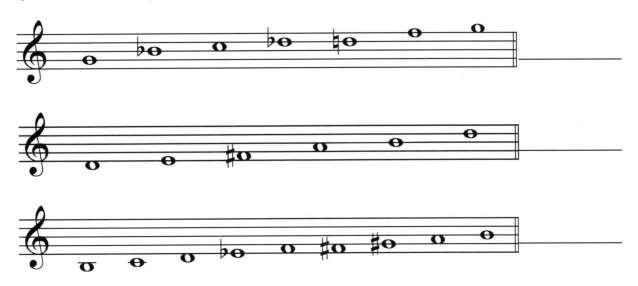

149

**9.** Match each musical term with its English definition.  (Not all definitions will be used.)

| Term | | Definition |
|------|---|-----------|
| *largo* | _____ | a)  but |
| *ritardando, rit.* | _____ | b)  above |
| *ottava, $8^{va}$* | _____ | c)  second; second or lower part of a duet |
| *ma* | _____ | d)  not too much |
| *meno* | _____ | e)  very slow |
| *sopra* | _____ | f)  with expression |
| *comodo* | _____ | g)  less |
| *secondo, seconda* | _____ | h)  at a comfortable, easy tempo |
| *non troppo* | _____ | i)  slowing down gradually |
| *con espressione* | _____ | j)  quiet, tranquil |
| | | k)  the interval of an octave |

**10.** Analyze the following excerpt by answering the questions below.

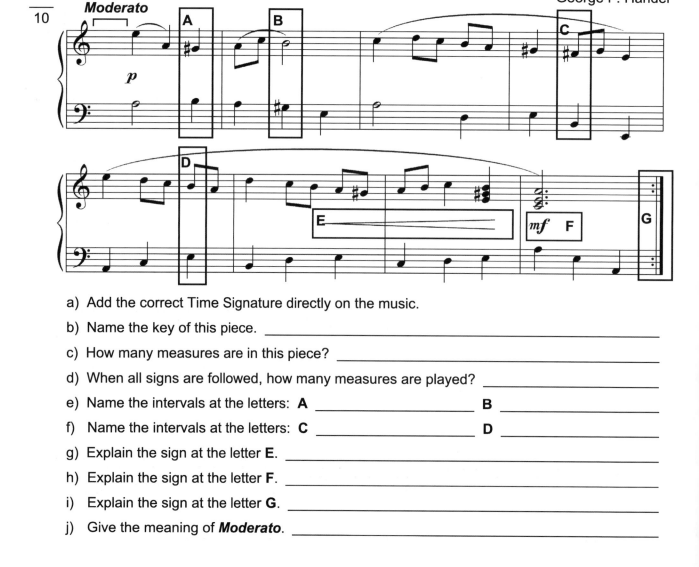

# Minuet

George F. Handel

a) Add the correct Time Signature directly on the music.

b) Name the key of this piece. _____

c) How many measures are in this piece? _____

d) When all signs are followed, how many measures are played? _____

e) Name the intervals at the letters:  **A** _____  **B** _____

f)  Name the intervals at the letters:  **C** _____  **D** _____

g) Explain the sign at the letter **E**. _____

h) Explain the sign at the letter **F**. _____

i)  Explain the sign at the letter **G**. _____

j)  Give the meaning of **Moderato**. _____

# Lesson 7 Triads - Major, Minor, Augmented, Diminished and 7ᵗʰ Chords

## SOLID ROOT POSITION TRIADS

A **TRIAD** is a three note chord:  the Root (the lowest note),
a third above the Root and a fifth above the Root.
A **SOLID** (blocked) triad is written one note above the other
(three notes played together).

F Major triad

♫ **Note:** A **ROOT** position triad is ALL lines or ALL spaces.  The lowest note names the Root.

1.  Copy the following solid root position triads.  Name the Root.

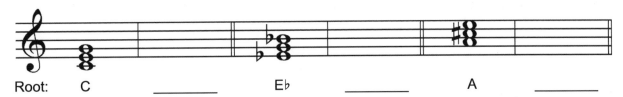

Root:    C    _____    E♭    _____    A    _____

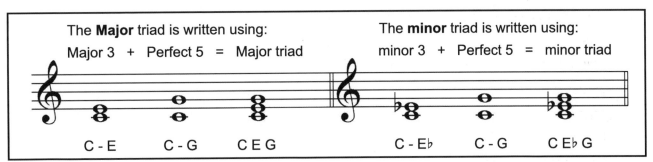

| The **Major** triad is written using: | The **minor** triad is written using: |
|---|---|
| Major 3  +  Perfect 5  =  Major triad | minor 3  +  Perfect 5  =  minor triad |
| C - E    C - G    C E G | C - E♭    C - G    C E♭ G |

2.  Following the example, write the intervals above the given notes.  Write the Major triads.

Maj 3 + Per 5 = D Major     Maj 3 + Per 5 = G Major     Maj 3 + Per 5 = A Major
                   triad                        triad                        triad

3.  Following the example, write the intervals above the given notes.  Write the minor triads.

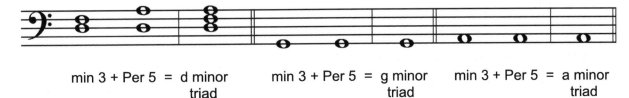

min 3 + Per 5 = d minor     min 3 + Per 5 = g minor     min 3 + Per 5 = a minor
                   triad                        triad                        triad

4.  Identify the type/quality of the following triads as Major or minor.

_____    _____    _____    _____    _____

## TONIC TRIADS and SUBDOMINANT TRIADS

**TRIADS** are built on any degree of a scale.  Roman Numerals are used to indicate the scale degree of the Root (lowest note).  Use UPPER case for Major triads and lower case for minor triads.

**Tonic triad** - first degree of the scale    I Major    i minor
**Subdominant triad** - fourth degree of the scale    IV Major    iv minor
**Dominant triad** - fifth degree of the scale    V Major    V Major

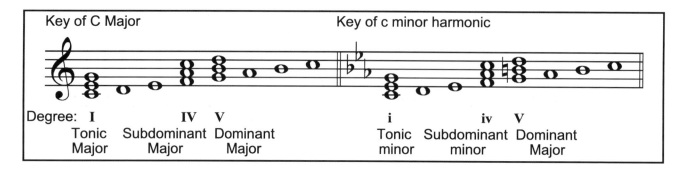

A **TONIC** triad is built on the first degree of the scale.
A Tonic triad uses the $\hat{1}$ (Tonic), $\hat{3}$ (Mediant) and $\hat{5}$ (Dominant) degrees of the scale.

1. a) Write the following Tonic triads in root position.  Use a Key Signature.  Use whole notes.
   b) Name the Tonic note.  Label the Tonic triad as **I** (Major) or **i** (minor).

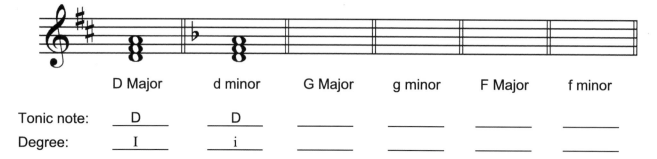

| | D Major | d minor | G Major | g minor | F Major | f minor |
|---|---|---|---|---|---|---|
| Tonic note: | D | D | | | | |
| Degree: | I | i | | | | |

A **SUBDOMINANT** triad is built on the fourth degree of the scale.  Count **UP** 4 notes from the Tonic.
A Subdominant triad uses the $\hat{4}$ (Subdominant), $\hat{6}$ (Submediant) and $\hat{1}$ (Tonic) degrees of the scale.

2. a) Write the following Subdominant triads in root position.  Use a Key Signature.  Use whole notes.
   b) Name the Subdominant note.  Label the Subdominant triad as **IV** (Major) or **iv** (minor).

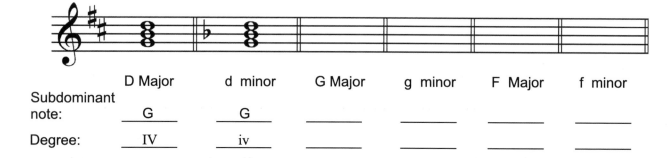

| | D Major | d minor | G Major | g minor | F Major | f minor |
|---|---|---|---|---|---|---|
| Subdominant note: | G | G | | | | |
| Degree: | IV | iv | | | | |

## DOMINANT TRIADS

A **DOMINANT** triad is built on the fifth degree of the scale.  Count **UP** 5 notes from the Tonic.
A Dominant triad uses the $\hat{5}$ (Dominant), $\hat{7}$ (Leading note) and $\hat{2}$ (Supertonic) degrees of the scale.

♫ **Note:**  Use the musical alphabet to find the fifth note above each Tonic.

**A   B   C   D   E   F   G   A   B   C   D   E   F   G**

1. a) Write the following Dominant triads in root position.  Use a Key Signature.  Use whole notes.
   b) Name the Dominant note.  Label the Dominant triad as **V** (Major).

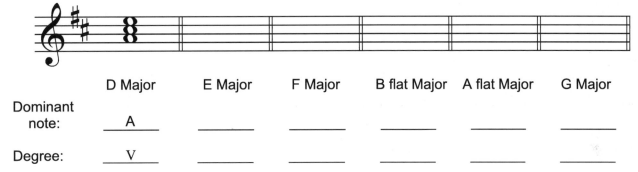

|  | D Major | E Major | F Major | B flat Major | A flat Major | G Major |
|---|---|---|---|---|---|---|
| Dominant note: | A | _____ | _____ | _____ | _____ | _____ |
| Degree: | V | _____ | _____ | _____ | _____ | _____ |

---

Key of f minor harmonic   Dominant triad is built on the:

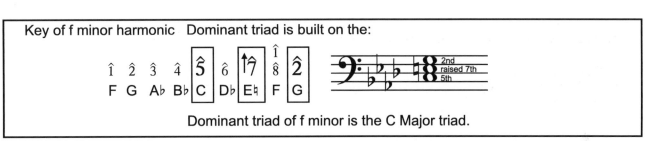

| $\hat{1}$ | $\hat{2}$ | $\hat{3}$ | $\hat{4}$ | $\boxed{\hat{5}}$ | $\hat{6}$ | $\boxed{\uparrow\hat{7}}$ | $\hat{1}$ $\hat{8}$ | $\boxed{\hat{2}}$ |
|---|---|---|---|---|---|---|---|---|
| F | G | A♭ | B♭ | C | D♭ | E♮ | F | G |

Dominant triad of f minor is the C Major triad.

---

♫ **Note**:  A Dominant triad of a minor key uses the raised 7th note of the harmonic minor scale.
When using a Key Signature, the raised Leading note of the harmonic minor scale will be
written using an accidental.  A Dominant triad is **ALWAYS** Major.

2. a) Write the following solid Dominant triads in root position.  Use a Key Signature and any
   necessary accidentals.  Use whole notes.
   b) Name the Dominant note.  Label the Dominant triad as **V** (Major).  Name the raised 7th note.

|  | d minor | e minor | f minor | b flat minor | a flat minor | g minor |
|---|---|---|---|---|---|---|
| Dominant note: | A | _____ | _____ | _____ | _____ | _____ |
| Degree: | V | _____ | _____ | _____ | _____ | _____ |
| Raised 7th note: | C♯ | _____ | _____ | _____ | _____ | _____ |

## WRITING TRIADS USING ACCIDENTALS

When the triad contains **TWO** accidentals, the accidental is written closest to the higher note and further away from the lower note.

When the triad contains **THREE** accidentals, the highest and lowest accidentals are written the same as above. The middle accidental is written furthest away from the middle note.

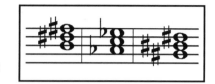

1. Copy the following Dominant triads. Name the Root (lowest note).

Root: _____    _____    _____

Each Dominant triad belongs to a Major key and a minor key. To identify the key of the Dominant triad, count **DOWN** 5 notes from the Dominant (a Perfect fifth) to find the Tonic note. This names BOTH the Tonic Major key and the Tonic minor key.

The Tonic Major key and the Tonic minor key have the **SAME Tonic note** and the **SAME Dominant triad**.

Dominant note: A    Tonic note: D
This is the Dominant triad of:
D Major and d minor
(Tonic Major and Tonic minor)

♫ **Note:** When using **accidentals**, the Dominant triad belongs to **BOTH** the Tonic Major key and the Tonic minor key.

2. Name both the Tonic Major key and Tonic minor key for each of the following Dominant triads.

Major key:  A Maj    _____   _____   _____   _____   _____

minor key:  a min    _____   _____   _____   _____   _____

♫ **Note:** When using a **Key Signature**, the Dominant triad belongs to only **ONE** key. If the Dominant triad contains an accidental (the raised 7th note of the harmonic minor scale), it belongs to the minor key.

3. Name the correct key (Major or minor) for each of the following Dominant triads.

Key:    c sharp minor    _____   _____   _____   _____   _____

## SOLID and BROKEN TRIADS

A **SOLID (BLOCKED) TRIAD** is written one note above the other (together).
A **BROKEN TRIAD** is written one note after the other. The notes are played one at a time (separately).

| C Major Tonic triad | | | c minor Tonic triad | | |
|---|---|---|---|---|---|
| Solid | Broken | Broken | Solid | Broken | Broken |
| Root: C | C | C | Root: C | C | C |

♫ **Note:** Broken triads in ROOT position may be written in the SKIPPING UP pattern or the SKIPPING DOWN pattern. The lowest note is ALWAYS the Root of the triad.

1. a) Name the Major key for each of the following broken triads. Name the Root.
   b) Label the triad degree as: I (Tonic Major), IV (Subdominant Major) or V (Dominant Major).

| Major key: | A Maj | D Maj | _____ | _____ | _____ |
|---|---|---|---|---|---|
| Root: | E | D | _____ | _____ | _____ |
| Degree: | V | I | _____ | _____ | _____ |

2. a) Name the minor key for each of the following broken triads. Name the Root.
   b) Label the triad degree as: i (Tonic minor), iv (Subdominant minor) or V (Dominant Major).

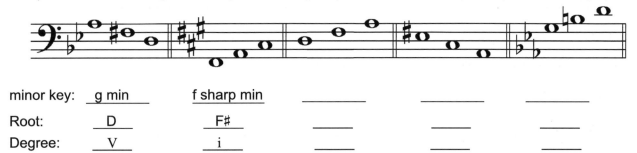

| minor key: | g min | f sharp min | _____ | _____ | _____ |
|---|---|---|---|---|---|
| Root: | D | F# | _____ | _____ | _____ |
| Degree: | V | i | _____ | _____ | _____ |

3. Name the Root. Label the triad degree as: I (Tonic Major), i (Tonic minor),
   IV (Subdominant Major), iv (Subdominant minor) or V (Dominant Major).

| Key: | A Major | g minor | E flat Major | f minor | c sharp minor |
|---|---|---|---|---|---|
| Root: | A | C | _____ | _____ | _____ |
| Degree: | I | iv | _____ | _____ | _____ |

## TRIADS and INVERSIONS

An **INVERSION** of a triad occurs when the Root (Key note) of the triad is moved to a new position.
A root position triad is all LINES or all SPACES. The Root of a root position triad is the lowest note.
In **ANY INVERSION**, the position of a triad is always determined by the LOWEST note.

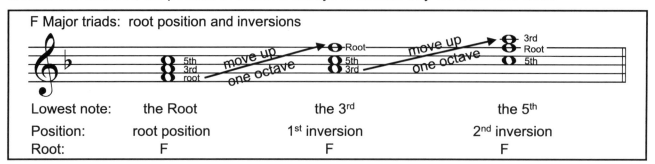

| | F Major triads: root position and inversions | | |
|---|---|---|---|
| Lowest note: | the Root | the 3rd | the 5th |
| Position: | root position | 1st inversion | 2nd inversion |
| Root: | F | F | F |

♫ **Note:** The name of the Root of the triad remains the same in root position, 1st inv. and 2nd inv.

Proper placement of accidentals in triads and inversions are as follows:
1- closest to the top note, 2- further away from the bottom note, 3- furthest away from the middle note.

1. a) Write the following root position triads in 1st inversion (inv) and 2nd inversion (inv) by moving the lowest note up one octave. Use whole notes. Use accidentals.
   b) Name the Root.

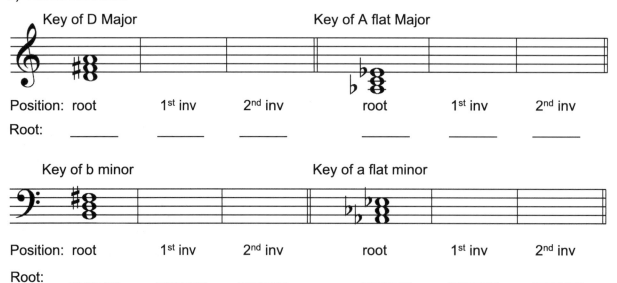

Key of D Major

Key of A flat Major

| Position: root | 1st inv | 2nd inv | root | 1st inv | 2nd inv |
|---|---|---|---|---|---|
| Root: ____ | ____ | ____ | ____ | ____ | ____ |

Key of b minor

Key of a flat minor

| Position: root | 1st inv | 2nd inv | root | 1st inv | 2nd inv |
|---|---|---|---|---|---|
| Root: ____ | ____ | ____ | ____ | ____ | ____ |

2. Invert the following triads. Use whole notes. a) Name the position. b) Name the Root.

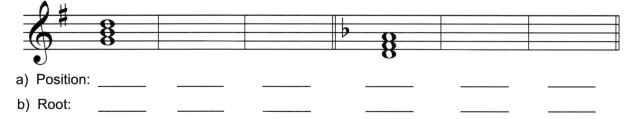

a) Position: ____  ____  ____    ____  ____  ____

b) Root: ____  ____  ____    ____  ____  ____

# MAJOR and MINOR TRIADS

A root position Major triad consists of the Root, Major 3rd and Perfect 5th.

A root position minor triad consists of the Root, minor 3rd and Perfect 5th.

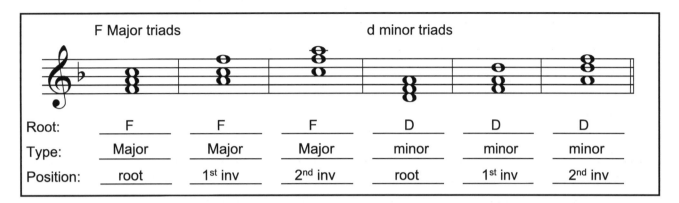

| Root: | F | F | F | D | D | D |
|-------|---|---|---|---|---|---|
| Type: | Major | Major | Major | minor | minor | minor |
| Position: | root | 1st inv | 2nd inv | root | 1st inv | 2nd inv |

1. Invert the following triads.  Use whole notes.  For each triad, name:
   a) the Root (Key note).
   b) the type/quality (Major or minor).
   c) the position (root, 1st inv or 2nd inv).

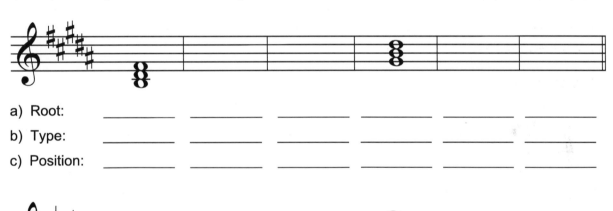

a) Root: _____ _____ _____ _____ _____ _____

b) Type: _____ _____ _____ _____ _____ _____

c) Position: _____ _____ _____ _____ _____ _____

a) Root: _____ _____ _____ _____ _____ _____

b) Type: _____ _____ _____ _____ _____ _____

c) Position: _____ _____ _____ _____ _____ _____

a) Root: _____ _____ _____ _____ _____ _____

b) Type: _____ _____ _____ _____ _____ _____

c) Position: _____ _____ _____ _____ _____ _____

## INVERSIONS of TONIC TRIADS

When writing an inversion of a triad, write it in root position first and then write the inversion.

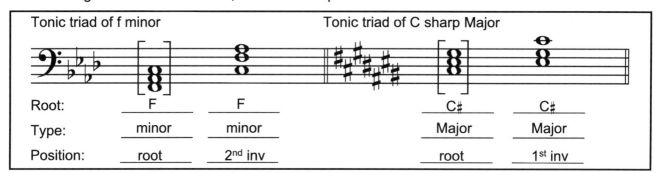

| | Tonic triad of f minor | | | Tonic triad of C sharp Major | |
|---|---|---|---|---|---|
| Root: | F | F | | C# | C# |
| Type: | minor | minor | | Major | Major |
| Position: | root | 2nd inv | | root | 1st inv |

1. Write the following triads in the Bass Clef, using a Key Signature.  Write the triad in root position in the [square bracket], then write the correct inversion.  Use whole notes.  Name the Root (Key note).

   a) the **TONIC** triad of E flat Major in second inversion
   b) the **TONIC** triad of d minor in first inversion
   c) the **TONIC** triad of c sharp minor in second inversion
   d) the **TONIC** triad of B flat Major in first inversion
   e) the **TONIC** triad of f sharp minor in root position
   f) the **TONIC** triad of A Major in second inversion

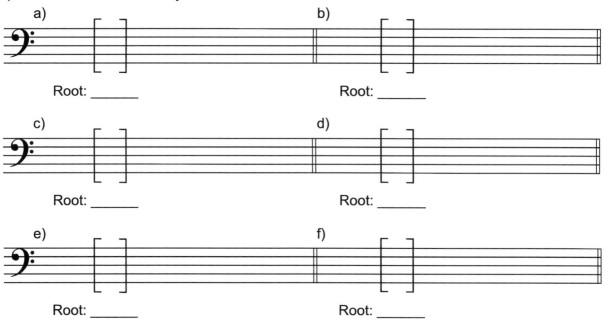

a)

Root: _____

b)

Root: _____

c)

Root: _____

d)

Root: _____

e)

Root: _____

f)

Root: _____

2. For each triad, name:  a) the Root.  b) the type/quality.  c) the position.

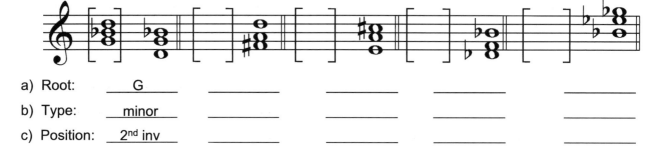

a) Root:      G      _____   _____   _____   _____

b) Type:    minor    _____   _____   _____   _____

c) Position:  2nd inv   _____   _____   _____   _____

## TRIADS and INVERSIONS

1. Invert the following triads into 1<sup>st</sup> inv and 2<sup>nd</sup> inv. Use whole notes. a) Name the position.
   b) Name the Root.

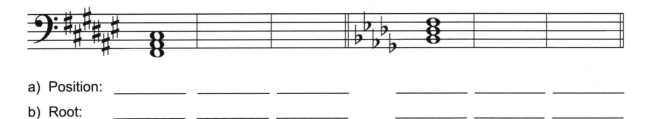

   a) Position: _____ _____ _____    _____ _____ _____

   b) Root: _____ _____ _____    _____ _____ _____

2. Invert the following triads. Use whole notes. For each triad, name:
   a) the Root (Key note).
   b) the type/quality (Major or minor).
   c) the position (root, 1<sup>st</sup> inv or 2<sup>nd</sup> inv).

   a) Root: _____ _____ _____    _____ _____ _____

   b) Type: _____ _____ _____    _____ _____ _____

   c) Position: _____ _____ _____    _____ _____ _____

   a) Root: _____ _____ _____    _____ _____ _____

   b) Type: _____ _____ _____    _____ _____ _____

   c) Position: _____ _____ _____    _____ _____ _____

3. For each triad, name: a) the Root. b) the type/quality. c) the position.

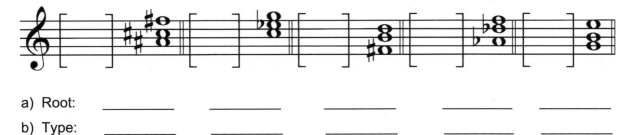

   a) Root: _____    _____    _____    _____    _____

   b) Type: _____    _____    _____    _____    _____

   c) Position: _____    _____    _____    _____    _____

## TRIADS BUILT on MAJOR SCALE DEGREES

**TRIADS** are built on any degree of a **MAJOR** scale. Roman Numerals are used to indicate the scale degree of the Root note of the triad. Roman Numerals (R.N.) in **UPPER** case indicate the type as a **Major triad**. Roman Numerals (R.N.) in **lower** case indicate the type as a **minor triad**.

Major and minor triads built on the scale degrees of D Major (using accidentals).

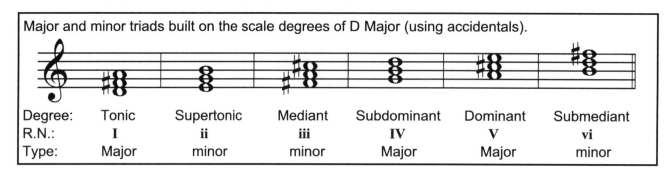

| Degree: | Tonic | Supertonic | Mediant | Subdominant | Dominant | Submediant |
|---|---|---|---|---|---|---|
| R.N.: | I | ii | iii | IV | V | vi |
| Type: | Major | minor | minor | Major | Major | minor |

♫ **Note:** In the **MAJOR** scale, only triads built on the Tonic, Supertonic, Mediant, Subdominant, Dominant and Submediant are Major or minor triads.

1. Write a root position triad above each of the following notes using the E Major Scale. Use whole notes. Use accidentals. For each triad, name: a) the technical degree (lowest note). b) the Roman Numeral (R.N.) for each degree. c) the type/quality (Major or minor).

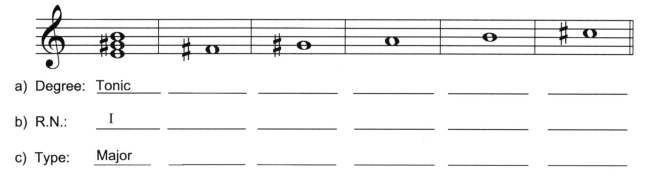

a) Degree:  <u>Tonic</u>  _____  _____  _____  _____  _____

b) R.N.:  <u>I</u>  _____  _____  _____  _____  _____

c) Type:  <u>Major</u>  _____  _____  _____  _____  _____

2. Write the following triads. Use whole notes. Use accidentals. Write the degree of each Major or minor triad using Roman Numerals (R.N.). Name the type/quality of the triad as Major or minor.

    a) the **DOMINANT** triad of G Major in 2nd inversion
    b) the **MEDIANT** triad of D Major in 2nd inversion
    c) the **TONIC** triad of B flat Major in 1st inversion
    d) the **SUPERTONIC** triad of C Major in root position
    e) the **SUBMEDIANT** triad of A flat Major in 1st inversion
    f) the **SUBDOMINANT** triad of F Major in root position

    a)      b)      c)      d)      e)      f)

R.N.:  <u>V</u>  _____  _____  _____  _____  _____

Type:  <u>Major</u>  _____  _____  _____  _____  _____

## TRIADS BUILT on HARMONIC MINOR SCALE DEGREES

**TRIADS** are built on any degree of a harmonic **MINOR** scale. Roman Numerals are used to indicate the scale degree of the Root note of the triad. Roman Numerals (R.N.) in **UPPER case** indicate the type as a **Major triad**. Roman Numerals (R.N.) in **lower case** indicate the type as a **minor triad**.

Major and minor triads built on the scale degrees of d minor harmonic (using accidentals).

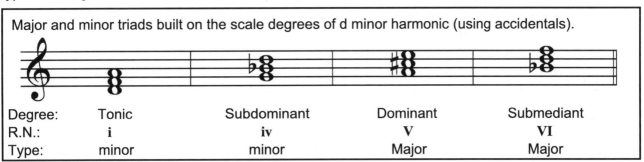

| Degree: | Tonic | Subdominant | Dominant | Submediant |
|---|---|---|---|---|
| R.N.: | i | iv | V | VI |
| Type: | minor | minor | Major | Major |

♫ **Note:** In the **HARMONIC MINOR** scale, only triads built on the Tonic, Subdominant, Dominant and Submediant are Major or minor triads.

1. Write a root position triad above each of the following notes using the e minor harmonic scale. Use whole notes. Use accidentals. For each triad, name: a) the technical degree (lowest note). b) the Roman Numeral for each degree. c) the type/quality (Major or minor).

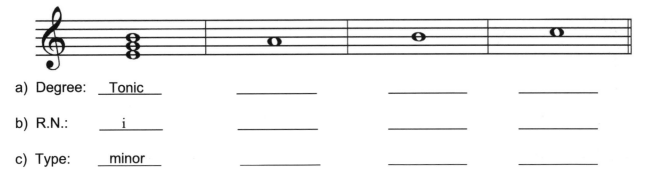

a) Degree:   <u>Tonic</u>   _____   _____   _____

b) R.N.:   <u>i</u>   _____   _____   _____

c) Type:   <u>minor</u>   _____   _____   _____

♫ **Note:** Use proper placement of accidentals when writing triads using accidentals.

2. Write the following triads. Use whole notes. Use accidentals. Write the degree of each Major or minor triad using Roman Numerals (R.N.). Name the type/quality of the triad as Major or minor.

   a) the **SUBDOMINANT** triad of b flat minor harmonic in 1st inversion
   b) the **DOMINANT** triad of f sharp minor harmonic in 2nd inversion
   c) the **TONIC** triad of e flat minor harmonic in 1st inversion
   d) the **SUBMEDIANT** triad of a sharp minor harmonic in 2nd inversion

   a)                    b)                    c)                    d)

R.N.:   <u>iv</u>   _____   _____   _____

Type:   <u>minor</u>   _____   _____   _____

## TRIADS in CLOSE POSITION

A triad in **CLOSE POSITION** is written as close together as possible. NO interval is larger than a 6th.
A triad in close position may be written as broken or solid; and in root position or an inversion.

♫ **Note:** The POSITION of a triad is ALWAYS determined by the LOWEST note.

| | Lowest note: | Root (Key note) | 3rd above the Root | 5th above the Root |
|---|---|---|---|---|
| | Position: | root position | 1st inversion | 2nd inversion |

Triads in Close Position

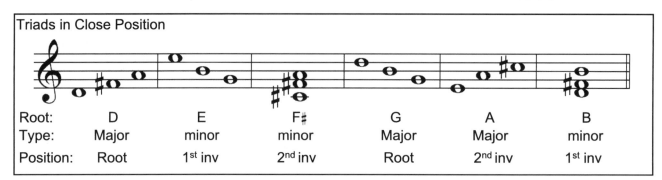

| Root: | D | E | F♯ | G | A | B |
|---|---|---|---|---|---|---|
| Type: | Major | minor | minor | Major | Major | minor |
| Position: | Root | 1st inv | 2nd inv | Root | 2nd inv | 1st inv |

1. For each triad in close position, name: a) the Root. b) the type/quality. c) the position.

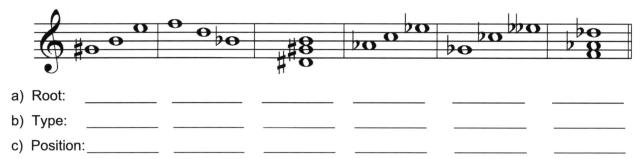

a) Root: _____  _____  _____  _____  _____  _____

b) Type: _____  _____  _____  _____  _____  _____

c) Position: _____  _____  _____  _____  _____  _____

♫ **Note:** A triad in CLOSE position may be written on the Grand Staff, divided between the
Treble Clef and the Bass Clef, as long as the distance from the lowest to highest note is
no larger than a 6th.

2. Rewrite the given triad in close root position in the [square] brackets. For each of the following
triads name: a) the Root. b) the type/quality. c) the position of the given triad.

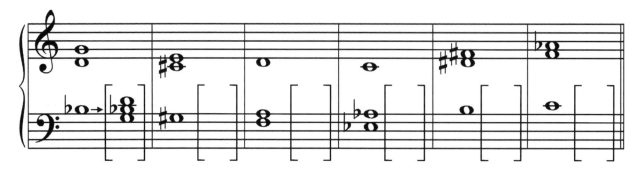

a) Root: _____G_____  _____  _____  _____  _____  _____

b) Type: ___minor___  _____  _____  _____  _____  _____

c) Position: __1st inv__  _____  _____  _____  _____  _____

## TRIADS in OPEN POSITION

A triad in **OPEN POSITION** is written with intervals larger than a 6th. An OPEN position triad may be written on a single staff or on the Grand Staff. One of the notes (usually the Root) may be doubled. A triad in open position may be written as broken or solid; and in root position or an inversion.

♫ **Note:** The position of a triad is ALWAYS determined by the LOWEST note.

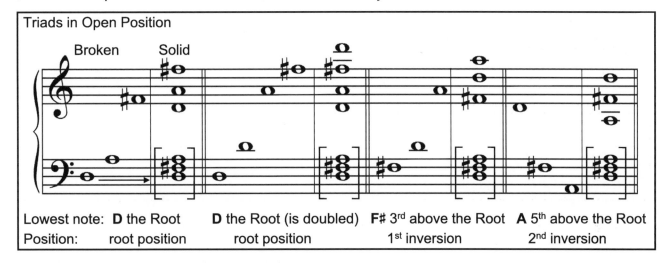

Lowest note:  **D** the Root     **D** the Root (is doubled)     **F#** 3rd above the Root    **A** 5th above the Root
Position:      root position       root position                 1st inversion               2nd inversion

1. Rewrite the given triad in close root position in the [square] brackets.  For each of the following triads name:  a) the Root.  b) the type/quality.  c) the position of the given triad.

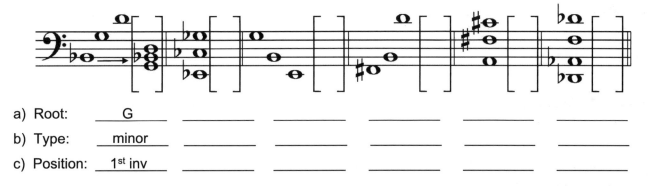

a) Root:      ___G___    _____    _____    _____    _____    _____

b) Type:      __minor__   _____    _____    _____    _____    _____

c) Position:  __1st inv__   _____    _____    _____    _____    _____

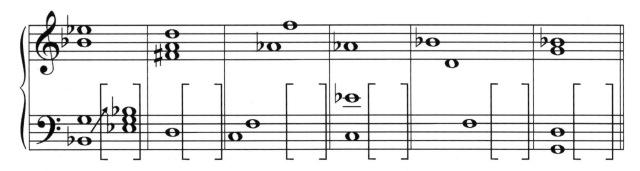

a) Root:      ___E♭___    _____    _____    _____    _____    _____

b) Type:      __Major__   _____    _____    _____    _____    _____

c) Position:  __2nd inv__   _____    _____    _____    _____    _____

## MAJOR, MINOR, AUGMENTED and DIMINISHED TRIADS

A **TRIAD** is a three note chord.  The lowest note of a root position triad (all lines or all spaces) is called the **Root**.  A root position triad consists of a third and a fifth above the Root.  The type/quality of the triad (Major, minor, Augmented or diminished) is determined by the type/quality of the intervals above the Root (Major or minor 3; Perfect, Augmented or diminished 5).

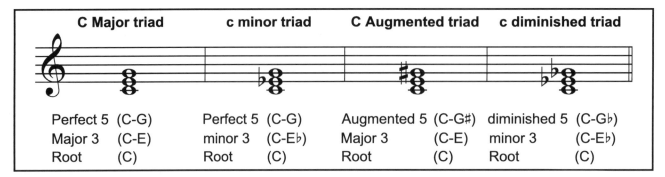

| C Major triad | c minor triad | C Augmented triad | c diminished triad |
|---|---|---|---|
| Perfect 5 (C-G) | Perfect 5 (C-G) | Augmented 5 (C-G♯) | diminished 5 (C-G♭) |
| Major 3 (C-E) | minor 3 (C-E♭) | Major 3 (C-E) | minor 3 (C-E♭) |
| Root (C) | Root (C) | Root (C) | Root (C) |

♪ **Note:**   **Major** triad: Root, Maj 3, Per 5          **minor** triad: Root, min 3, Per 5
        **Augmented** triad: Root, Maj 3, Aug 5          **diminished** triad: Root, min 3, dim 5

1.  Copy the chart to determine the type/quality of a Major, minor, Augmented or diminished triad.

Maj 3 + Per 5  = **Major triad**          _____ 3 +  _____ 5 = **Major triad**

min 3 + Per 5  = **minor triad**          _____ 3 +  _____ 5 = **minor triad**

Maj 3 + Aug 5  = **Augmented triad**          _____ 3 +  _____ 5 = **Augmented triad**

min 3 + dim 5  = **diminished triad**          _____ 3 +  _____ 5 = **diminished triad**

2.  a)  Name the type/quality of the interval of a fifth above the Root as Per, Aug or dim.
    b)  Name the type/quality of the interval of a third above the Root as Maj or min.
    c)  Name the type/quality of the triad as Major, minor, Augmented or diminished.

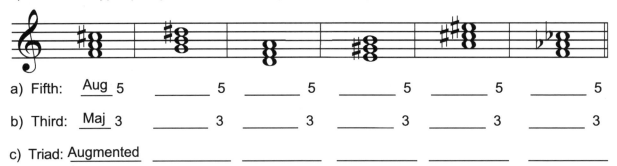

a) Fifth:  <u>Aug</u> 5      _____ 5      _____ 5      _____ 5      _____ 5      _____ 5

b) Third:  <u>Maj</u> 3      _____ 3      _____ 3      _____ 3      _____ 3      _____ 3

c) Triad: <u>Augmented</u>      _____      _____      _____      _____      _____

a) Fifth:  <u>dim</u> 5      _____ 5      _____ 5      _____ 5      _____ 5      _____ 5

b) Third:  <u>min</u> 3      _____ 3      _____ 3      _____ 3      _____ 3      _____ 3

c) Triad: <u>diminished</u>      _____      _____      _____      _____      _____

# TRIADS on SCALE DEGREES

**TRIADS** may be built on any scale degree of a Major or minor scale. **Functional Chord Symbols** are Roman Numerals that are used to identify the type/quality and scale degree of a triad (chord).

♫ **Note:**  **Major** (**Maj**) triads:  Upper case Roman Numerals.
**Minor** (**min**) triads:  lower case Roman Numerals.
**Augmented** (**Aug**) triads:  Upper case Roman Numerals and an ˣ or + sign.
**Diminished** (**dim**) triads:  lower case Roman Numerals and a ° degree sign.

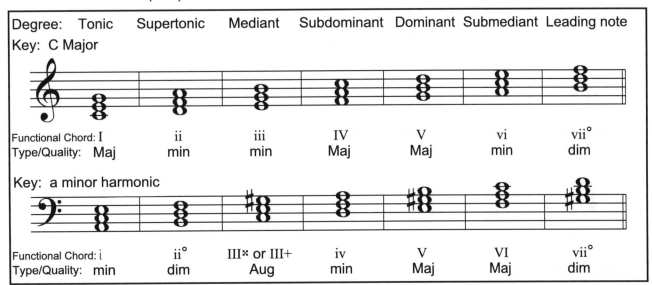

| Degree: | Tonic | Supertonic | Mediant | Subdominant | Dominant | Submediant | Leading note |
|---|---|---|---|---|---|---|---|
| Key: C Major | | | | | | | |
| Functional Chord: | I | ii | iii | IV | V | vi | vii° |
| Type/Quality: | Maj | min | min | Maj | Maj | min | dim |
| Key: a minor harmonic | | | | | | | |
| Functional Chord: | i | ii° | III˟ or III+ | iv | V | VI | vii° |
| Type/Quality: | min | dim | Aug | min | Maj | Maj | dim |

♫ **Note:**  Triads built on the Mediant, Dominant and Leading note of the harmonic minor scale always contain the raised 7ᵗʰ note.

1. Write a solid root position triad above each note of the g minor harmonic scale.  Use whole notes. Name the type/quality as Major (Maj), minor (min), Augmented (Aug) or diminished (dim).

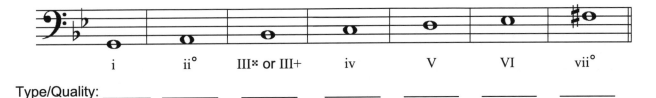

i          ii°        III˟ or III+        iv          V          VI          vii°

Type/Quality: _____  _____  _____  _____  _____  _____  _____

2. Write the following solid root position triads using accidentals, in the Bass Clef.  Use whole notes. Name the type/quality as Major, minor, Augmented or diminished.

   a) the **SUPERTONIC** triad (ii) of E flat Major
   b) the **LEADING NOTE** triad (vii°) of d sharp minor harmonic
   c) the **DOMINANT** triad (V) of f minor harmonic
   d) the **MEDIANT** triad (III˟ or III+) of b minor harmonic
   e) the **SUBMEDIANT** triad (VI) of a flat minor harmonic

a)          b)          c)          d)          e)

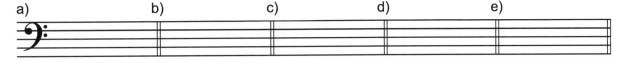

Type/Quality: _____  _____  _____  _____  _____

## TRIADS IN CLOSE POSITION

**TRIADS** in **CLOSE POSITION** are written as close together as possible. NO interval is larger than a sixth. **Figured bass** (chord position) numbers are used to indicate the position of a triad. Each number represents interval distance of the notes ABOVE the lowest note of the triad.

♫ **Note:** In **CLOSE POSITION**, the **position** (root, 1st inv or 2nd inv) of a triad is determined by the lowest note. The lowest note of a **root position triad** names the Root of the triad.

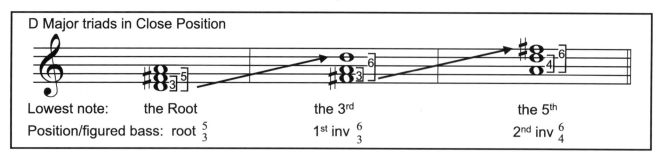

D Major triads in Close Position

| Lowest note: | the Root | the 3rd | the 5th |
|---|---|---|---|
| Position/figured bass: | root $\frac{5}{3}$ | 1st inv $\frac{6}{3}$ | 2nd inv $\frac{6}{4}$ |

1. For each of the following triads, name:
   a) the Root. Write the triad in root position in [square brackets]. (Lowest note names the Root.)
   b) the type/quality (Major, minor, Augmented or diminished).
   c) the position and figured bass (root $\frac{5}{3}$, 1st inv $\frac{6}{3}$ or 2nd inv $\frac{6}{4}$).

a) Root:    C♭ _____   _____   _____   _____   _____

b) Type:    Aug _____   _____   _____   _____   _____

c) Position: 1st inv $\frac{6}{3}$ _____   _____   _____   _____   _____

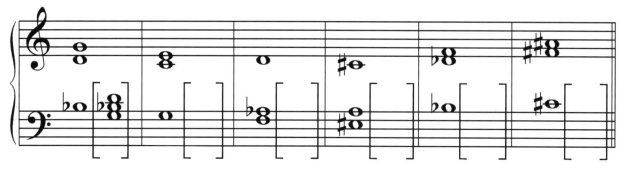

a) Root:    G _____   _____   _____   _____   _____

b) Type:    min _____   _____   _____   _____   _____

c) Position: 1st inv $\frac{6}{3}$ _____   _____   _____   _____   _____

## TRIADS in OPEN POSITION

**TRIADS** in **OPEN POSITION** are written on one staff or on the Grand Staff. The triad is spread out over more than an octave. When one of the notes (usually the root) is doubled, the triad is in four note form. Open position and closed position triads use the same chord positions and figured bass.

♫ **Note:** In **OPEN POSITION**, the **position** of a triad is determined by the lowest note. The other notes may be written in ANY order above the lowest note.

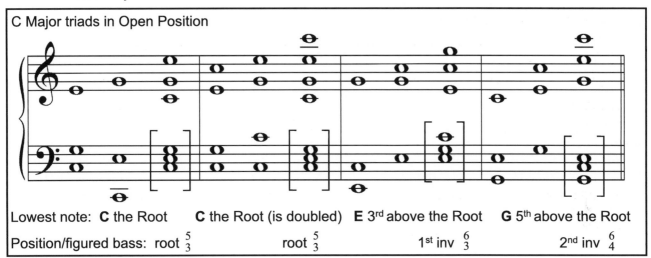

C Major triads in Open Position

| Lowest note: | **C** the Root | **C** the Root (is doubled) | **E** 3rd above the Root | **G** 5th above the Root |
|---|---|---|---|---|
| Position/figured bass: | root $\frac{5}{3}$ | root $\frac{5}{3}$ | 1st inv $\frac{6}{3}$ | 2nd inv $\frac{6}{4}$ |

1. Fill in the blanks:

   a) When in root position (Close or Open position), the lowest note names the _____.

   b) The position of a triad (Close or Open position) is determined by the _____ note.

   c) Write the figured bass for:  root position - _____;  1st inv - _____;  2nd inv - _____.

2. For each of the following triads, name:

   a) the Root. Write the triad in root position in [square brackets]. (Lowest note names the Root.)

   b) the type/quality (Major, minor, Augmented or diminished).

   c) the position and figured bass (root $\frac{5}{3}$, 1st inv $\frac{6}{3}$ or 2nd inv $\frac{6}{4}$).

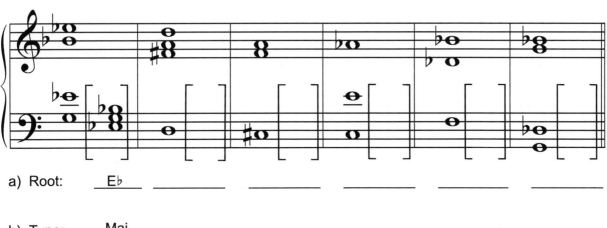

a) Root:  ___E♭___  _____  _____  _____  _____  _____

b) Type:  ___Maj___  _____  _____  _____  _____  _____

c) Position: 1st inv $\frac{6}{3}$  _____  _____  _____  _____  _____

# WRITING MAJOR, MINOR, AUGMENTED and DIMINISHED TRIADS and INVERSIONS

When writing **MAJOR, MINOR, AUGMENTED** or **DIMINISHED** triads, always start with root position. Determine the intervals above the Root to create the triad. The third and fifth above the Root determine the type/quality of the triad. Then write the triad in the inverted position.

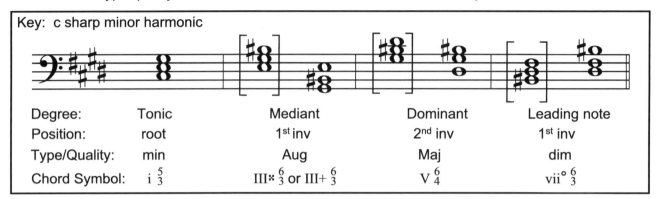

| Degree: | Tonic | Mediant | Dominant | Leading note |
|---|---|---|---|---|
| Position: | root | 1st inv | 2nd inv | 1st inv |
| Type/Quality: | min | Aug | Maj | dim |
| Chord Symbol: | i $^5_3$ | III✺ $^6_3$ or III+ $^6_3$ | V $^6_4$ | vii° $^6_3$ |

♫ **Note:** The **CHORD SYMBOL** will show the **Functional Chord Symbol** (Roman Numeral) and the **Figured bass** (position numbers).

1. Write the following triads in close position using the correct Key Signature. Use whole notes. Name the type/quality. Write the chord symbol for each triad.

   a) the **MEDIANT** triad of g minor harmonic in second inversion
   b) the **LEADING NOTE** triad of b minor harmonic in first inversion
   c) the **DOMINANT** triad of A flat Major in second inversion
   d) the **SUPERTONIC** triad of B Major in root position
   e) the **SUBMEDIANT** triad of e minor harmonic in first inversion

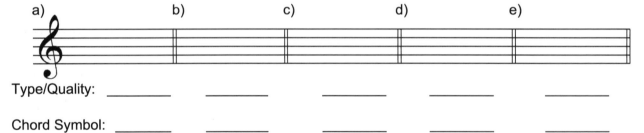

Type/Quality: _____   _____   _____   _____   _____

Chord Symbol: _____   _____   _____   _____   _____

2. Write the following triads in close position using accidentals. Use whole notes. Name the type/quality. Write the chord symbol for each triad.

   a) the **TONIC** triad of a flat minor harmonic in second inversion
   b) the **SUBDOMINANT** triad of f sharp minor harmonic in root position
   c) the **MEDIANT** triad of G flat Major in first inversion
   d) the **DOMINANT** triad of c sharp minor harmonic in first inversion
   e) the **LEADING NOTE** triad of D flat Major in root position

a)     b)     c)     d)     e)

Type/Quality: _____   _____   _____   _____   _____

Chord Symbol: _____   _____   _____   _____   _____

# IDENTIFYING a SCALE WHICH CONTAINS a GROUP of TRIADS

When **IDENTIFYING** a **SCALE WHICH CONTAINS** a **GROUP** of **TRIADS**, write the accidentals in the order of the Key Signature. If the triads are written using accidentals in correct Key Signature order, the scale will be Major and its relative natural minor. If the accidentals are not in correct Key Signature order, a triad will contain the raised 7th note, and the scale will be the harmonic minor.

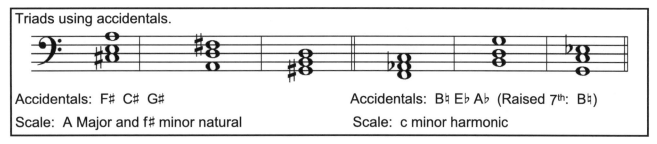

Triads using accidentals.

Accidentals: F# C# G#

Scale: A Major and f# minor natural

Accidentals: B♮ E♭ A♭  (Raised 7th: B♮)

Scale: c minor harmonic

1. For each of the triads, name: a) the accidentals. b) the scale which contains all of the triads.

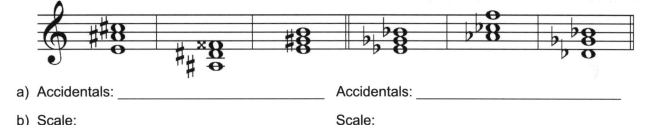

a) Accidentals: _____    Accidentals: _____

b) Scale: _____    Scale: _____

♫ **Note:** If a Key Signature is used and no accidental appears with a triad, the scale which contains a group of triads (Major, minor or diminished) belongs to a Major scale and its relative natural minor scale. If an accidental (raised 7th note) is used, the scale which contains a group of triads (Major, minor, Augmented or diminished) belongs to a harmonic minor scale.

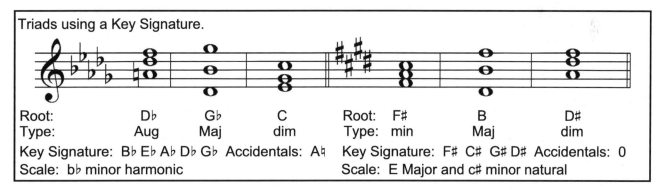

Triads using a Key Signature.

| Root: | D♭ | G♭ | C | Root: | F# | B | D# |
|-------|-----|-----|-----|-------|-----|-----|-----|
| Type: | Aug | Maj | dim | Type: | min | Maj | dim |

Key Signature: B♭ E♭ A♭ D♭ G♭  Accidentals: A♮    Key Signature: F# C# G# D#  Accidentals: 0

Scale: b♭ minor harmonic    Scale: E Major and c# minor natural

2. For each of the triads, name: a) the Root. b) the type. c) the Key Signature and any accidentals. d) the scale which contains all of the triads.

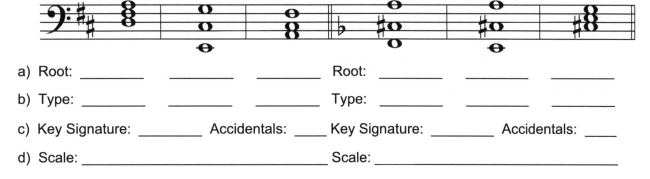

a) Root: _____  _____  _____    Root: _____  _____  _____

b) Type: _____  _____  _____    Type: _____  _____  _____

c) Key Signature: _____ Accidentals: ____    Key Signature: _____ Accidentals: ____

d) Scale: _____    Scale: _____

## POLYCHORD, QUARTAL CHORD and CLUSTER CHORD

A **POLYCHORD** is a combination of two or more different chords. They can be in root position or in any inversion. The chords may have notes in common, or none at all.

A **QUARTAL CHORD** is built on intervals of fourths. The fourths can be a combination of Perfect, Augmented and/or diminished. The Quartal chord has three or more notes.

 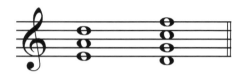

A **CLUSTER CHORD** or **TONE CLUSTER** is a chord consisting of three or more adjacent notes of a scale.

1. Identify the following chords as polychord, quartal chord or cluster chord.

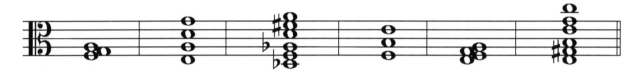

_____  _____  _____  _____  _____  _____

2. Match each chord description with the correct chord.

quartal chord        _____          a) 

Major triad          _____          b) 

polychord            _____          c) 

minor triad          _____          d) 

cluster chord        _____          e)

# DOMINANT SEVENTH CHORDS

The **DOMINANT SEVENTH** chord is a four note chord that is built on the fifth degree of a scale.  It consists of a Root, Major 3, Perfect 5 and a minor 7.  The symbol for the **Dominant 7th** chord is **V7**.  The Roman Numeral V indicates the Dominant triad.  The number 7 after the Roman Numeral ( **V7** ) indicates the interval of a minor 7th above the Root of the Dominant triad.

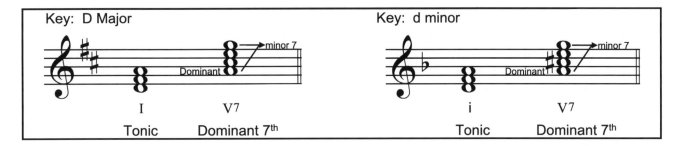

♫ **Note:**  Tonic Major and minor keys have the SAME Dominant 7th chord.  The Dominant 7th chord of a minor key always contains the raised 7th note of the harmonic minor scale.

1.  For each of the following keys, write the Dominant seventh chord in root position.  Use accidentals.  Use whole notes.

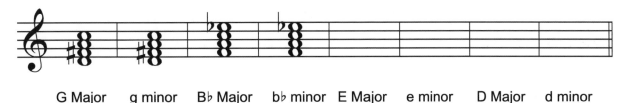

Dominant 7th chords written using a Key Signature belong to either the Major or relative minor key. (The minor key contains the raised 7th note.)  To identify the Major or minor key of a Dominant chord, count DOWN a Perfect fifth from the bottom note (the Root) of the Dominant 7th chord.

2.  Name the key (Major or minor) to which the following Dominant seventh chords belong.

Dominant seventh chords written using accidentals belong to BOTH the Major and Tonic minor keys.

3.  Name the TWO keys (Major and Tonic minor) to which the following Dominant 7th chords belong.

# DOMINANT 7th CHORDS in CLOSE POSITION

**DOMINANT 7th chords in CLOSE POSITION** are written as close together as possible. NO interval is larger than a seventh. **Figured bass** (chord position) numbers are used to indicate the position of a chord. Each number represents the interval distance ABOVE the lowest note of the chord. There are **3 inversions** of the Dominant 7th chord. The position of a chord is determined by the lowest note.

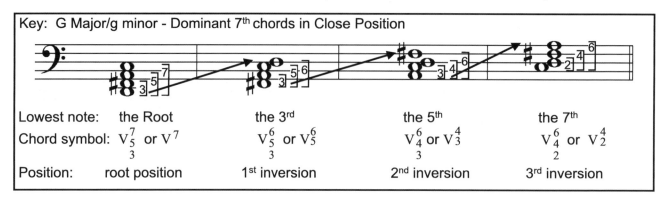

Key: G Major/g minor - Dominant 7th chords in Close Position

| Lowest note: | the Root | the 3rd | the 5th | the 7th |
|---|---|---|---|---|
| Chord symbol: | $V_5^7$ or $V^7$ | $V_5^6$ or $V_5^6$ | $V_4^6$ or $V_3^4$ | $V_4^6$ or $V_2^4$ |
| Position: | root position | 1st inversion | 2nd inversion | 3rd inversion |

1. For each of the following Dominant seventh chords, name:
   a) the Root. Write the chord in root position in [square brackets]. (Lowest note names the Root.)
   b) the keys to which it belongs (Major and Tonic minor).
   c) the position (root position, 1st inv, 2nd inv or 3rd inv); the chord symbol ($V^7$, $V_5^6$, $V_3^4$ or $V_2^4$).

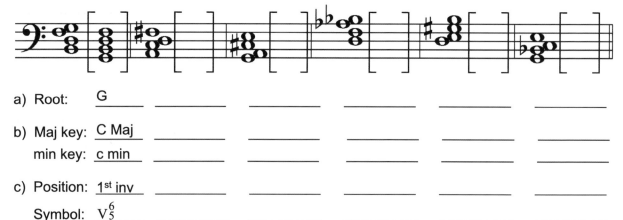

a) Root:     G     _____  _____  _____  _____  _____

b) Maj key:  C Maj  _____  _____  _____  _____  _____

   min key:  c min  _____  _____  _____  _____  _____

c) Position: 1st inv  _____  _____  _____  _____  _____

   Symbol:   $V_5^6$  _____  _____  _____  _____  _____

2. Write the following Dominant seventh chords in the Bass Clef. Use the correct Key Signature. Use whole notes. Write the chord symbol for each.
   a) the Dominant seventh chord of e minor harmonic in 2nd inversion
   b) the Dominant seventh chord of b minor harmonic in 1st inversion
   c) the Dominant seventh chord of D Major in root position
   d) the Dominant seventh chord of c sharp minor harmonic in 2nd inversion
   e) the Dominant seventh chord of G flat Major in 3rd inversion
   f) the Dominant seventh chord of a minor harmonic in 1st inversion

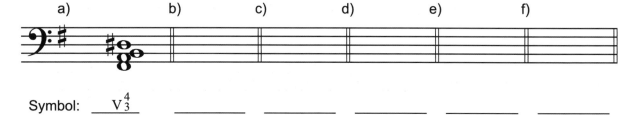

Symbol:     $V_3^4$     _____  _____  _____  _____  _____

# DOMINANT 7th CHORDS in OPEN POSITION

**DOMINANT 7th chords in OPEN POSITION** are written on one staff or on the Grand Staff. The chord is spread out over more than an octave. Open Position and Closed Position Chords use the same chord symbols. The position of a chord is determined by the lowest note. The UPPER notes may be written in ANY order and do not affect the position of the chord.

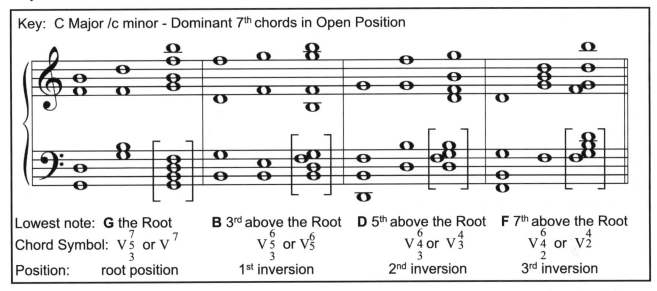

Key: C Major /c minor - Dominant 7th chords in Open Position

| Lowest note: | **G** the Root | **B** 3rd above the Root | **D** 5th above the Root | **F** 7th above the Root |
|---|---|---|---|---|
| Chord Symbol: | $V_5^7$ or $V^7$ | $V_5^6$ or $V_5^6$ | $V_3^6$ or $V_3^4$ | $V_4^6$ or $V_2^4$ |
| Position: | root position | 1st inversion | 2nd inversion | 3rd inversion |

1. For each of the following Dominant 7th chords, name:
   a) the Root. Write the chord in root position in [square brackets].
   b) the key to which it belongs.
   c) the position (root position, 1st inv, 2nd inv or 3rd inv); the chord symbol ($V^7$, $V_5^6$, $V_3^4$ or $V_2^4$).

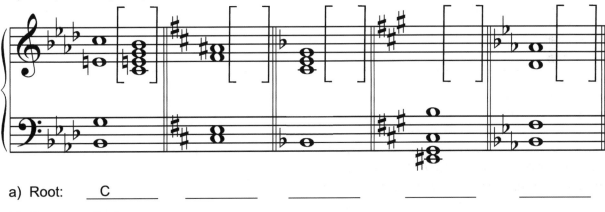

|  |  |  |  |  |  |
|---|---|---|---|---|---|
| a) Root: | C | _____ | _____ | _____ | _____ |
| b) Key: | f min | _____ | _____ | _____ | _____ |
| c) Position: | 3rd inv | _____ | _____ | _____ | _____ |
| Symbol: | $V_2^4$ | _____ | _____ | _____ | _____ |

2. Add accidentals to each of the following chords to form Dominant 7th chords. Name the keys to which it belongs (Major and minor).

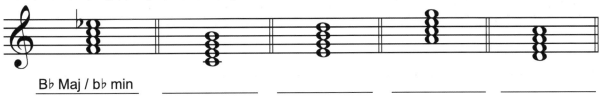

Bb Maj / bb min      _____      _____      _____

173

## DIMINISHED SEVENTH CHORDS

The **DIMINISHED SEVENTH** chord is a four note chord that is built on the raised seventh degree of a harmonic minor scale. It consists of a Root, minor 3, diminished 5 and a diminished 7. The symbol for the **diminished 7th** chord is **vii°7**. The Roman Numeral vii indicates the seventh scale degree above the Tonic. The symbol °7 after the Roman Numeral (vii°7) indicates the diminished Leading note triad with an interval of a diminished 7th above the Root. The chord notes are all a minor 3 apart.

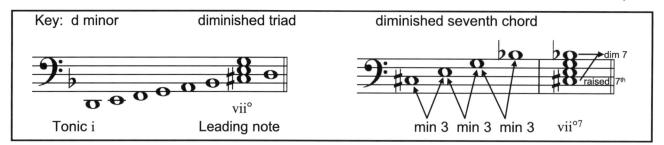

♪ **Note:** The raised 7th note is a diatonic semitone BELOW the Tonic of the harmonic minor key.
A root position diminished 7th chord is written as all line notes or all space notes.

1. For each of the following minor keys, write the diminished seventh chord in root position. Use accidentals. Use whole notes.

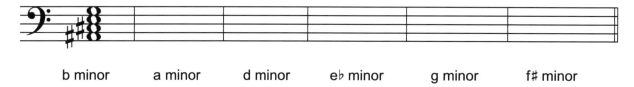

b minor        a minor        d minor        e♭ minor        g minor        f♯ minor

When using a Key Signature, an accidental is used to raise the 7th note, the Root of the chord.

♪ **Note:** The raised 7th note (the raised Leading note) is the Root of a diminished 7th chord.
The raised 7th note is the third above the Root of a Dominant 7th chord.

2. Name the minor key to which the following diminished seventh chords belong.

a♭ minor _____    _____    _____    _____    _____

♪ **Note:** The abbreviation for Dominant 7th is Dom 7th or V7.
The abbreviation for diminished 7th is dim 7th or vii°7.

3. a) Name the following chords as a Dominant 7th (V7) or a diminished 7th (vii°7) chord.
   b) Name the minor key to which each chord belongs.

a)  _____    _____    _____    _____    _____    _____

b)  _____    _____    _____    _____    _____    _____

174

# THREE COMBINATIONS of DIMINISHED 7th CHORDS

There are only **THREE COMBINATIONS** of a **DIMINISHED 7th CHORD**. When a diminished 7th chord is inverted, some notes will be changed to their enharmonic equivalent, creating the root position diminished 7th (vii°7) chord of another minor key.

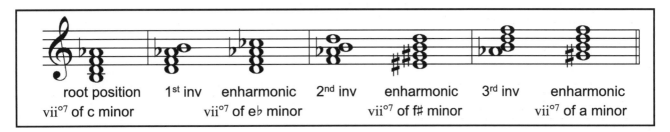

root position    1st inv   enharmonic    2nd inv   enharmonic    3rd inv   enharmonic

vii°7 of c minor     vii°7 of e♭ minor     vii°7 of f# minor     vii°7 of a minor

Five different root position diminished 7th chords can be built using the 4 notes on the keyboard of one diminished 7th chord. The notes will be used in different orders (inversions). Two diminished 7th chords will be enharmonic equivalents (same pitch/keys on the keyboard, different letter names).

There are **3 enharmonic minor keys**: g#/a♭, d#/e♭ and a#/b♭.

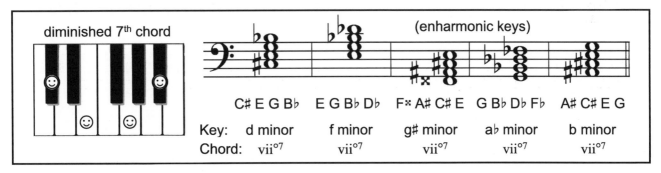

|  | C# E G B♭ | E G B♭ D♭ | F✕ A# C# E | G B♭ D♭ F♭ | A# C# E G |
|---|---|---|---|---|---|
| Key: | d minor | f minor | g# minor | a♭ minor | b minor |
| Chord: | vii°7 | vii°7 | vii°7 | vii°7 | vii°7 |

1. a) Identify the minor key for each of the following diminished 7th chords.
   b) Label each vii°7 chord.

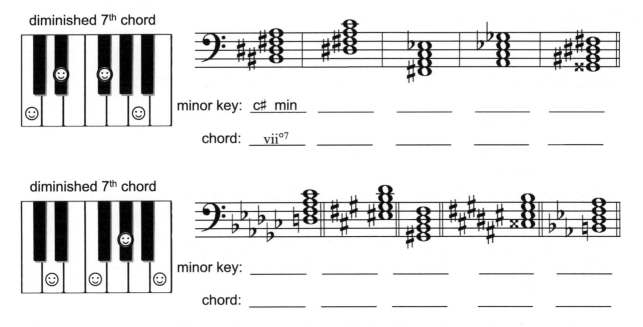

minor key:   <u>c#   min</u>     _____     _____     _____     _____

chord:   <u>vii°7</u>     _____     _____     _____     _____

minor key:   _____     _____     _____     _____     _____

chord:   _____     _____     _____     _____     _____

♫ **Note:** The type/quality of a triad is Major, minor, Augmented or Diminished. The type/quality of a Dominant 7th chord or a diminished 7th chord is Dominant 7th or diminished 7th.

# CIRCLE OF FIFTHS and TERM REVIEW

1.  Complete the Circle of Fifths with Major keys and minor keys.

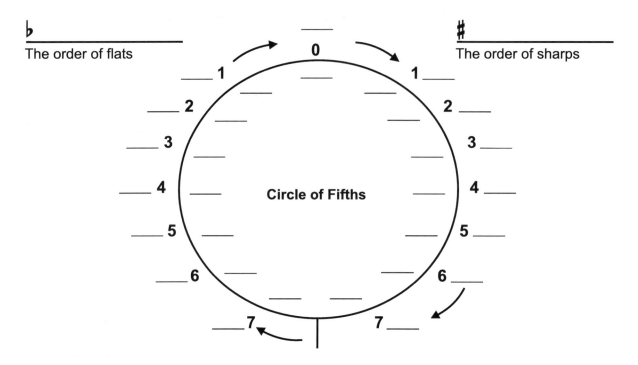

The order of flats                       The order of sharps

2.  Match each musical term with its English definition.  (Not all definitions will be used.)

a)  **Term**

| Term | | **Definition** |
|------|---|------------|
| *langsam* | _____ | a)  sad |
| *ad libitum, ad lib.* | _____ | b)  humorous, jocose |
| *con fuoco* | _____ | c)  agitated |
| *giocoso* | _____ | d)  slow; slowly |
| *mässig* | _____ | e)  with grace |
| *agitato* | _____ | f)  very |
| *schnell* | _____ | g)  playful |
| *con grazia* | _____ | h)  moderate; moderately |
| *scherzando* | _____ | i)  at the liberty of the performer |
| *dolente* | _____ | j)  fast |
| | | k)  with fire |

b)  **Term**

| Term | | **Definition** |
|------|---|------------|
| *grandioso* | _____ | a)  broadly |
| *vivo* | _____ | b)  with vigor, spirit |
| *largamente* | _____ | c)  soft, subdued, under the breath |
| *mesto* | _____ | d)  dying, fading away |
| *semplice* | _____ | e)  sonorous |
| *sotto voce* | _____ | f)  lively |
| *morendo* | _____ | g)  quiet, tranquil |
| *sonore* | _____ | h)  sad, mournful |
| *tranquillo* | _____ | i)  with expression |
| *con brio* | _____ | j)  grand, grandiose |
| | | k)  simple |

# Lesson 7       Review Test

Total Score: _____
100

Write the Circle of Fifths on a blank piece of paper. Use it as a reference when doing the review test.

1.  a) Name the following harmonic intervals.

10

_____  _____  _____  _____  _____

     b) Invert the above intervals in the Bass Clef. Use whole notes. Name the inversions.

_____  _____  _____  _____  _____

2.  Add the necessary accidentals to form Dominant seventh chords. For each chord, name:
    a) the keys to which it belongs (Major and minor).
    b) the position (root, 1st inversion, 2nd inversion or 3rd inversion).

10

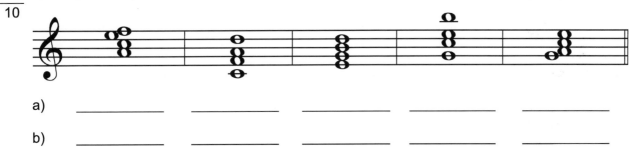

a) _____  _____  _____  _____  _____

b) _____  _____  _____  _____  _____

3.  For each of the following triads, name:
    a) the Root.
    b) the type/quality (Major, minor, Augmented or diminished).
    10  c) the position (root, 1st inversion or 2nd inversion).

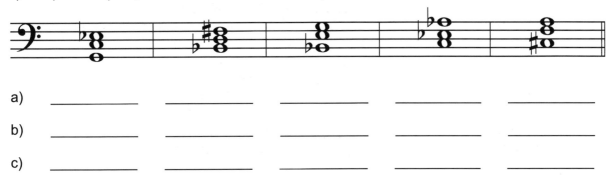

a) _____  _____  _____  _____  _____

b) _____  _____  _____  _____  _____

c) _____  _____  _____  _____  _____

**4.** a) Name the key of the following melody.

b) Rewrite the given melody at the **SAME PITCH** in the Tenor Clef. Use the correct Key Signature.

Key: _____

**5.** Write the Basic Beat and the pulse below each measure. Add rests below each bracket to complete the measure. Cross off the Basic Beat as each beat is completed.

Basic Beat: _____

Pulse:

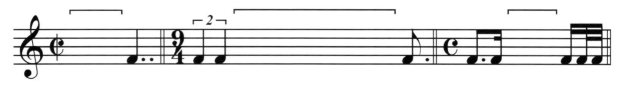

Basic Beat: _____

Pulse:

Basic Beat: _____

Pulse:

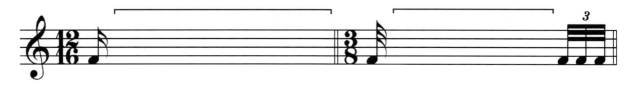

Basic Beat: _____

Pulse:

**6.** Match each description with the correct chord.

**Description**                                              **Chord**

cluster chord                    _____            a)

diminished seventh chord    _____            b)

Dominant seventh chord      _____            c)

polychord                         _____            d)

quartal chord                    _____            e)

f) Circle the scale which contains all of these chords:

b minor melodic          d♯ minor natural          f♯ minor harmonic

**7.** Match each musical term with its English definition. (Not all definitions will be used.)

| Term | | Definition |
|---|---|---|
| *tempo* | _____ | a) slow and solemn |
| *prima volta* | _____ | b) held, sustained |
| *loco* | _____ | c) smooth |
| *grave* | _____ | d) speed at which music is performed |
| *tenuto* | _____ | e) as fast as possible |
| *volti subito, v.s.* | _____ | f) the end |
| *legato* | _____ | g) left hand |
| *mano sinistra, M.S.* | _____ | h) return to the normal register |
| *prestissimo* | _____ | i) right hand |
| fine | _____ | j) turn the page quickly |
| | | k) first time |

179

**8.** Name the following scales as Major, harmonic minor, melodic minor, natural minor, chromatic, whole tone, octatonic, blues, Major pentatonic or minor pentatonic.

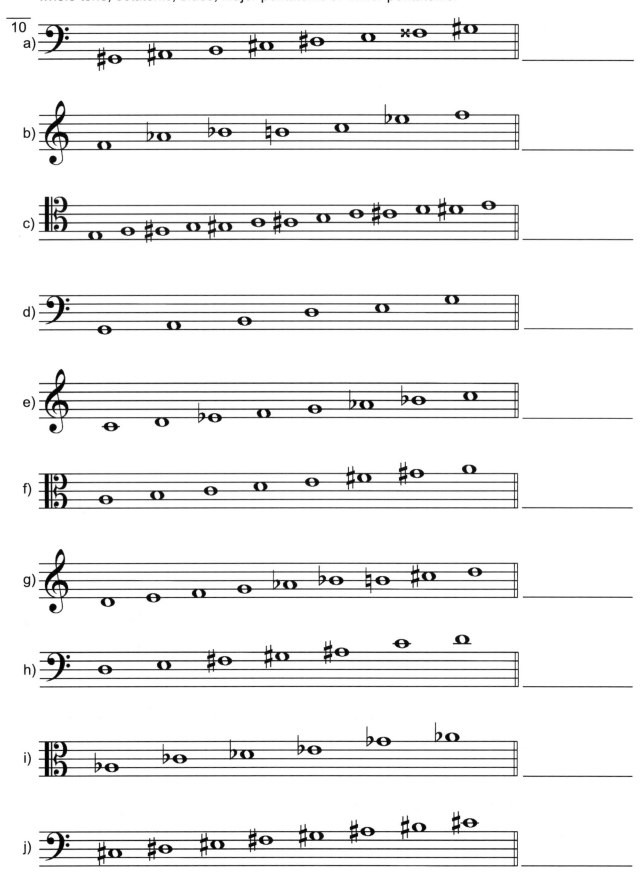

**9.** Match each musical term with its English definition.  (Not all definitions will be used.)

**Term**                                                **Definition**

bewegt                _____                a) with expression

sehr                  _____                b) moving

léger                 _____                c) sweet, gentle

cédez                 _____                d) at a moderate tempo

diminuendo, dim.      _____                e) slowly

mit Ausdruck          _____                f) yield; hold the tempo back

modéré                _____                g) light; lightly

mouvement             _____                h) tempo; motion

vite                  _____                i) very

lentement             _____                j) becoming softer

                                             k) fast

**10.** Analyze the following piece of music by answering the questions below.

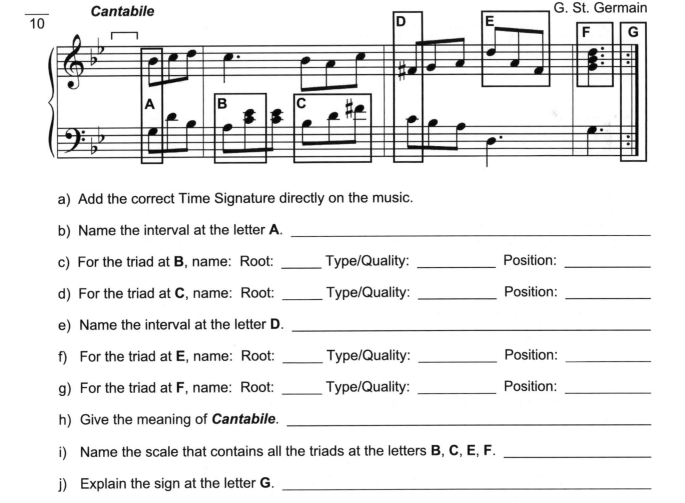

a) Add the correct Time Signature directly on the music.

b) Name the interval at the letter **A**. _____

c) For the triad at **B**, name:  Root: _____ Type/Quality: _____ Position: _____

d) For the triad at **C**, name:  Root: _____ Type/Quality: _____ Position: _____

e) Name the interval at the letter **D**. _____

f) For the triad at **E**, name:  Root: _____ Type/Quality: _____ Position: _____

g) For the triad at **F**, name:  Root: _____ Type/Quality: _____ Position: _____

h) Give the meaning of **Cantabile**. _____

i) Name the scale that contains all the triads at the letters **B, C, E, F**. _____

j) Explain the sign at the letter **G**. _____

# Lesson 8   Rewriting a Melody using a Key Signature and Cadences

A **Melody** may be written using accidentals or a Key Signature.  A melody usually ends on the Tonic.

### REWRITING a MAJOR KEY MELODY

To determine the key when a melody is written with accidentals, name the accidentals in order of the Key Signature.  When accidentals are in the correct Key Signature order, the key is usually Major.

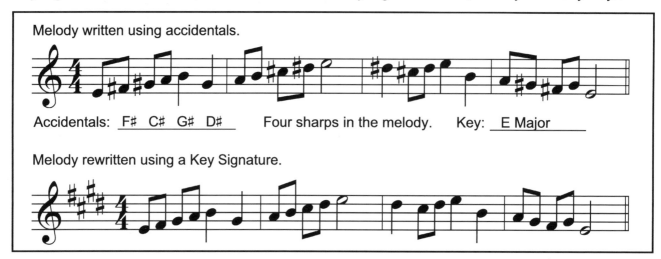

Melody written using accidentals.

Accidentals:  F#  C#  G#  D#        Four sharps in the melody.     Key:   E Major

Melody rewritten using a Key Signature.

♫ **Note:**  When rewriting a melody in a Major key using a Key Signature, accidentals are not used.
The Key Signature is written directly after the clef and before the Time Signature.

1. Name the accidentals in the order of the Key Signature.  Name the key.  Rewrite the following melodies using a Key Signature.

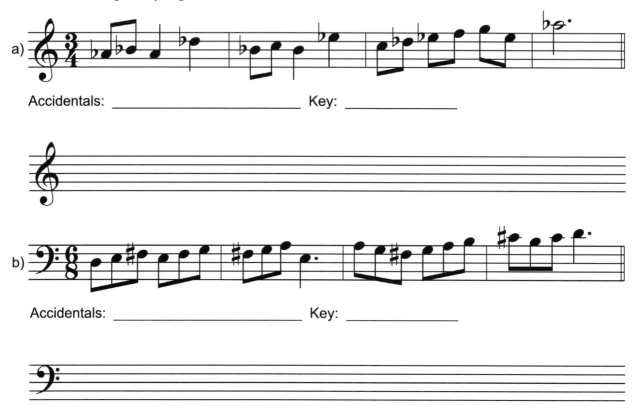

a)

Accidentals: _____  Key: _____

b)

Accidentals: _____  Key: _____

# REWRITING a HARMONIC MINOR MELODY USING FLATS

A **Melody** written using accidentals with flats may NOT have all the flats in order of the Key Signature. The melody below is written using accidentals of flats. To determine the key, name the accidentals in the order of the Key Signature with flats. The missing flat indicates the raised 7th note of the harmonic minor key.

♪ **Note:** An accidental (natural) is used for the raised 7th note of the harmonic minor key.

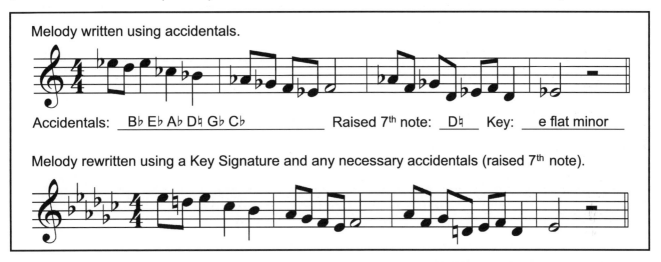

Melody written using accidentals.

Accidentals:   B♭ E♭ A♭ D♮ G♭ C♭          Raised 7th note:   D♮   Key:   e flat minor

Melody rewritten using a Key Signature and any necessary accidentals (raised 7th note).

♪ **Note:** When rewriting a melody in a minor key, the flats are written in the Key Signature. An accidental (natural) is used for the raised 7th note of the harmonic minor key.

1. Name the accidentals in the order of the Key Signature. Name the raised 7th note. Name the key. Rewrite the following melodies using a Key Signature and any necessary accidentals.

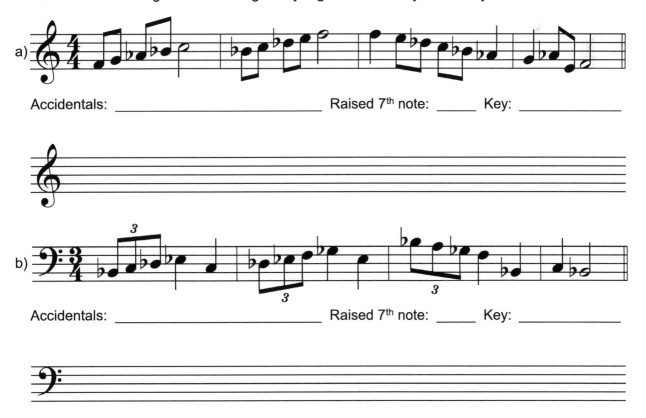

a) Accidentals: _____ Raised 7th note: _____ Key: _____

b) Accidentals: _____ Raised 7th note: _____ Key: _____

## REWRITING a HARMONIC MINOR MELODY USING FLATS and a SHARP

A **Melody** written using accidentals may have flats AND a sharp. The melody below is written using accidentals of flats and a sharp. To determine the key, name the accidentals in the order of the Key Signature with flats. The sharp indicates the raised 7th note of the harmonic minor key.

♫ **Note:** There are only two harmonic minor keys that contain flats and a sharp: g minor and d minor.

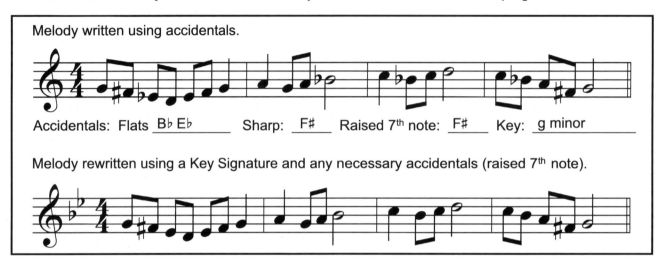

Accidentals: Flats __Bb Eb__    Sharp: __F#__    Raised 7th note: __F#__    Key: __g minor__

Melody rewritten using a Key Signature and any necessary accidentals (raised 7th note).

♫ **Note:** When rewriting a melody in a minor key, the flats are written in the Key Signature. An accidental (sharp) is used for the raised 7th note of the harmonic minor key.

1. Name the accidentals in the order of the Key Signature. Name the raised 7th note. Name the key. Rewrite the following melodies using a Key Signature and any necessary accidentals.

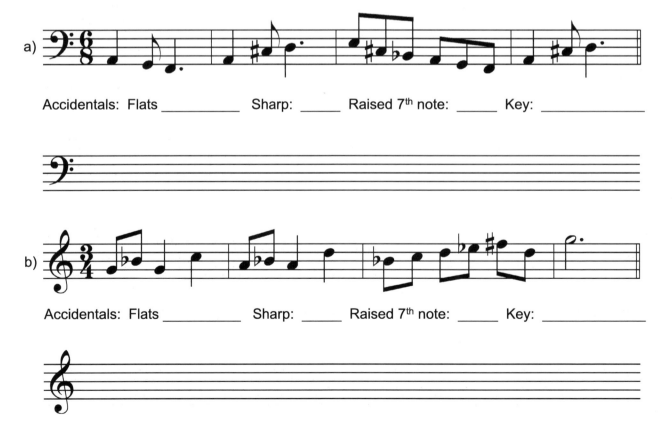

a)

Accidentals: Flats _____    Sharp: _____    Raised 7th note: _____    Key: _____

b)

Accidentals: Flats _____    Sharp: _____    Raised 7th note: _____    Key: _____

# REWRITING a HARMONIC MINOR MELODY USING SHARPS

A **Melody** written using accidentals with sharps may contain an extra sharp that is NOT in the Key Signature. The melody below is written using accidentals of sharps. To determine the key, name the accidentals in the order of the Key Signature with sharps. The extra sharp indicates the raised 7th note of the harmonic minor key.

♫ **Note:** An accidental (sharp) is used for the raised 7th note of the harmonic minor key.

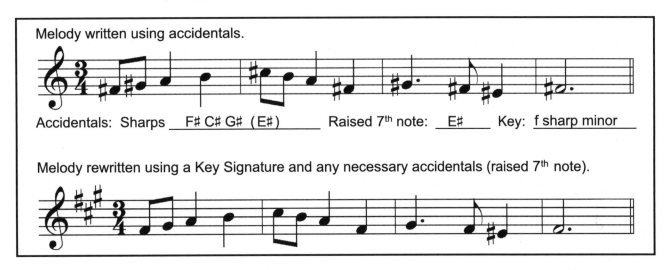

1. Name the accidentals in the order of the Key Signature. Name the raised 7th note. Name the key. Rewrite the following melodies using a Key Signature and any necessary accidentals.

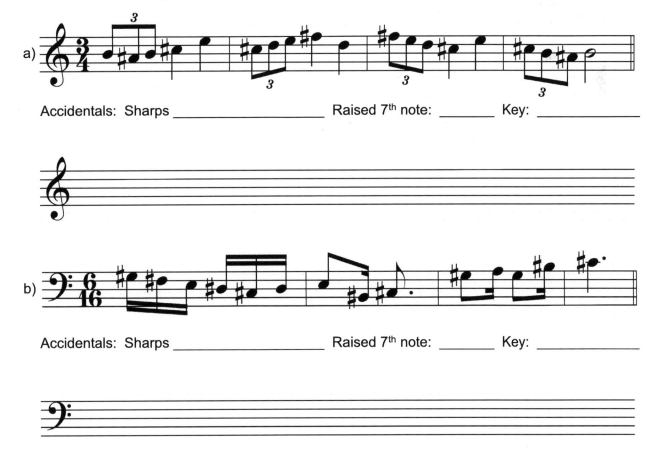

# REWRITING a HARMONIC MINOR MELODY USING SHARPS and a DOUBLE SHARP

A **Melody** written using accidentals may have sharps AND a double sharp.  The melody below is written using accidentals of sharps and a double sharp.  To determine the key, name the accidentals in the order of the Key Signature with sharps.  The double sharp indicates the raised 7th note of the harmonic minor key.

♫ **Note:**  There are only three harmonic minor keys that contain a double sharp as the raised 7th note:
g sharp minor (F✕);  d sharp minor (C✕);  and a sharp minor (G✕).

1.  Name the accidentals in the order of the Key Signature.  Name the raised 7th note.  Name the key. Rewrite the following melodies using a Key Signature and any necessary accidentals.

a) Accidentals: Sharps _____  Double Sharp: ___  Raised 7th note: ___  Key: _____

b) Accidentals: Sharps _____  Double Sharp: ___  Raised 7th note: ___  Key: _____

c) Accidentals: Sharps _____  Double Sharp: ___  Raised 7th note: ___  Key: _____

186

## REWRITING a MELODIC MINOR MELODY

A **Melody** written using accidentals may contain two accidentals NOT in the Key Signature. The melody below is written using accidentals. To determine the key, name the accidentals in the order of the Key Signature. The two extra accidentals indicate the raised 6th and 7th notes of the melodic minor key.

♫ **Note:** In the melodic minor form, the 6th and 7th notes are raised in the ascending melody and may be lowered in the descending melody.

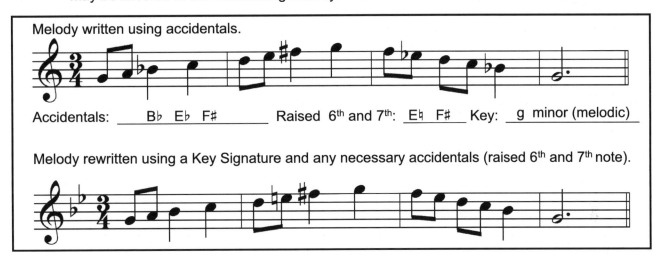

1. Name the accidentals in the order of the Key Signature. Name the raised 6th and 7th notes. Name the key. Rewrite the following melodies using a Key Signature and any necessary accidentals.

a) Accidentals: _____ Raised 6th and 7th: _____ Key: _____

b) Accidentals: _____ Raised 6th and 7th: _____ Key: _____

## CADENCES - PERFECT, PLAGAL and IMPERFECT

A **CADENCE** is a progression of two chords that ends a phrase or section of music.
There are three types of cadences:  **Perfect** (authentic), **Plagal** and **Imperfect** (half cadence).
Roman Numerals identify the degree and type of chord:  UPPER case - Major; lower case - minor.

A **Keyboard Style** Cadence is written with the Root of each chord in the Bass Clef and the Root, 3$^{rd}$ and 5$^{th}$ notes of each chord in the Treble Clef.  A cadence is often written over 2 measures.

| Cadence | Major keys | minor keys | |
|---|---|---|---|
| Perfect (authentic): | V - I | V - i | |
| Plagal: | IV- I | iv - i | |
| Imperfect (half cadence): | I - V, IV - V | i - V, iv - V | V - I |

## IDENTIFYING PERFECT and PLAGAL CADENCES

Perfect and Plagal Cadences (final cadences) end on the Tonic.  They are often found at the end of a piece of music.  The last note in the Bass Clef is the Tonic note and identifies the key.  The Key Signature determines if the key is Major or minor.  The bass notes determine the type of cadence.

♩ **Note:**  Count **UP** from the Tonic note in the last measure, to the bass note in the first measure, to determine the degree of the note and identify the cadence as Perfect or Plagal.

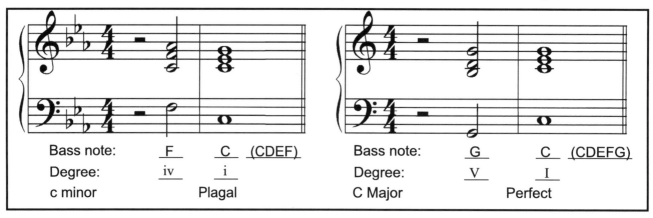

| Bass note: | F | C | (CDEF) |
|---|---|---|---|
| Degree: | iv | i | |
| c minor | | Plagal | |

| Bass note: | G | C | (CDEFG) |
|---|---|---|---|
| Degree: | V | I | |
| C Major | | Perfect | |

1. For each of the following cadences, name:
   a) the bass note in each measure; write the Tonic note UP to the next degree note (in brackets).
   b) the degree of each bass note (Use Roman Numerals:  Upper case - Major; lower case - minor).
   c) the key (Major or minor).
   d) the cadence (Perfect or Plagal).

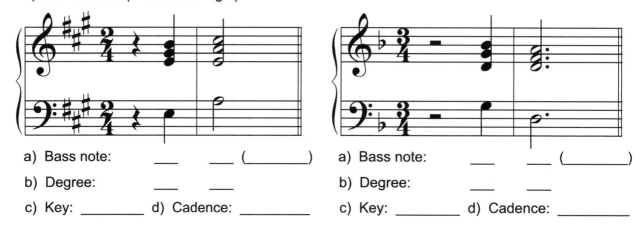

a) Bass note: ___ ___ (_____)
b) Degree: ___ ___
c) Key: _____ d) Cadence: _____

a) Bass note: ___ ___ (_____)
b) Degree: ___ ___
c) Key: _____ d) Cadence: _____

## IDENTIFYING KEYBOARD STYLE CADENCES - MAJOR KEYS

| Keyboard Style Cadence | Major keys | Cadence ending |
|---|---|---|
| Perfect (authentic): | V - I | Tonic |
| Plagal: | IV - I | Tonic |
| Imperfect (half cadence): | I - V, IV - V | Dominant |

♫ **Note:** An **Imperfect Cadence**, (**I - V**) or (**IV - V**), begins on the Tonic (**I**) or the Subdominant (**IV**) and ends on the Dominant (**V**). It is often found ending a phrase in the middle of a section.

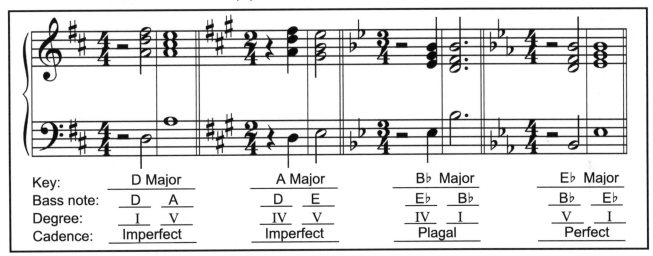

| Key: | D Major | | A Major | | B♭ Major | | E♭ Major | |
|---|---|---|---|---|---|---|---|---|
| Bass note: | D | A | D | E | E♭ | B♭ | B♭ | E♭ |
| Degree: | I | V | IV | V | IV | I | V | I |
| Cadence: | Imperfect | | Imperfect | | Plagal | | Perfect | |

♫ **Note:** The notes in the Bass Clef determine if the cadence is Perfect, Plagal or Imperfect. Determine the key and the Tonic note. Count UP from the Tonic note to determine the degree of the notes in the Bass Clef.

1. For each of the following cadences, name:
   a) the Major key.
   b) the bass note in each measure.
   c) the degree of each bass note (Use Roman Numerals).
   d) the cadence (Perfect, Plagal or Imperfect).

a) Key: _____ _____ _____ _____

b) Bass note: ___ ___ ___ ___ ___ ___ ___ ___

c) Degree: ___ ___ ___ ___ ___ ___ ___ ___

d) Cadence: _____ _____ _____ _____

## IDENTIFYING KEYBOARD STYLE CADENCES - MINOR KEYS

| Keyboard Style Cadence | minor keys | Cadence ending |
|---|---|---|
| Perfect (authentic): | V - i | Tonic |
| Plagal: | iv - i | Tonic |
| Imperfect (half cadence): | i - V, iv - V | Dominant |

♫ **Note:** The Dominant (**V**) chord of the harmonic minor key ALWAYS contains the raised 7th note. The Dominant (**V**) chord is ALWAYS Major.

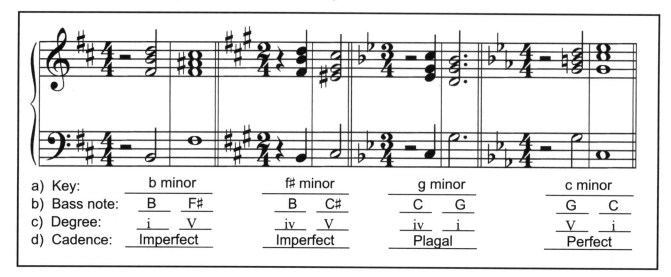

| a) Key: | b minor | | f# minor | | g minor | | c minor | |
|---|---|---|---|---|---|---|---|---|
| b) Bass note: | B | F# | B | C# | C | G | G | C |
| c) Degree: | i | V | iv | V | iv | i | V | i |
| d) Cadence: | Imperfect | | Imperfect | | Plagal | | Perfect | |

♫ **Note:** An accidental is used for the raised 7th note of the harmonic minor key. An UPPER case Roman Numeral is used for the Dominant (**V**) Major chord. Lower case Roman Numerals are used for the Subdominant (**iv**) and Tonic (**i**) minor chords.

1. For each of the following cadences, name:
   a) the minor key.
   b) the bass note in each measure.
   c) the degree of each bass note (Use Roman Numerals).
   d) the cadence (Perfect, Plagal or Imperfect).

a) Key: _____   _____   _____   _____

b) Bass note: ____ ____   ____ ____   ____ ____   ____ ____

c) Degree: ____ ____   ____ ____   ____ ____   ____ ____

d) Cadence: _____   _____   _____   _____

## IDENTIFYING the KEY for PERFECT and IMPERFECT CADENCES

When **IDENTIFYING the KEY for PERFECT and IMPERFECT CADENCES**, if the cadence contains an accidental (raised 7th note), the key is minor. (Perfect V - i or Imperfect i - V.) If the cadence does NOT contain an accidental (raised 7th note), the key is Major. (Perfect V - I or Imperfect I - V.)

♫ **Note:** A Perfect Cadence ends on the Tonic. An Imperfect Cadence ends on the Dominant.

1. Identify the following cadences using Roman Numerals.

| Cadence | Major keys | minor keys |
|---|---|---|
| Perfect (authentic): | ____ - ____ | ____ - ____ |
| Imperfect (half cadence): | ____ - ____ OR ____ - ____ | ____ - ____ OR ____ - ____ |

2. For each of the following cadences, name:
   a) the key.
   b) the bass note in each measure.
   c) the degree of each bass note.
   d) the cadence.

a) Key: _____ _____ _____ _____

b) Bass note: ____ ____ ____ ____ ____ ____ ____ ____

c) Degree: ____ ____ ____ ____ ____ ____ ____ ____

d) Cadence: _____ _____ _____ _____

a) Key: _____ _____ _____ _____

b) Bass note: ____ ____ ____ ____ ____ ____ ____ ____

c) Degree: ____ ____ ____ ____ ____ ____ ____ ____

d) Cadence: _____ _____ _____ _____

**IDENTIFYING the KEY for PLAGAL CADENCES**

When **IDENTIFYING the KEY for PLAGAL CADENCES**, the cadence will NOT contain an accidental (raised 7th note) of the harmonic minor key. Plagal Cadence (minor) iv - i; (Major) IV - I.

♫ **Note:** To determine if the Plagal Cadence belongs to the Major key or the minor key, check the Key Signature. Determine if the Tonic note belongs to the Major key or the minor key.

1. Identify the following cadences using Roman Numerals.

| Cadence | Major keys | minor keys |
|---------|-----------|-----------|
| Plagal: | ____ - ____ | ____ - ____ |

2. For each of the following cadences, name:
   a) the key.
   b) the bass note in each measure.
   c) the degree of each bass note.
   d) the cadence.

a) Key: _____  _____      _____  _____

b) Bass note: ____ ____   ____ ____      ____ ____   ____ ____

c) Degree: ____ ____   ____ ____      ____ ____   ____ ____

d) Cadence: _____  _____      _____  _____

3. For each of the following cadences, name:  a) the key.  b) the type (Perfect, Plagal or Imperfect).

a) Key: _____  _____  _____  _____

b) Cadence: _____  _____  _____  _____

192

# WRITING A CADENCE IN KEYBOARD STYLE

**A CADENCE in KEYBOARD STYLE** is written with the Root of each triad in the Bass Clef and the Root, 3rd and 5th notes of each triad in the Treble Clef. A cadence is often written over 2 measures.

| Cadence | Major keys | minor keys | |
|---|---|---|---|
| Perfect (authentic): | V - I | V - i | |
| Plagal: | IV - I | iv - i | |
| Imperfect (half cadence): | I - V, IV - V | i - V, iv - V | |
| Final cadence ends on the Tonic, a non final cadence ends on the Dominant. | | | V - I |

♪ **Note:** In all cadences (except IV-V and iv- V) there is one note that is the same in both triads. This is called the **COMMON NOTE**. (When possible, it is written at the same pitch.)

When writing a Perfect cadence in keyboard style BELOW a melodic fragment, follow these 3 steps:

1. Name the key. Label the Perfect cadence (**V - I**). Write the note names below the triad.

2. Underline the bass notes and write them in the Bass Clef. (Same note value as the melody.)

3. Write the two remaining notes of each triad in the Treble Clef BELOW the given melody.

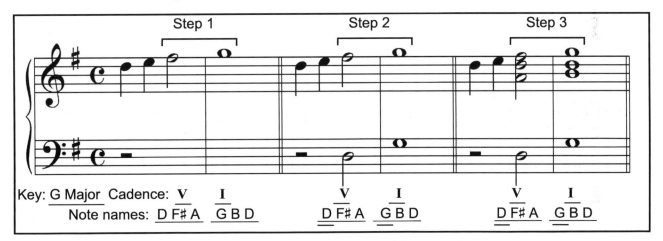

1. As in the example above, write a Perfect cadence in keyboard style BELOW the bracketed notes:
a) Name the key. Label the Perfect cadence (**V - I**). Write the note names below the triad.
b) Underline the bass notes and write them in the Bass Clef. (Same note value as the melody.)
c) Write the two remaining notes of each triad in the Treble Clef BELOW the given melody.

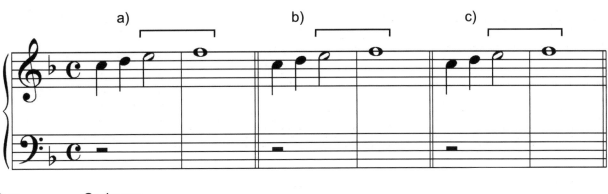

Key: _____ Cadence: ____ ____      ____ ____      ____ ____

   Note names: _____ _____      _____ _____      _____ _____

## PERFECT CADENCES - MAJOR KEY (V - I) and MINOR KEY (V - i)

When **WRITING a PERFECT CADENCE**, identify the key based on the given melodic fragment. In a minor key, the Perfect cadence (**V - i**) will contain the raised 7th note of the harmonic minor.

♫ **Note:** The notes in the Treble Clef triads must be written in CLOSE POSITION (as close together as possible, either in root position, 1st inversion or 2nd inversion) below the given note.

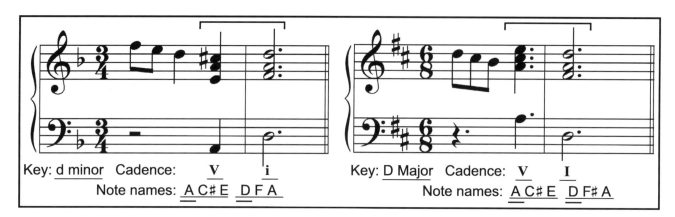

Key: d minor   Cadence:   **V**   **i**
Note names: A C♯ E  D F A

Key: D Major   Cadence:   **V**   **I**
Note names: A C♯ E  D F♯ A

1. Write a Perfect cadence in keyboard style BELOW the bracketed notes following these steps:

a) Name the key. Label the Perfect cadence **V-I** or **V-i**. Write the note names below the triad.

b) Underline the bass notes and write them in the Bass Clef.

c) Write the two remaining notes of each triad in the Treble Clef BELOW the given melody.

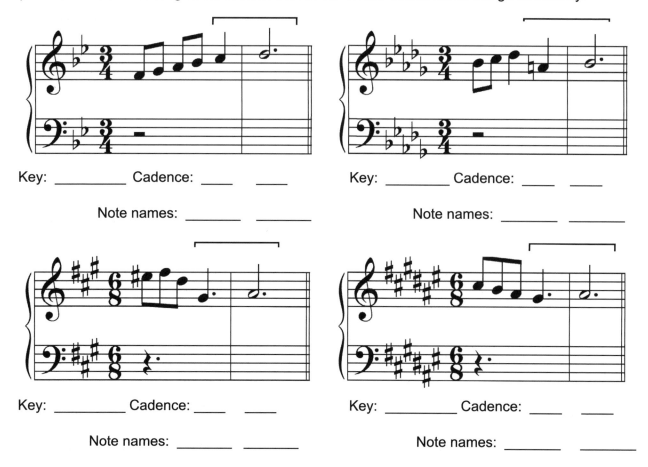

Key: _____   Cadence: ____   ____

Note names: _____  _____

Key: _____   Cadence: ____   ____

Note names: _____  _____

Key: _____   Cadence: ____   ____

Note names: _____  _____

Key: _____   Cadence: ____   ____

Note names: _____  _____

194

## PLAGAL CADENCES - MAJOR KEY (IV - I) and MINOR KEY (iv - i)

When **WRITING a PLAGAL CADENCE**, identify the key based on the given melodic fragment. In a minor key, the Plagal cadence (**iv - i**) will NOT contain the raised 7th note of the harmonic minor.

♫ **Note:** The bass note may move up a Perfect 5 or down a Perfect 4 to the Tonic.
The notes in the Treble Clef are written BELOW the given notes.

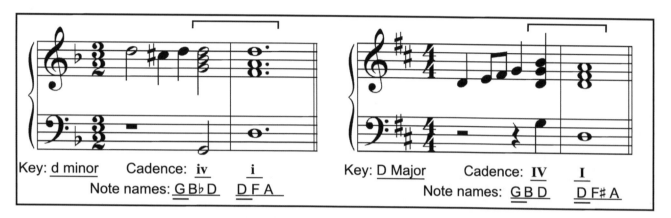

Key: d minor     Cadence: **iv**     **i**

Note names: G B♭ D     D F A

Key: D Major     Cadence: **IV**     **I**

Note names: G B D     D F♯ A

1. Write a Plagal cadence in keyboard style BELOW the bracketed notes following these steps:

a) Name the key. Label the Plagal cadence **IV- I** or **iv-i**. Write the note names below the triad.

b) Underline the bass notes and write them in the Bass Clef.

c) Write the two remaining notes of each triad in the Treble Clef BELOW the given melody.

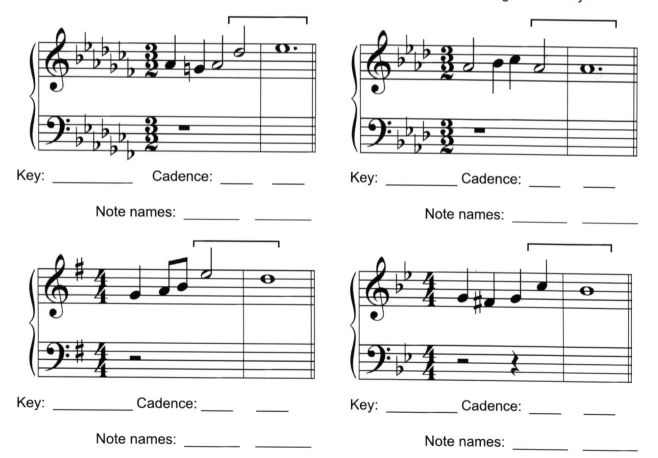

Key: _____     Cadence: ____     ____

Note names: _____     _____

Key: _____     Cadence: ____     ____

Note names: _____     _____

Key: _____     Cadence: ____     ____

Note names: _____     _____

Key: _____     Cadence: ____     ____

Note names: _____     _____

195

# IMPERFECT CADENCES - MAJOR KEY (**I - V**) and MINOR KEY (**i - V**)

When **WRITING an IMPERFECT CADENCE**, identify the key based on the given melodic fragment. In a minor key, the Imperfect cadence (**i - V**) will contain the raised 7th note of the harmonic minor.

♫ **Note:** A melody written in a minor key may or may not include the raised 7th note of the harmonic minor. If there is no raised 7th, look at the given notes of the cadence to determine if they belong to the I, IV or V triads of the Major key or the i, iv or V triads of the relative minor key.

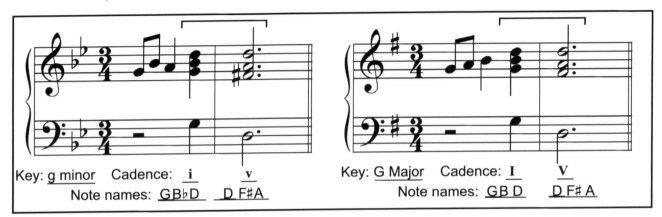

1. Write an Imperfect cadence in keyboard style BELOW the bracketed notes following these steps:
a) Name the key. Label the Imperfect cadence **I-V** or **i-V**. Write the note names below the triad.
b) Underline the bass notes and write them in the Bass Clef.
c) Write the two remaining notes of each triad in the Treble Clef BELOW the given melody.

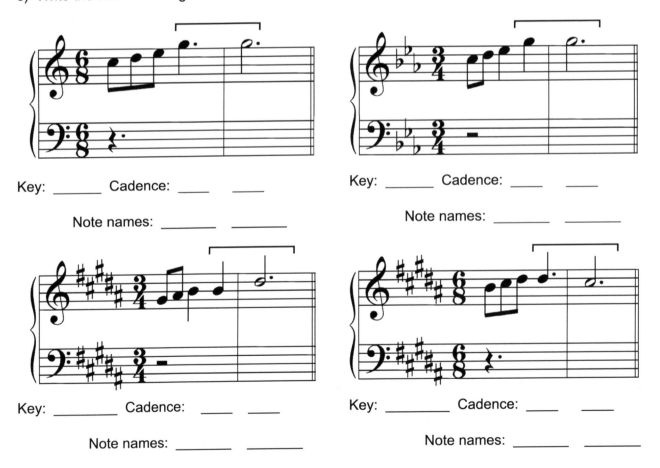

## IMPERFECT CADENCES - MAJOR KEY (IV - V) and MINOR KEY (iv- V)

When **WRITING an IMPERFECT CADENCE**, identify the key based on the given melodic fragment.
In a minor key, the Imperfect cadence (**iv - V**) will contain the raised 7th note of the harmonic minor.

♪ **No**te:  There is NO common note in the IV - V (iv - V) Imperfect cadence.  The Treble Clef notes
move in contrary motion to the Bass Clef notes.  Bass notes ASCEND (move up a Major 2);
Treble Clef notes DESCEND (move down).

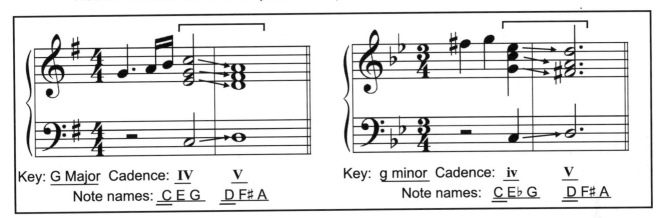

Key: G Major  Cadence: **IV**  **V**
Note names: C E G  D F♯ A

Key: g minor  Cadence: **iv**  **V**
Note names: C E♭ G  D F♯ A

1.  Write an Imperfect cadence in keyboard style BELOW the bracketed notes following these steps:

a)  Name the key.  Label the Imperfect cadence **IV-V** or **iv-V**.  Write the note names below the triad.

b)  Underline the bass notes and write them in the Bass Clef (ascending a Major 2).

c)  Write the two remaining notes of each triad in the Treble Clef BELOW the given melody.

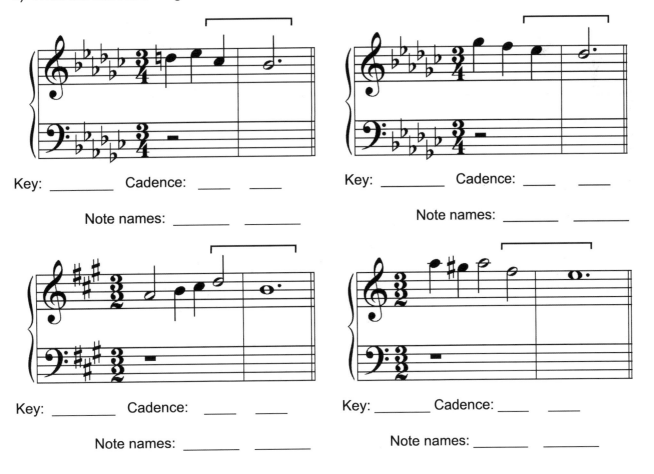

Key: _____  Cadence: ____  ____

Note names: _____  _____

Key: _____  Cadence: ____  ____

Note names: _____  _____

Key: _____  Cadence: ____  ____

Note names: _____  _____

Key: _____  Cadence: ____  ____

Note names: _____  _____

# PERFECT, PLAGAL and IMPERFECT CADENCES

When writing a **PERFECT, PLAGAL or IMPERFECT CADENCE** in keyboard style, the given melodic fragment will contain notes from the I, i, IV, iv or V chords.

To write a cadence in keyboard style below the bracketed notes, follow these 5 steps:

1. Name the key. Write the note names for the triads: I (i) _____, IV (iv) _____ and V _____.

2. Look at the notes under the bracket. Find the note in the I (i), IV (iv) or V chord.
   Write the chord symbols and note names for the cadence below the staff.

3. Underline the bass notes and write them in the Bass Clef. (Same note value as the melody.)

4. Write the two remaining notes of each triad in the Treble Clef BELOW the given melody.

5. Name the type of cadence (Perfect, Plagal or Imperfect).

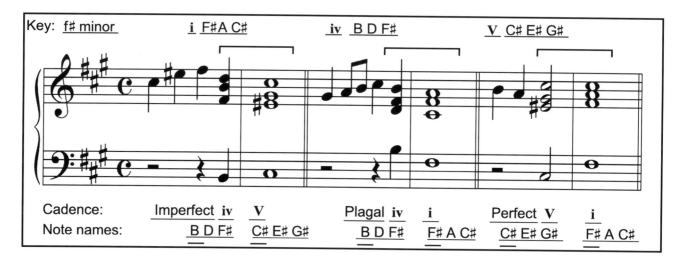

| Cadence: | Imperfect iv | V | Plagal iv | i | Perfect V | i |
|---|---|---|---|---|---|---|
| Note names: | B D F# | C# E# G# | B D F# | F# A C# | C# E# G# | F# A C# |

1. Write a cadence in keyboard style BELOW the bracketed notes following these steps:
   a) Name the key. Write the note names for the triads I (i), IV (iv) and V.
   b) Write the chord symbols and note names for the cadence below the staff.
   c) Underline the bass notes and write them in the Bass Clef.
   d) Write the two remaining notes of each triad in the Treble Clef BELOW the given melody.
   e) Name the type of cadence (Perfect, Plagal or Imperfect).

Key: _____    ___ _____    ___ _____    ___ _____

Cadence: _____ _____    _____ _____    _____ _____

Note names: _____ _____    _____ _____    _____ _____

198

## PERFECT, PLAGAL and IMPERFECT CADENCES

1. For each melodic fragment, write a cadence in keyboard style BELOW the bracketed notes.
   a) Name the key.  Write the note names for the triads I (i), IV (iv) and V.
   b) Name the type of cadence (Perfect, Plagal or Imperfect) and write the chord symbols.
   c) Name the notes in each of the triads of the cadence.

a) Key: _____   __  _____   __  _____  __  _____

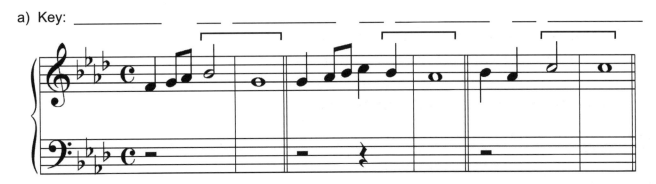

b) Cadence: _____  __  __  _____  ____  ____  __

c) Note names: _____  _____   _____  _____  _____

a) Key: _____   __  _____   __  _____  __  _____

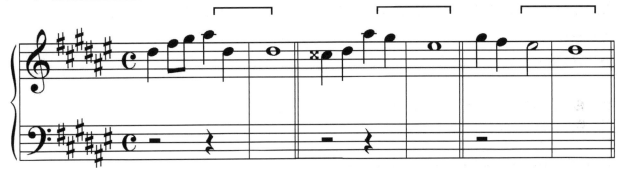

b) Cadence: _____  __  __  _____  __  _____  __

c) Note names: _____  _____   _____  _____  __

a) Key: _____   __  _____   __  _____  __  _____

b) Cadence: _____  __  _____   _____  _____  __

c) Note names: _____  _____   _____  _____  __

## PERFECT CADENCES USING THE V7 CHORD

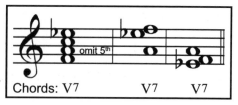

A **V7 Chord** is the Dominant triad plus a minor 7th.

A PERFECT Major Cadence is a **V - I** or **V7 - I** chord progression.

A PERFECT minor cadence is a **V - i** or **V7 - i** chord progression.

When a Dominant 7th (**V7**) chord is used in a Perfect Cadence, the 5th note above the Dominant may be omitted. The **V7** chord ALWAYS contains the added 7th note. The **V7** chord contains a tritone.

♫ **Note:** The raised 7th note "hugs" the Dominant note (interval of a 2nd).

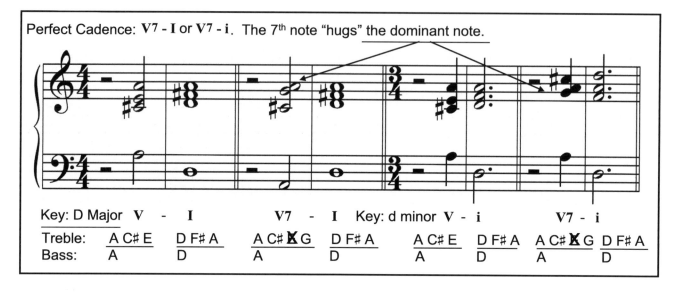

1. Name the key. Use chord symbols to identify the following Perfect Cadences.
   Major keys: **V - I** or **V7 - I**. Minor keys: **V - i** or **V7 - i**.

Key: _____ ___ - ___   _____ ___ - ___   _____ ___ - ___

Key: _____ ___ - ___   _____ ___ - ___   _____ ___ - ___

200

**6.** Write the following scales, ascending and descending, in the clefs indicated. Use the correct Key Signature. Use whole notes.

a) enharmonic relative minor, melodic form, of C flat Major
b) e flat minor harmonic, from supertonic to supertonic
c) b flat minor natural, from subdominant to subdominant
d) enharmonic Tonic Major of B Major
e) Lydian mode starting on G
f) Phrygian mode starting on C sharp

10

a)

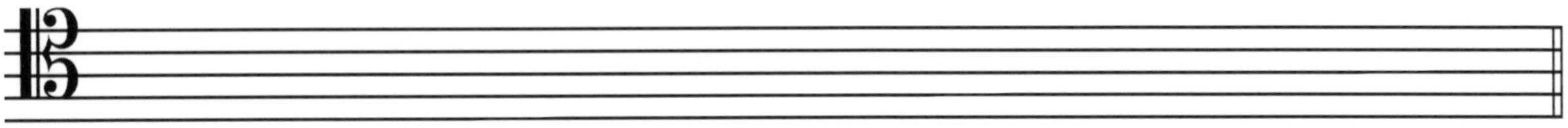

b)

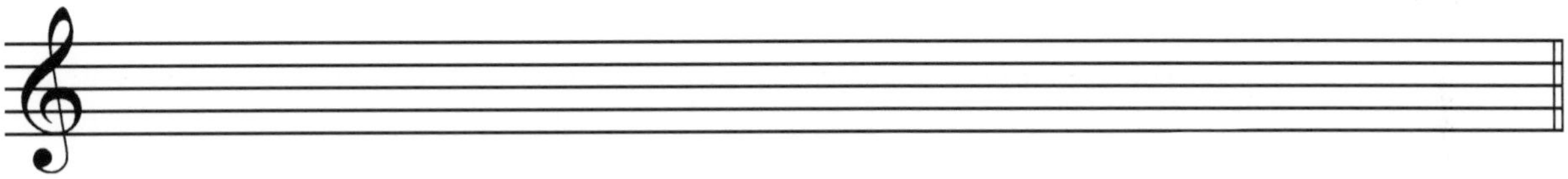

c)

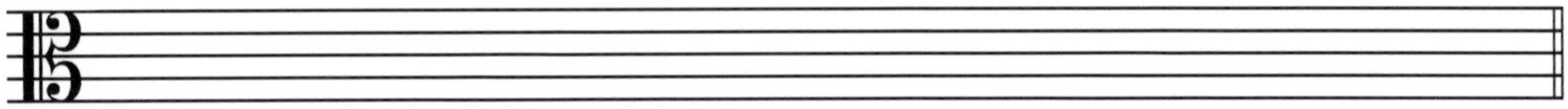

d)

e)

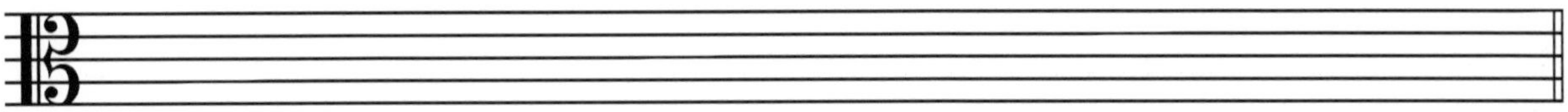

f)

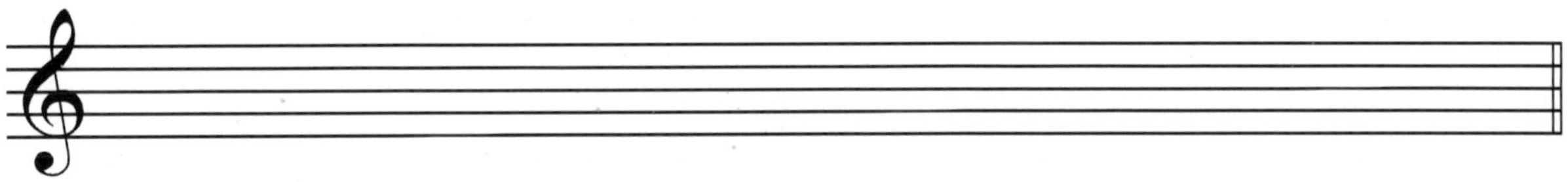

7. a) Name the key for the following melodic fragments. Write a cadence (keyboard style) **BELOW** the bracketed notes. Name the type of cadence (Perfect, Plagal or Imperfect).

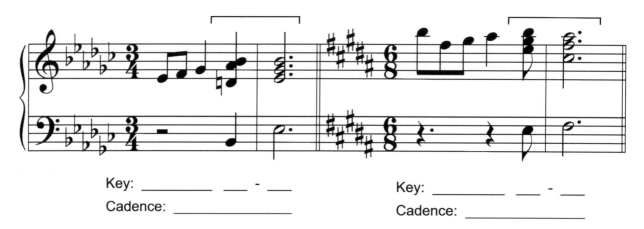

Key: _____ ___ - ___          Key: _____ ___ - ___

Cadence: _____          Cadence: _____

b) Name the key for each of the following cadences. Use chord symbols to identify the cadence. Name the type of cadence (Perfect, Plagal or Imperfect).

Key: _____ ___ - ___          Key: _____ ___ - ___

Cadence: _____          Cadence: _____

8. Match each musical term with its English definition. (Not all definitions will be used.)

**Term**

martellato          _____

pesante             _____

calando             _____

sostenuto           _____

andante             _____

rubato              _____

accelerando, accel. _____

cantabile           _____

dolce               _____

maestoso            _____

**Definition**

a) becoming slower and softer

b) in a singing style

c) majestic

d) weighty, with emphasis

e) becoming quicker

f) sweet, gentle

g) moderately slow; at a walking pace

h) strongly accented, hammered

i) graceful

j) sustained

k) with some freedom of tempo to enhance musical expression

**9.** Add the correct Time Signature below the bracket for each of the following rhythms.

**10.** Analyze the following piece of music by answering the questions below.

a) Add the correct Time Signature directly on the music.

b) Name the key of this piece. _____

c) Name the intervals at the letters:  **A** _____  **B** _____  **C** _____

d) For the chord at **D**, name:  Root: _____  Type/Quality: _____  Position: _____

e) Name the mode at the letter **E**. _____

f) For the chord at **F**, name:  Root: _____  Type/Quality: _____  Position: _____

g) Name the mode at the letter **G**. _____

h) Name the type of cadence formed by the chords at the letter **H**. _____

i) Explain the meaning of ***Andantino***. _____

j) When observing the repeat sign, how many measures of music are played? _____

# Lesson 9  Transposing Keys - Major, Minor and Concert Pitch

**TRANSPOSITION from MAJOR KEY to MAJOR KEY** occurs when music is written or played at a different pitch. When **transposing** a melody UP a given interval, name the original key first. Starting from the original Tonic, use the given interval to count UP to determine the interval note name. The TOP note names the NEW Major key. All the notes move up the same interval.

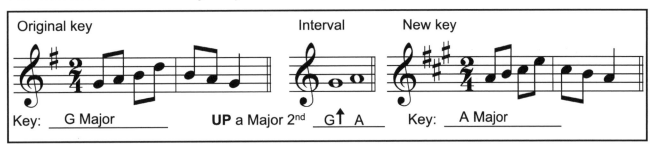

Key: ___G Major___   **UP** a Major 2nd ___G↑A___   Key: ___A Major___

1.  a) Name the key of the given melody.

    b) Write the interval of a melodic Major 2nd ABOVE the Tonic note (D). Name the note.

    c) Name the new key. Transpose the given melody **UP** a Major 2nd using the correct

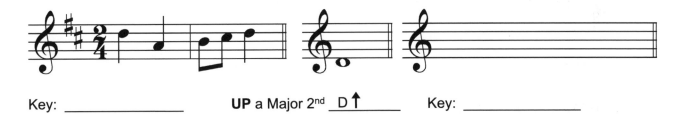

Key: _____   **UP** a Major 2nd ___D↑___   Key: _____

♫ **Note:** When a Major key is transposed to a new key, the key will ALWAYS remain MAJOR.

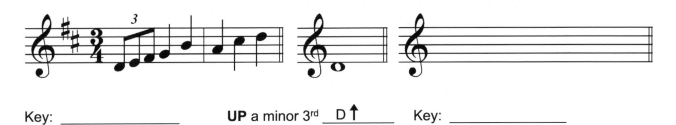

Key: ___G Major___   **UP** a minor 3rd ___G↑B♭___   Key: ___B flat Major___

2.  a) Name the key of the given melody.

    b) Write the interval of a melodic minor 3rd ABOVE the Tonic note (D). Name the note.

    c) Name the new key. Transpose the given melody **UP** a minor 3rd using the correct

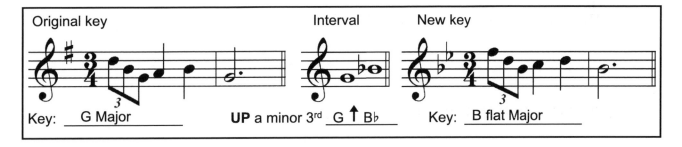

Key: _____   **UP** a minor 3rd ___D↑___   Key: _____

## TRANSPOSING a MELODY with ACCIDENTALS

When **TRANSPOSING a MELODY with ACCIDENTALS**: if the original melody contains accidentals, the transposed melody will contain accidentals. If an accidental raises or lowers a note in the original melody, the transposed melody must contain an accidental to raise or lower the note as well.

♪ **Note:** When adding accidentals, observe the Key Signature. Example: Key of G Major, F sharp is lowered to F natural in the original key. Transposing to the new key of C Major, the same degree is the note B. B natural is lowered to B flat.

♪ **Note:** When transposing a melody UP to a new key, always determine the interval first. The bottom note names the original key. The top note names the new key.

1. The following melody is in the key of F Major.

   a) Transpose the given melody **UP** a Major 3rd, using the correct Key Signature. Name the key.

   b) Transpose the given melody **UP** a minor 2nd, using the correct Key Signature. Name the key.

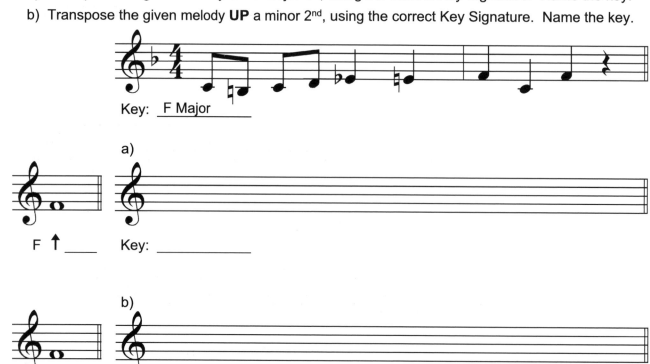

## TRANSPOSING a MELODY UP an INTERVAL

When **TRANSPOSING a MELODY UP an INTERVAL**, write the interval ABOVE the Tonic note of the given melody. The TOP note determines the new key.

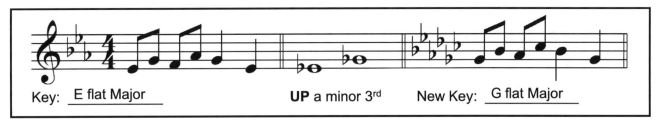

Key: __E flat Major__          **UP** a minor 3rd          New Key: __G flat Major__

1. For each of the following:
   a) Name the key of the given melody.
   b) Write the Tonic note and the given interval ABOVE the Tonic note.
   c) Name the new key. Transpose the melody UP by the given interval, using the correct Key Signature.

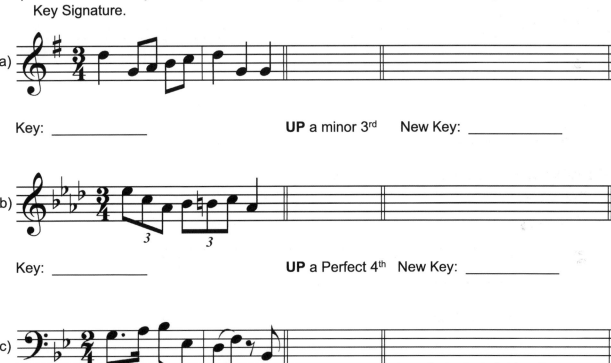

a)

Key: _____          **UP** a minor 3rd          New Key: _____

b)

Key: _____          **UP** a Perfect 4th          New Key: _____

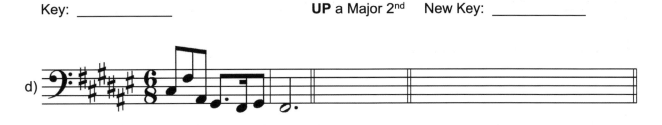

c)

Key: _____          **UP** a Major 2nd          New Key: _____

d)

Key: _____          **UP** a minor 6th          New Key: _____

## TRANSPOSING a MELODY to a NEW KEY

When **TRANSPOSING a MELODY to a NEW KEY**, a Major key will ALWAYS remain a Major key. All the notes will move the SAME interval.

♪ **Note:** Draw a staff in the margin. Write the interval above the Tonic note of the given melody. The top note names the new key.

1. The following melody is in the key of G flat Major. Transpose the given melody UP an Augmented 2nd using the correct Key Signature. Name the new key.

Key: _____

2. The following melody is in the key of F Major. Transpose the given melody UP a minor 3rd using the correct Key Signature. Name the new key.

Key: _____

3. The following melody is in the key of C sharp Major. Transpose the given melody UP a Perfect 4th using the correct Key Signature. Name the new key.

Key:_____

# TRANSPOSITION - MINOR KEY to MINOR KEY

**TRANSPOSITION from MINOR KEY to MINOR KEY** occurs when music is written or played at a different pitch. When **transposing** a melody UP or DOWN a given interval, name the original key first. Starting from the original Tonic, use the given interval to count UP or DOWN to determine the interval note name. That note names the NEW minor key. All the notes move the same interval.

♩ **Note:** If the given melody contains an accidental, so will the transposed melody. The accidental used in the given melody may or may not be the same accidental used in the transposed melody, but must perform the same function of raising or lowering the note.

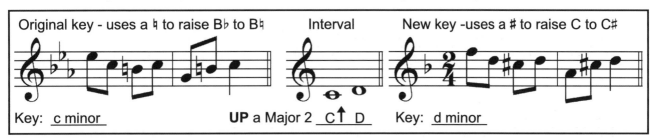

1. a) Name the key of the given melody.
   b) Write the interval of a melodic Major 2 ABOVE the Tonic note (B♭). Name the note.
   c) Name the new key. Transpose the given melody **UP** a Major 2 in the Treble Clef, using the correct Key Signature.

Key: _____    **UP** a Major 2  B♭↑_____    Key: _____

♩ **Note:** When a minor key is transposed to a new key, the new key will ALWAYS be minor.

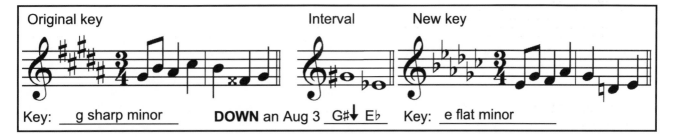

2. a) Name the key of the given melody.
   b) Write the interval of a melodic Aug 3 BELOW the Tonic note (C♯). Name the note.
   c) Name the new key. Transpose the given melody **DOWN** an Aug 3 in the Treble Clef, using the correct Key Signature.

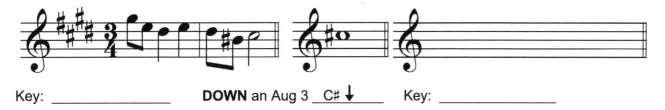

Key: _____    **DOWN** an Aug 3 _C♯ ↓_____    Key: _____

## TRANSPOSING a MELODY with ACCIDENTALS

When **TRANSPOSING a MELODY with ACCIDENTALS**, if the original melody contains accidentals, the transposed melody will contain accidentals. If an accidental raises or lowers a note in the original melody, the transposed melody must contain an accidental to raise or lower the note as well.

♫ **Note:** When adding accidentals, observe the Key Signature. Example: Key of **e minor**, F# is lowered to F♮ and then raised to F# in the original key. Transposing to the new key of **a minor**, the same degree is the note B. B natural is lowered to B♭ and then raised to B♮.

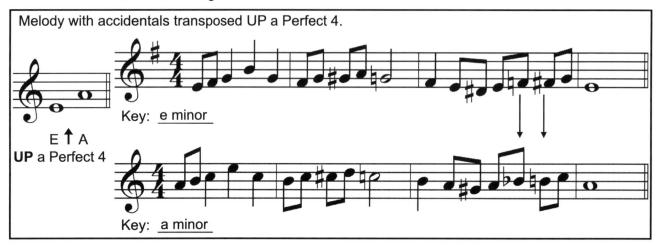

♫ **Note:** When transposing a melody UP or DOWN to a new key, always determine the interval first. That note names the new key.

1. The following melody is in the key of f minor. Transpose the melody and name the new key.
   a) Transpose the given melody **UP** a Perfect 4, using the correct Key Signature.
   b) Transpose the given melody **DOWN** a minor 2, using the correct Key Signature.

## TRANSPOSING a MELODY - MAJOR KEY to MAJOR KEY and MINOR KEY to MINOR KEY

When **TRANSPOSING a MELODY** UP or DOWN an interval, write the interval ABOVE or BELOW the Tonic note of the given melody as indicated.  That note determines the new key.

♫ **Note:**  Transpose a **MAJOR** key to a **MAJOR** key and a **MINOR** key to a **MINOR** key.

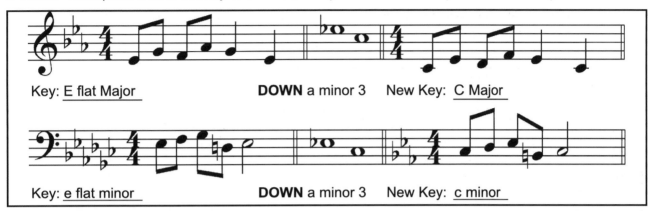

Key: E flat Major                **DOWN** a minor 3    New Key:  C Major

Key: e flat minor                 **DOWN** a minor 3    New Key:  c minor

♫ **Note:**  A double bar line cancels a Key Signature.

1. For each of the following:
   a) Name the key of the given melody.
   b) Write the Tonic note and the given interval ABOVE or BELOW the Tonic note as indicated.
   c) Name the new key.  Transpose the melody UP or DOWN by the given interval, using the correct Key Signature.

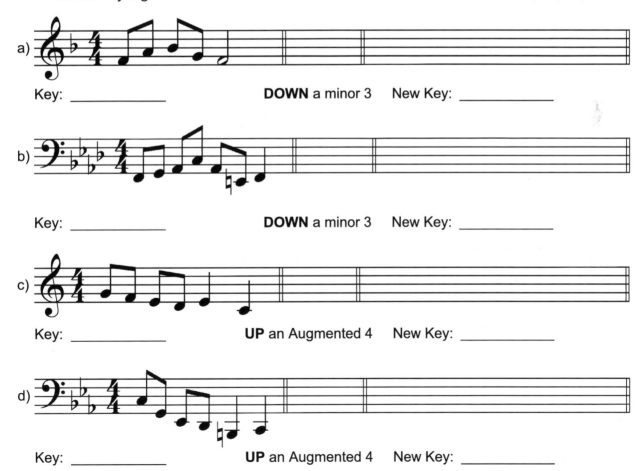

a) Key: _____          **DOWN** a minor 3    New Key: _____

b) Key: _____          **DOWN** a minor 3    New Key: _____

c) Key: _____          **UP** an Augmented 4    New Key: _____

d) Key: _____          **UP** an Augmented 4    New Key: _____

213

## TRANSPOSING a MELODY to a NEW KEY

When **TRANSPOSING a MELODY to a NEW KEY**, a Major key will ALWAYS remain a Major key and a minor key will ALWAYS remain a minor key. All the notes move UP or DOWN the SAME interval.

There are 2 possible keys for each melody: the Major Key and the relative minor key. If the 7th note of the minor key appears and it is raised, the key is minor. However, the 7th note of the minor key may not appear in the melody.

♫ **Note:** If there is no 7th note, look for the overall tonality: does the melody use more Tonic notes of the Major or minor key; is there a Tonic triad from the Major or minor key; is the final note the Tonic note of the Major or minor key? (The melody MAY NOT end on a Tonic note.)

(No raised 7th; c minor triad)

Key:  __c minor__          **DOWN** a dim 4  _C_ ↓ _G#_     Key:  __g# minor__

♫ **Note:** Draw a staff in the margin. Write the interval ABOVE or BELOW the Tonic note of the given melody as indicated. That note names the new key.

1. Name the key of the following melody. Transpose it **UP** an Augmented 2 in the Bass Clef, using the correct Key Signature. Name the new key.

Key: _____

Key: _____

3. Name the key of the following melody. Transpose it **UP** a minor 3 in the Treble Clef, using the correct Key Signature. Name the new key.

Key: _____

Key: _____

214

## TRANSPOSING a MELODY from CLEF to SAME CLEF

When **TRANSPOSING a MELODY** from one key to another (Major to Major or minor to minor), the CLEF will remain the same.

♫ **Note:** Draw a staff in the margin. Use the SAME clef as the given melody. Write the interval ABOVE or BELOW the Tonic note as indicated. That note names the new key.

1. Name the key of the following melody. Transpose it **DOWN** a Major 2 in the Tenor Clef, using the correct Key Signature. Name the new key.

Key: _____

Key: _____

2. Name the key of the following melody. Transpose it **UP** a minor 2 in the Alto Clef, using the correct Key Signature. Name the new key.

Key: _____

Key: _____

3. Name the key of the following melody. Transpose it **DOWN** an Augmented 3 in the Alto Clef, using the correct Key Signature. Name the new key.

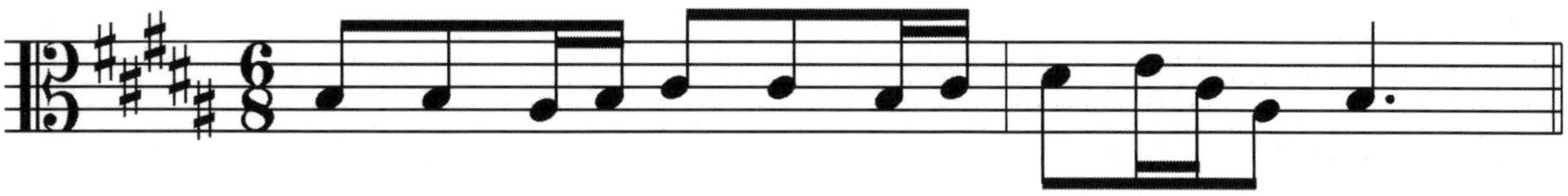

Key: _____

Key: _____

# TRANSPOSITION to CONCERT PITCH - ORCHESTRAL B flat INSTRUMENTS

**CONCERT PITCH** is the sounding pitch of an instrument.

**NON-TRANSPOSING** instruments, such as piano and violin, sound the SAME pitch as the written pitch. These non-transposing instruments are called "**C**" instruments because the sounding pitch (concert pitch) of C is the SAME as the written pitch of C.

A **TRANSPOSING** instrument is an orchestral instrument, such as Trumpet, Clarinet, English Horn and French Horn, whose sounding pitch (concert pitch) is DIFFERENT from the written pitch.

The name of a transposing instrument gives the interval of transposition between the written pitch and the concert pitch. The written pitch of C, in B♭ instruments, will be heard at the concert pitch of B♭, an interval distance of a Major 2 below C (C down to B♭).

When transposing a melody written for B♭ Clarinet or B♭ Trumpet to concert pitch, transpose the melody **DOWN** a Major 2.

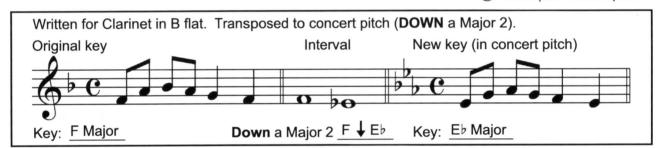

1. The following melody is written for Clarinet in B flat. Name the key in which it is written. Transpose it to concert pitch, using the correct Key Signature. Name the new key.

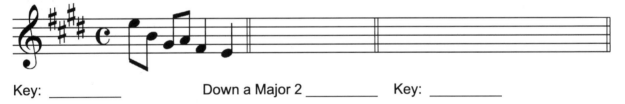

Key: _____        Down a Major 2 _____        Key: _____

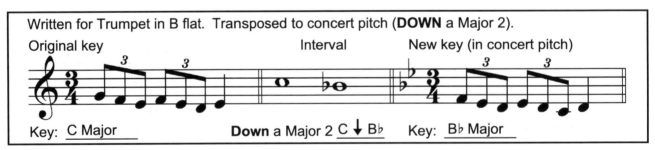

2. The following melody is written for Trumpet in B flat. Name the key in which it is written. Transpose it to concert pitch, using the correct Key Signature. Name the new key.

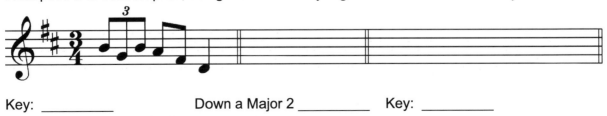

Key: _____        Down a Major 2 _____        Key: _____

## TRANSPOSITION to CONCERT PITCH - ORCHESTRAL F INSTRUMENTS

| Transposing Instruments | Written Pitch | Concert Pitch | Transpose |
|---|---|---|---|
| Clarinet in B♭ and Trumpet in B♭ | C | B♭ | DOWN a Major 2 |
| English Horn in F and French Horn in F | C | F | DOWN a Perfect 5 |

♫ **Note:** Written pitch is what you see.  Concert pitch is what you hear.

The name of a transposing instrument gives the interval of transposition between the written pitch and the concert pitch.  The written pitch of C, in F instruments, will be heard at the concert pitch of F, an interval distance of a Perfect 5 below C (C down to F).

When transposing a melody written for English Horn or French Horn in F to concert pitch, transpose the melody **DOWN** a Perfect 5.

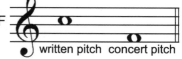

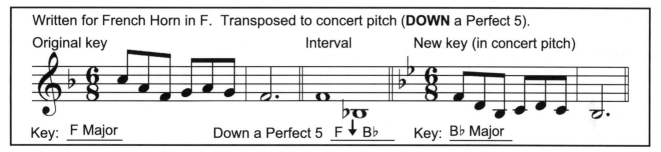

1.  The following melody is written for French Horn in F.  Name the key in which it is written.
    Transpose it to concert pitch, using the correct Key Signature.  Name the new key.

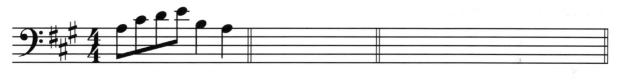

Key: _____          Down a Perfect 5 _____          Key: _____

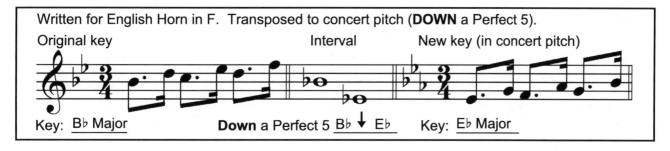

2.  The following melody is written for English Horn in F.  Name the key in which it is written.
    Transpose it to concert pitch, using the correct Key Signature.  Name the new key.

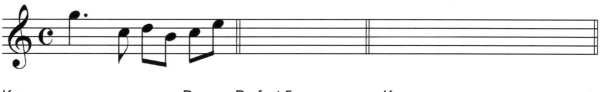

Key: _____          Down a Perfect 5 _____          Key: _____

## WRITTEN RANGE for ORCHESTRAL INSTRUMENTS

The **WRITTEN RANGE** for **ORCHESTRAL INSTRUMENTS** varies depending on the instrument. Each orchestral instrument has a specific range of sound.

♫ **Note:** Written Range to Concert Pitch for:
        French Horn in F and English Horn in F transposed DOWN a Perfect 5
        Clarinet in B♭ and Trumpet in B♭ transposed DOWN a Major 2.

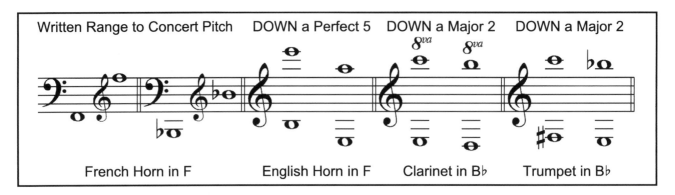

1. The following melody is written for French Horn in F. Name the key in which it is written. Transpose it to concert pitch in the Bass Clef, using the correct Key Signature. Name the new key.

Key: _____

Key: _____

2. The following melody is written for Clarinet in B flat. Name the key in which it is written. Transpose it to concert pitch in the Treble Clef, using the correct Key Signature. Name the new key.

Key: _____

Key: _____

# Lesson 9      Review Test

Total Score: ____
100

Write the Circle of Fifths on a blank piece of paper. Use it as a reference when doing the review test.

**1.**    a) Name the following melodic intervals.

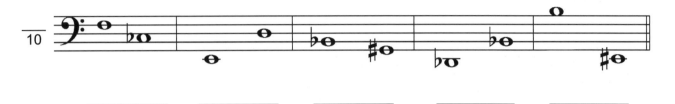

10

_____  _____  _____  _____  _____

     b) Change the **LOWER** note of each interval **ENHARMONICALLY**. Rename the interval.

_____  _____  _____  _____  _____

**2.**    For each of the following seventh chords, name:
     a) the key to which each chord belongs (Major or minor).
     b) the type (Dominant seventh, $V^7$, or diminished seventh, $vii^{o7}$).
     c) the position (root, 1st inversion, 2nd inversion or 3rd inversion).

10

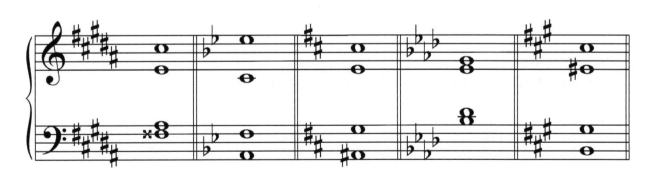

a)   _____  _____  _____  _____  _____

b)   _____  _____  _____  _____  _____

c)   _____  _____  _____  _____  _____

**3.** Write the following triads using accidentals. Use whole notes.
Name the type/quality (Major, minor, Augmented or diminished).

10
a) the **LEADING NOTE** triad of C Major in second inversion
b) the **SUBMEDIANT** triad of b flat minor harmonic in root position
c) the **SUPERTONIC** triad of e flat minor harmonic in second inversion
d) the **MEDIANT** triad of F Major in first inversion
e) the **MEDIANT** triad of d minor harmonic in root position

a)                 b)                 c)                 d)                 e)

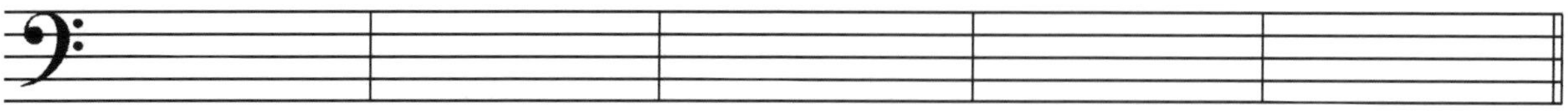

Type: _____     _____     _____     _____     _____

**4.**  a) The following melody is written for Trumpet in B flat. Name the key in which it is written.
Transpose it to concert pitch in the Treble Clef. Use the correct Key Signature.
Name the new key.

10

Key: _____

Key: _____

b) The following melody is written for English Horn in F. Name the key in which it is written.
Transpose it to concert pitch in the Treble Clef. Use the correct Key Signature.
Name the new key.

Key: _____

Key: _____

**5.** Write the Basic Beat and the pulse below each measure.  Add rests below each bracket to complete the measure.  Cross off the Basic Beat as each beat is completed.

Basic Beat: _____

Pulse:

Basic Beat: _____

Pulse:

**6.** Identify the following scales as:  Dorian, Phrygian, Lydian, Mixolydian, Aeolian, Major pentatonic, minor pentatonic, blues or whole tone.

7.  a) Name the key for the following melodic fragments.  Use chord symbols to identify the
       cadence.  Write a cadence (keyboard style) **BELOW** the bracketed notes.  Name the type
       of cadence (Perfect, Plagal or Imperfect).

10

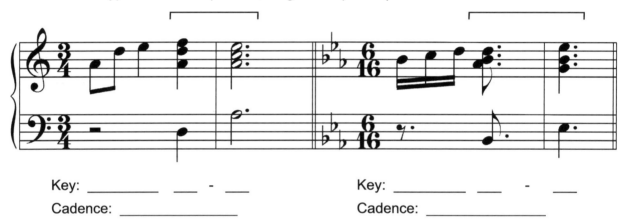

Key: _____ __ - __          Key: _____ __ - __

Cadence: _____          Cadence: _____

   b) Name the key for each of the following cadences.  Use chord symbols to identify the cadence.
      Name the type of cadence (Perfect, Plagal or Imperfect).

Key: _____ __ - __          Key: _____ __ - __

Cadence: _____          Cadence: _____

8.  Match each musical term with its English definition.  (Not all definitions will be used.)

| Term | | Definition |
|------|------|------------|
| subito pianissimo | _____ | a) three strings; release the left (piano) pedal |
| senza pedale | _____ | b) more spirited |
| lento | _____ | c) smooth |
| adagio | _____ | d) fast |
| presto | _____ | e) with movement |
| più spiritoso | _____ | f) suddenly very soft |
| allegro | _____ | g) the same tempo |
| con moto | _____ | h) very fast |
| tre corde | _____ | i) slow |
| l'istesso tempo | _____ | j) without pedal |
| | | k) a slow tempo; slower than *andante* but not as slow as *largo* |

**9.** a) Name the key. Rewrite the following melody in the **ALTO** Clef at the **SAME PITCH**.

**Andantino**

Key: _____

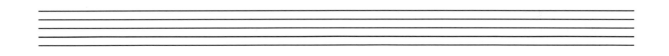

b) Name the key. Rewrite the following melody in the **TENOR** Clef at the **SAME PITCH**.

Key: _____

c) Name the key. Rewrite the following melody one octave **HIGHER** in the **TREBLE** Clef.

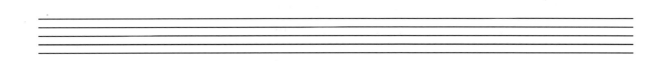

Key: _____

223

**10.** Complete the Circle of Fifths.  a)  Write the order of flats and the order of sharps.
b)  Write the Major keys and their relative minor keys.
c)  Write the Key Signature for all the flats and sharps in each clef.

___
10

# Circle of Fifths

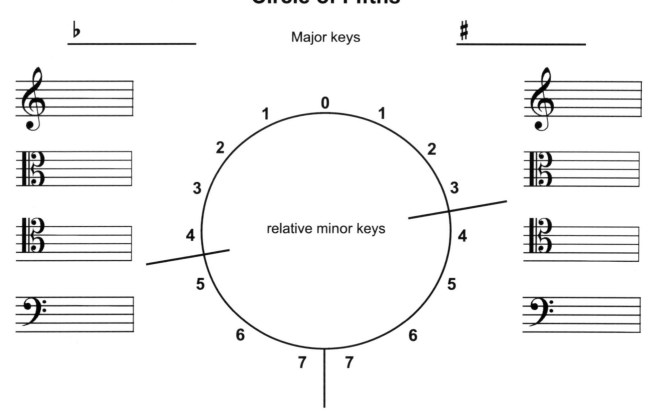

Name the type of scale for each of the following definitions.

a) _____ Major and minor scales - same Key Signature.

b) _____ Major and minor scales - same Tonic note.

c) _____ Major scale - same pitch, different letter name.

d) _____ minor scale - same pitch, different letter name.

e) _____ minor scale - same pitch as the relative minor, different letter name.

f) _____ scale - 6 consecutive whole tones beginning and ending on same note.

g) _____ scale - alternates tones and semitones or semitones and tones.

h) _____ scale - Major scale omitting the 4th and 7th degrees.

i) _____ scale - natural minor scale omitting the 2nd and 6th degrees.

j) _____ scale - minor pentatonic scale add the raised 4th or lowered 5th degree.

k) _____ scale - 12 consecutive semitones.

# Lesson 10  Scores - Short, Modern Vocal and String Quartet

A **SHORT SCORE** (Condensed score or Close score) is written for **FOUR** voices or instruments on two staves, Treble and Bass.  A short score may be written in Keyboard Style or Chorale Style.

**Keyboard Style**: Four part texture. Three notes in the Treble Clef and one note in the Bass Clef.

**Chorale Style**: Four part texture.  Two notes in the Treble Clef and two notes in the Bass Clef.

♫ **Note:**  The melody is written in the highest voice for both Keyboard Style and Chorale Style.

In **Chorale Style** the four parts (voices) are written with:
the UPPER notes in the Treble Clef, stems UP and the LOWER notes, stems DOWN.
the UPPER notes in the Bass Clef, stems UP and the LOWER notes, stems DOWN.

In **OPEN SCORE** each voice or instrument is written on its own staff, one above the other.  Notes are lined up vertically and normal stem rules apply.  A straight bracket is used to join the 4 staves.

---

**MODERN VOCAL SCORE**
  (written for FOUR voices)

The **Soprano** is written in the Treble Clef.

The **Alto** is written in the Treble Clef.

The **Tenor** is written in the Treble Clef, one octave HIGHER than it sounds.  (In some publications a small "8" is written below the Treble Clef.) ——————→

The **Bass** is written in the Bass Clef.

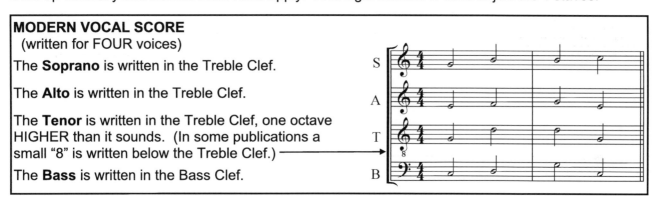

---

1.  Name the 4 voices in the Modern Vocal Score:

1. _____  2. _____  3. _____  4. _____

---

**STRING QUARTET SCORE**
  (written for FOUR instruments)

The **First Violin** (Vl.I) is written in the Treble Clef.

The **Second Violin** (Vl.II) is written in the Treble Clef.

The **Viola** (Vla.) is written in the Alto Clef.

The **Cello** (Vc.) is written in the Bass Clef.

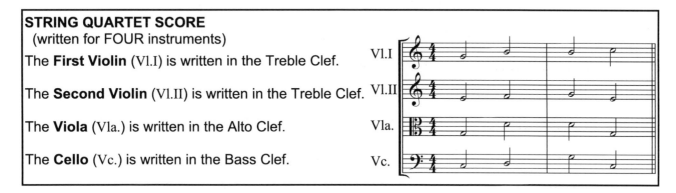

---

2.  Name the 4 instruments in the String Quartet Score:

1. _____  2. _____  3. _____  4. _____

# REWRITING a SHORT SCORE into OPEN SCORE for MODERN VOCAL SCORE

**REWRITING a SHORT SCORE for MODERN VOCAL SCORE into OPEN SCORE Rules:**

**Title** (center), **Tempo** (left) **and Composer** (right): written ONCE at the top of the score.
**Key Signature and Time Signature**: written at the beginning of each staff.
**Dynamics**: must be written ABOVE each staff where each voice begins when words are included.
**Fermata**: written ABOVE each staff.
**Bar Lines**: remain on the staff so as NOT to interfere with the words written below each staff.

♫ **Note:** Always use a ruler to keep all notes and bar lines vertically aligned.

The **MODERN VOCAL SCORE** is a CHORAL Score written for FOUR voices: (SATB)
**Soprano** (Treble Clef),   **Alto** (Treble Clef),   **Tenor** (Treble Clef),   **Bass** (Bass Clef).

The **Short Score** is written on TWO staves that are joined by a **BRACE** and a **LINE**. (Staves is the plural for Staff.)

The **Open Score** is written on FOUR staves that are joined by a **BRACKET** and a **LINE**.

In Open Score for **Modern Vocal Score**, the four voices (each written on its own staff) are in order of range from highest to lowest. Normal stem rules apply.

In Short Score, the **Tenor** voice is written where it sounds. In Open Score, the Tenor voice is written one octave **HIGHER** than it sounds.

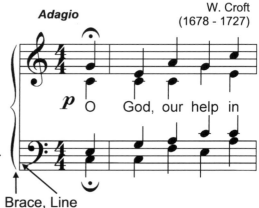

**O God, Our Help in Ages Past**

Brace, Line

1. Following the example, rewrite the Short Score above in Open Score for Modern Vocal Score. Name the four voices.

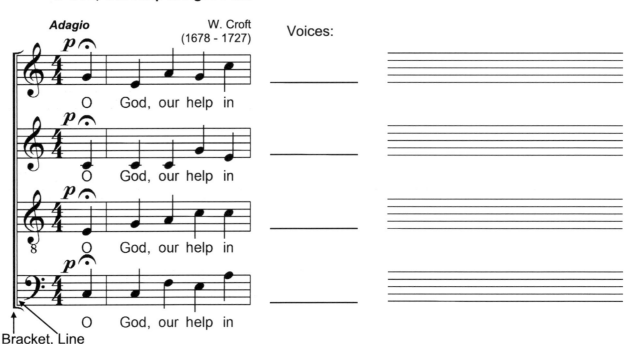

**O God, Our Help in Ages Past**

Voices:

Bracket, Line

## SHORT SCORE to MODERN VOCAL SCORE

In **SHORT SCORE**, a two note slur curves up in the Soprano and Tenor voices, and curves down in the Alto and Bass voices. Two note slurs are written in between the stems.
In **OPEN SCORE**, a two note slur is written on the notehead side when stems are in the same direction. For stems in opposite directions, the slur is written curved up in between the noteheads.

In **SHORT SCORE**, dotted line notes are written with the dot ABOVE the line in the Soprano and Tenor voices, and written with the dot BELOW the line in the Alto and Bass voices.
In **OPEN SCORE**, dotted line notes are written with the dot ABOVE the line.

♫ **Note:** An "excerpt" is a passage taken from a piece of music.

1. Rewrite the following excerpt in Open Score for Modern Vocal Score. Name the four voices.

**REWRITING a SHORT SCORE into OPEN SCORE for STRING QUARTET**

**REWRITING a SHORT SCORE for STRING QUARTET into Open Score Rules:**

**Title** (center), **Tempo** (left) **and Composer** (right): written ONCE at the top of the score.
**Key Signature and Time Signature:** written at the beginning of each staff.
**Dynamics:** written BELOW each staff, starting with the first note.
**Fermata:** written ABOVE each staff.
**Bar Lines:** run continuously through all four staves.

♫ **Note:** Ties in close score are drawn from notehead to notehead on the stem side.
Ties in open score are drawn on the notehead side of the notes.

The **STRING QUARTET** is an INSTRUMENTAL Score written for FOUR stringed instruments:

| **First Violin, Violin I** | **Second Violin, Violin II** | **Viola** | **Cello** |
|---|---|---|---|
| (Treble Clef) | (Treble Clef) | (Alto Clef) | (Bass Clef) |

The **Short Score** is written on TWO staves. If the same note is played by two instruments at the same time, it is given two stems; one up and one down.

In **Short Score**, staccato dots are written: ABOVE the stem for notes with stems up and BELOW the stem for notes with stems down.

In **Open Score** for String Quartet, each instrument has its own note. Normal stem rules apply. Correct placement of articulation is followed.

**Morning Glory**

1. Following the example, rewrite the Short Score above in Open Score for String Quartet. Name the four instruments.

**Morning Glory**

Instruments:

## SHORT SCORE to STRING QUARTET

In **SHORT SCORE**, rests may be written higher or lower than usual on the staff depending on which instrument or voice is having a rest. Rests may also be written outside the staff (use ledger lines for breve, whole rest and half rests). When BOTH instruments or voices written on the SAME staff have the same rest, only ONE rest is written for both instruments or voices.

In **OPEN SCORE** each instrument or voice has its own rest. Correct placement of rest rules apply.

1. Rewrite the following excerpt in Open Score for String Quartet. Name the four instruments.

229

**REWRITING an OPEN SCORE into SHORT SCORE**

**REWRITING an OPEN SCORE for Modern Vocal Score into SHORT SCORE Rules:**

**Short Score**: written on two staves, Treble and Bass. Stem direction identifies each voice.
**Soprano**: written in the Treble Clef, stems UP. **Alto**: written in the Treble Clef, stems DOWN.
**Tenor**: written in the Bass Clef, stems UP. **Bass**: written in the Bass Clef, stems DOWN.
If the same note is sung by two voices at the same time, it is given two stems: one up and one down.
**Words**: written in the middle of the Grand Staff. Space the notes to fit the syllables of the words.

**Fermata**: written ABOVE the soprano part and BELOW the bass part.
**Bar Lines**: remain on the staff and do NOT run continuously through both staves (as in piano music).

♫ **Note:** Always use a ruler to keep all notes and bar lines vertically aligned.

In **SHORT SCORE**, the **BRACE** and bar line are written at the beginning of the staves.

1. Rewrite the following excerpt in Short Score. Name the four voices.

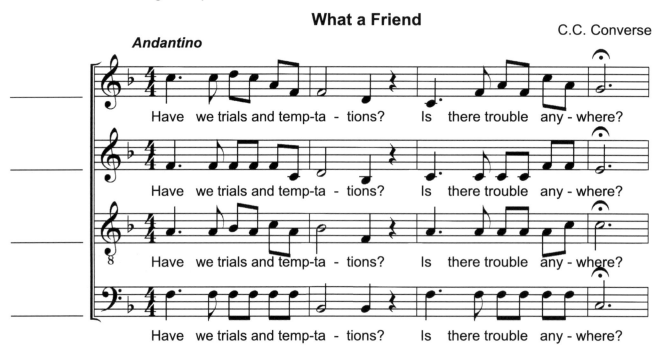

## OPEN SCORE to SHORT SCORE

When rewriting an **OPEN SCORE** into **SHORT SCORE**, write the UPPER notes in the Treble Clef first. Use a ruler to line up the other notes directly below the top notes.

1.  a)  Name the type of Open Scores. Name the four voices or instruments for each.
    b)  Rewrite the Open Scores into Short Scores.

a)  Type of Score: _____          a)  Type of Score: _____

b)  Short Score (of above)                     b)  Short Score (of above)

# Lesson 10        Review Test

Total Score: ____
/ 100

Write the Circle of Fifths on a blank piece of paper.  Use it as a reference when doing the review test.

**1.**    a)  Write the following harmonic intervals **BELOW** the given notes.  Use whole notes.

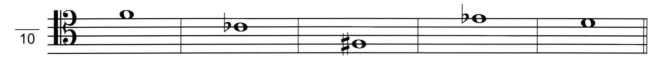

10

     Augmented 11      minor 6      Major 3      diminished 13      Perfect 12

b)  Invert the above intervals in the Bass Clef.  Name the inversions.

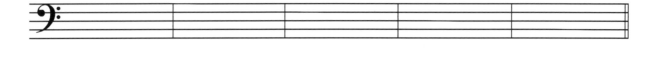

_____    _____    _____    _____    _____

**2.**    Write the following seventh chords in the Treble Clef.  Use whole notes.  Use the correct Key Signature.

____    a)  the **DIMINISHED SEVENTH** chord of g sharp minor harmonic in root position
10    b)  the **DOMINANT SEVENTH** chord of B flat Major in second inversion
      c)  the **DOMINANT SEVENTH** chord of c sharp minor harmonic in third inversion
      d)  the **DOMINANT SEVENTH** chord of A Major in first inversion
      e)  the **DIMINISHED SEVENTH** chord of e flat minor harmonic in root position

     a)            b)            c)            d)            e)

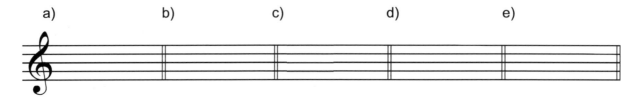

**3.**    Name each of the following chords as:  Major triad, minor triad,  Augmented triad, diminished triad, seventh chord, quartal chord, polychord or cluster chord.

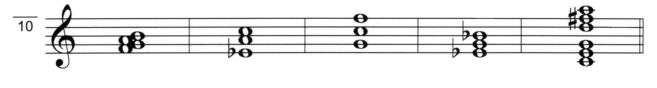

10

_____    _____    _____    _____    _____

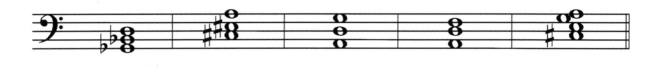

_____    _____    _____    _____    _____

**4.** The following melody is written for Trumpet in B flat.  Name the key in which it is written. Transpose it to concert pitch in the Treble Clef.  Use the correct Key Signature. Name the new key.

Key: _____

Key: _____

**5.** Name the key for the following melodic fragments.  Use chord symbols to identify the cadence.  Write a cadence (keyboard style) **BELOW** the bracketed notes.  Name the type of cadence (Perfect, Plagal or Imperfect).

Key: _____ ___ - ___          Key: _____ ___ - ___

Cadence: _____          Cadence: _____

**6.** Write the Basic Beat and the pulse below each measure.  Add rests below each bracket to complete the measure.  Cross off the Basic Beat as each beat is completed.

Basic Beat: _____

Pulse:

Basic Beat: _____

Pulse:

7. Write the following scales, ascending and descending, in the clefs indicated. Use whole notes. Use accidentals.

10     a) g sharp minor harmonic, from Subdominant to Subdominant
           b) a flat minor melodic, from Submediant to Submediant
           c) enharmonic Tonic Major of b minor
           d) Lydian mode starting on C flat

a)

b)

c)

d)

8. Match each musical term or sign with its English definition. (Not all definitions will be used.)

| Term | Definition |
|---|---|
| da capo, D.C. _____ | a) from the sign, 𝄋 |
| dal segno, D.S. _____ | b) play one octave above the written pitch |
| D.C. al Fine _____ | c) hold for the combined value of the tied notes |
| 𝄐 _____ | d) Maelzel's metronome |
| Tempo primo, Tempo I _____ | e) return to the original tempo |
| M.M. _____ | f) repeat from the beginning and end at *Fine* |
| 8va‑ ‑ ‑ ⌋ _____ | g) repeat the music within the double bars |
| 8va‑ ‑ ‑ ⌐ _____ | h) from the beginning |
| ♩♩ _____ | i) accent, a stressed note |
| 𝄆 𝄇 _____ | j) play one octave below the written pitch |
| | k) fermata, pause; hold the note or rest longer than its written value |

234

**9.** a) Name the type of Open Score below. _____

b) Name the four voices or instruments for the score below.  (Do not use abbreviations.)

10

_____ _____ _____ _____

c) Rewrite the following excerpt in Short Score (using the two staves below).

**10.** Analyze the following excerpt by answering the questions below.

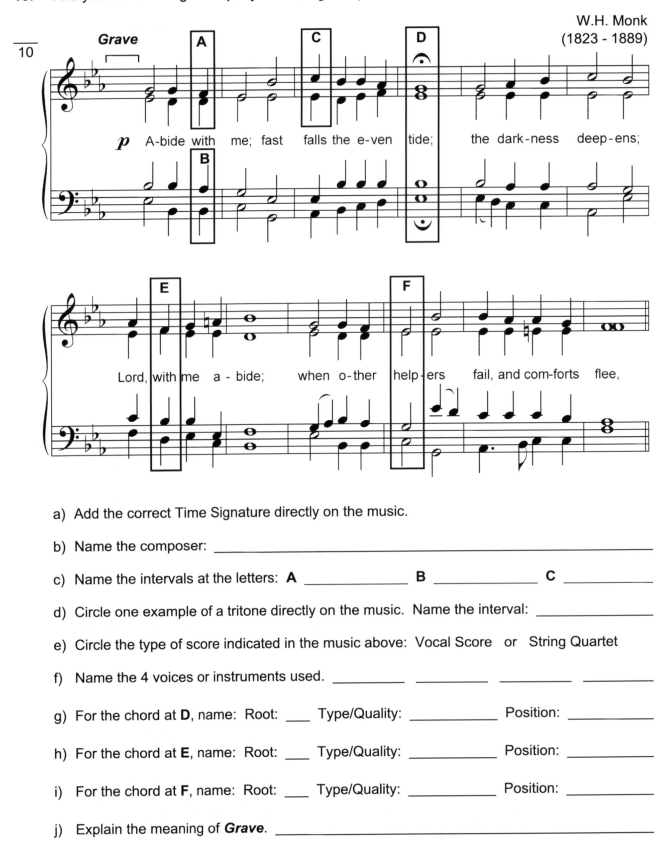

a) Add the correct Time Signature directly on the music.

b) Name the composer: _____

c) Name the intervals at the letters: **A** _____ **B** _____ **C** _____

d) Circle one example of a tritone directly on the music. Name the interval: _____

e) Circle the type of score indicated in the music above: Vocal Score  or  String Quartet

f) Name the 4 voices or instruments used. _____ _____ _____ _____

g) For the chord at **D**, name: Root: ___ Type/Quality: _____ Position: _____

h) For the chord at **E**, name: Root: ___ Type/Quality: _____ Position: _____

i) For the chord at **F**, name: Root: ___ Type/Quality: _____ Position: _____

j) Explain the meaning of **Grave**. _____

# Lesson 11          Analysis - Musical Compositions

**ANALYSIS** - relationship between the motive/phrase and **IMITATION**, **SEQUENCE** and **INVERSION**.

A **Motive** is the smallest unit of musical form that is used as a building block in music (2 - 7 notes, sometimes more).  A **Phrase** is a musical unit of 4 (more or less) measures, ending with a cadence.

♫ **Note:**   A musical idea may be a motive or larger, even a phase.

**Repetition** - the repeating of a musical idea by the **same** voice at the **same** pitch.

**Imitation** - the repetition of a musical idea (exact or varied) by **another** voice at the **same** pitch or at a **different** pitch.  The imitation may be in the same clef or a different clef.

**Sequence** - the repetition of a musical idea by the **same** voice at a **higher** or **lower** pitch. Melodic sequence is in one voice.  Harmonic sequence is in more than one voice.

**Inversion** - the musical idea is repeated "**upside-down**".
Melodic (interval) inversion occurs when interval directions of a single melodic line are reversed.
The inversion may not always be exact, as it is based on the melodic shape and chord structure.
Harmonic (voice) inversion occurs when one voice is transposed past another voice.

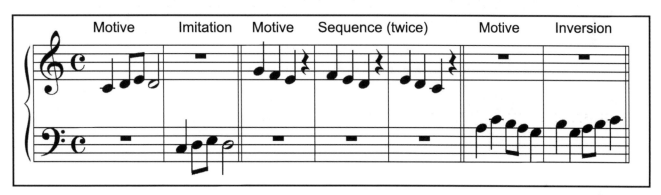

♫ **Note:**  An "excerpt" is a passage taken from a piece of music.

1. For the excerpts below, give the term for the relationship between each motive and the measures at the following letters **A**, **B**, **C**, **D** and **E** as: repetition, imitation, sequence or inversion.

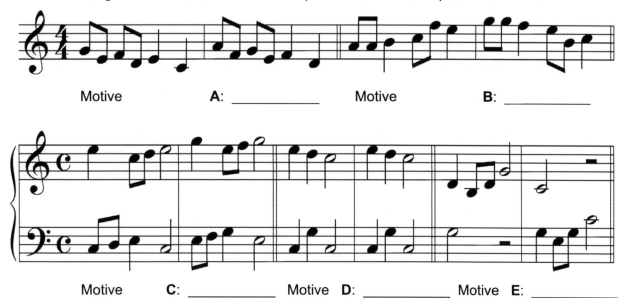

## ANALYSIS of a MUSICAL COMPOSITION

**ANALYSIS** of a piece of music develops a deeper understanding of the composers ideas.

1. Analyze the following piece of music by answering the questions below.

a) The **COMPOSER'S** name is written at the top right of the piece. The dates underneath are the year of his/her birth and death. If there is only one date, it is the year of birth and the composer is still alive.

Name the composer. _____ When did he/she live? _____

b) When naming the **KEY**, look at the Key Signature. Check for the raised 7th note of the harmonic minor key to determine if the key is Major or minor. The piece will often end on the Tonic.

Name the Key: _____ Tonic: _____ Dominant: _____ Leading note: _____

c) When writing the **TIME SIGNATURE** on the music, always write it in BOTH clefs. Look at several measures to determine if there is a pickup beat (anacrusis or incomplete measure).

Write the Time Signature directly on the music.

The **TEMPO** is written directly above the Time Signature.

Name and explain the tempo of this piece. _____

d) When counting the number of **MEASURES** in a piece, a repeat sign WILL NOT affect the number of measures.

How many measures are in this piece? _____

When all repeat signs are observed, how many measures of music are played? _____

Measure numbers may be written in a small square at the beginning of each line of music.

Write the measure number in the square at the letter **A**.

e) When naming a chord, the **ROOT** is determined by the lowest note of a root position chord. The **TYPE/QUALITY** of a chord may be a Major, minor, Augmented or diminished triad; or a Dominant seventh ($V^7$) or diminished seventh ($vii°^7$) chord. The chord is determined by the intervals above the Root. The **POSITION**, root position, first inversion, second inversion or third inversion (for seventh chords), is determined by the lowest note. Name the chord at the following letters:

**B**: Root: _____ Type/Quality: _____ Position: _____

**C**: Root: _____ Type/Quality: _____ Position: _____

f) When identifying **INTERVALS**, count ALL the lines and ALL the spaces. Check the Key Signature, changes in clefs and any accidentals in the measure that would affect the note.

Circle and label a tritone directly on the music. Name the interval. _____

Name the intervals at the following letters: **D**: _____ **E**: _____ **F**: _____

g) When adding a **REST(S)** to complete a measure, determine the Time Signature and follow the rest rules.

Write the appropriate rest(s) at the letter **G**. Name the type of rest used. _____

h) When analyzing an **OPEN SCORE**, check the clef signs to determine if it is written for Modern Vocal Score or String Quartet.

Is this piece written in open score or closed score for piano? _____

Name the clefs and voices/instruments for each of the following open scores.

Modern Vocal Score
Clef: _____ _____ _____ _____

Voice/Instrument: _____ _____ _____ _____

String Quartet
Clef: _____ _____ _____ _____

Voice/Instrument: _____ _____ _____ _____

i) Determining the relationship of the motive (musical idea or phrase) and other measures, look for:
**IMITATION** - the motive is repeated by another voice/instrument at the same or different pitch.
**INVERSION** - the motive is turned "upside-down". Interval directions (up or down) are reversed.
**SEQUENCE** - the motive is repeated (one or more times) at a higher or lower pitch.

Give the term for the relationship in the R.H between mm. 1 - 2 and mm. 3 - 4. _____

j) When identifying a **CADENCE** as Perfect, Plagal or Imperfect, determine the key. Count UP from the Tonic note to determine the degree of the bass notes. Look for the raised 7th note of the harmonic minor key.

Name the cadence at the letter **H**. _____

## ANALYSIS of a MUSICAL COMPOSITION

1. Analyze the following piece of music by answering the questions below.

# Lonely Waltz

*Larghetto* M.M. ♩ = 60 - 65  **A**

G. St. Germain

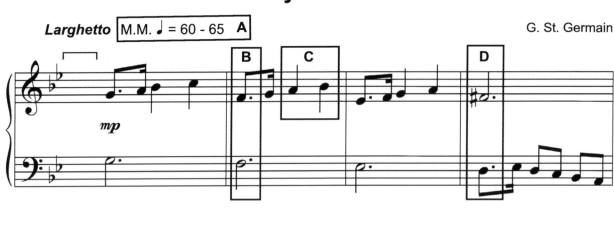

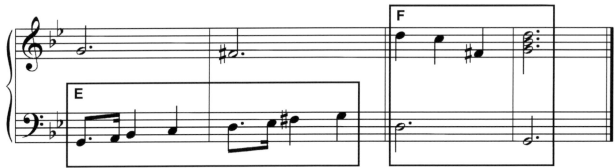

a) Add the correct Time Signature directly on the music.

b) Name the key of this piece. _____

c) Explain the meaning at the letter **A**. _____

d) Name the intervals at the letters: **B** _____ **C** _____ **D** _____

e) Name the scale at the letter **E**. _____

f) Circle one example of a tritone directly on the music.  Name the interval: _____

g) Circle the term for the relationship between mm. 1, 2 and 3.

   imitation     inversion     sequence

h) Circle the term for the relationship between the R.H. in m. 1 and the L.H. in m. 5.

   imitation     inversion     sequence

i) Name the type of cadence formed by the chords at the letter **F**. _____

j) Explain the meaning of *Larghetto.* _____

240

# Lesson 11                    Review Test

Write the Circle of Fifths on a blank piece of paper.  Use it as a reference when doing the review test.

**1.**   a) Name the following harmonic intervals.

10

_____   _____   _____   _____   _____

   b) Invert the above intervals in the Treble Clef.  Use whole notes.  Name the inversions.

_____   _____   _____   _____   _____

**2.**   Write the following triads using accidentals.  Use whole notes.  Name the type/quality (Major, minor, Augmented or diminished).

   a) the **LEADING NOTE** triad of c minor harmonic in first inversion

10   b) the **SUPERTONIC** triad of c minor harmonic in root position

   c) the **TONIC** triad of f minor harmonic in second inversion

   d) the **DOMINANT** triad of D flat Major in first inversion

   e) the **MEDIANT** triad of c minor harmonic in root position

   f) Name the scale which contains all of these chords: _____

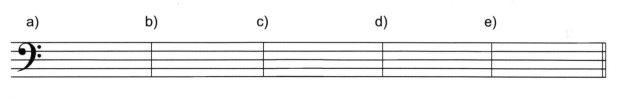

   a)            b)            c)            d)            e)

Type: _____   _____   _____   _____   _____

**3.**   For each of the following seventh chords, name:

   a) the key to which each chord belongs (Major or minor).

   b) the type (Dominant seventh, $V^7$, or diminished seventh, $vii°^7$).

10   c) the position (root, 1$^{st}$ inversion, 2$^{nd}$ inversion or 3$^{rd}$ inversion).

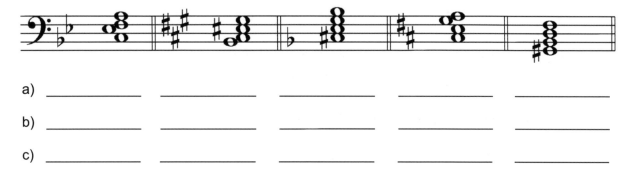

   a) _____   _____   _____   _____   _____

   b) _____   _____   _____   _____   _____

   c) _____   _____   _____   _____   _____

**4.** a) The following melody is written for French Horn in F.  Name the key in which it is written.
Transpose it to concert pitch in the Bass Clef.  Use the correct Key Signature.
Name the new key.

Key: _____

Key: _____

b) Transpose the given melody **UP** a augmented fourth in the Tenor Clef.  Use the correct
Key Signature.  Name the new key.

Key: _____

**5.** Write the Basic Beat and the pulse  below each measure.  Add rests below each bracket to
complete the measure.  Cross off the Basic Beat as each beat is completed.

Basic Beat: _____

Pulse:

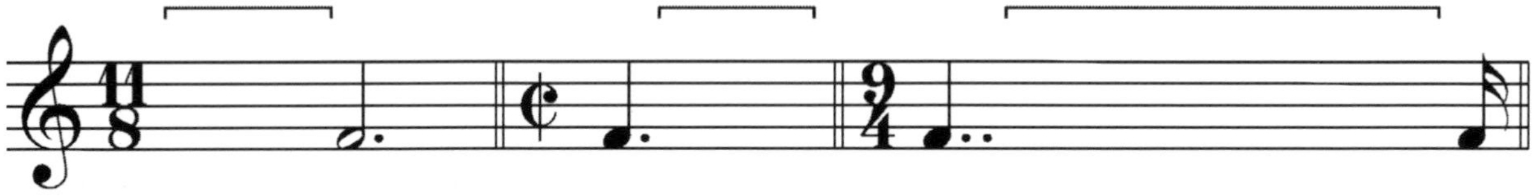

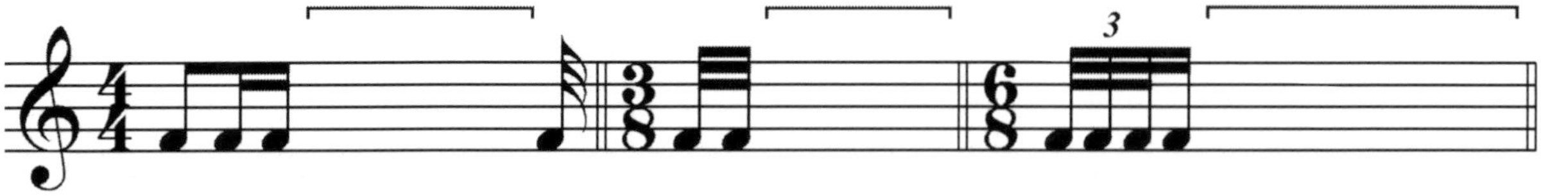

Basic Beat: _____

Pulse:

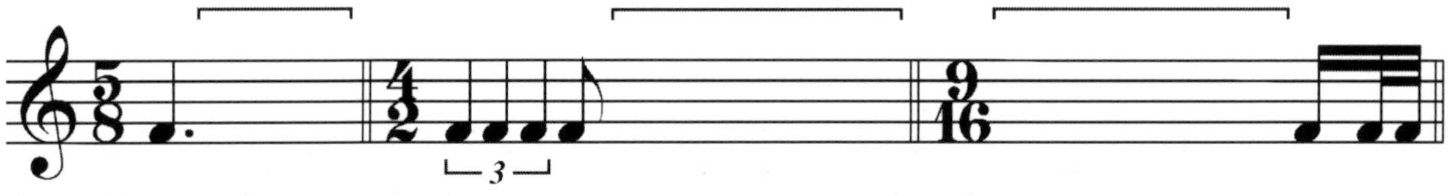

Basic Beat: _____

Pulse:

**6.** Write the following scales, ascending and descending, in the clefs indicated.  Use whole notes.

a) whole tone scale starting on E using any standard notation
b) a sharp minor melodic, from Leading note to Leading note, using the correct Key Signature
c) b flat minor harmonic, from Subdominant to Subdominant, using the correct Key Signature
d) Phrygian mode starting on A sharp using accidentals
e) enharmonic Tonic minor, melodic form, of C flat Major using accidentals
f) Dorian mode starting on C using accidentals

10

a)

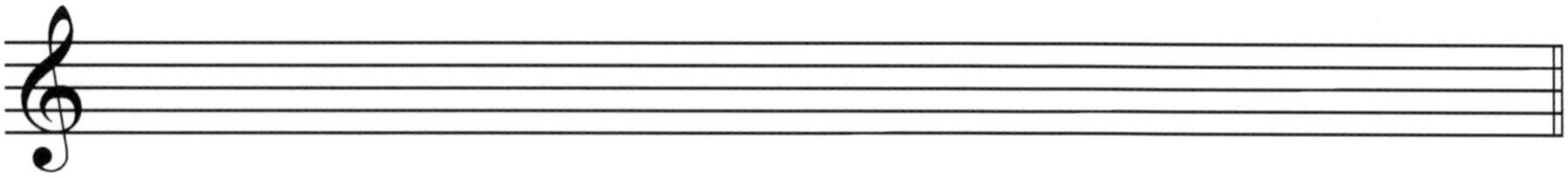

b)

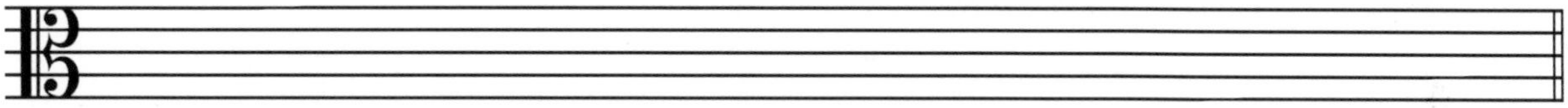

c)

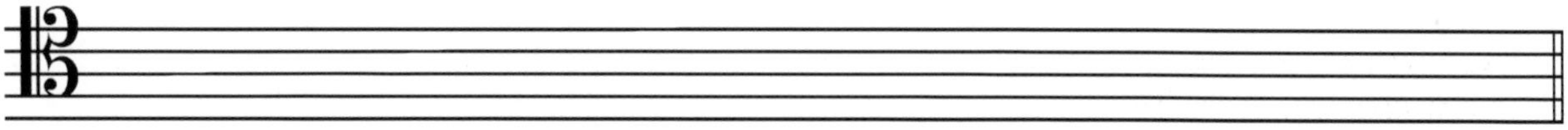

d)

e)

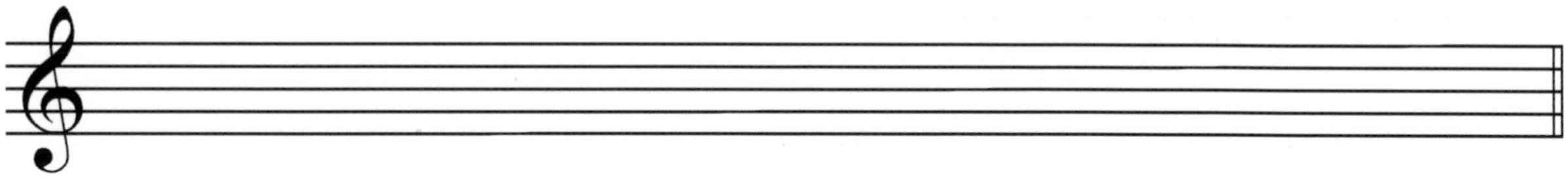

f)

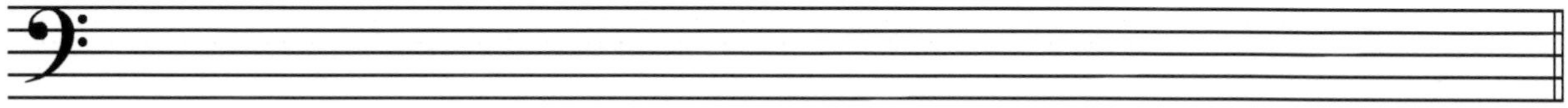

7. a) Name the key for the following melodic fragments. Use chord symbols to identify the cadence. Write a cadence (keyboard style) **BELOW** the bracketed notes. Name the type of cadence (Perfect, Plagal or Imperfect).

10

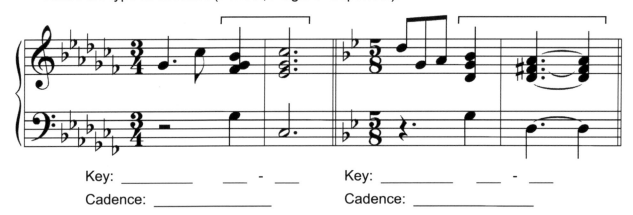

Key: _____ ___ - ___       Key: _____ ___ - ___

Cadence: _____       Cadence: _____

b) Name the key for each of the following cadences. Use chord symbols to identify the cadence. Name the type of cadence (Perfect, Plagal or Imperfect).

Key: _____ ___ - ___       Key: _____ ___ - ___

Cadence: _____       Cadence: _____

8. Match each musical term with its English definition. (Not all definitions will be used.)

| Term | | Definition | |
|------|---|------------|---|
| *mässig* | _____ | a) | with expression |
| *sehr schnell* | _____ | b) | slow, slowly |
| *mit Ausdruck* | _____ | c) | marked or stressed |
| *quasi* | _____ | d) | less movement, slower |
| *langsam* | _____ | e) | lively, brisk |
| *marcato, marc.* | _____ | f) | moderate, moderately |
| *meno mosso* | _____ | g) | with mute |
| *ritenuto, riten.* | _____ | h) | with spirit |
| *con sordino* | _____ | i) | almost, as if |
| *vivace* | _____ | j) | very fast |
| | | k) | suddenly slower, held back |

10

**9.**   a) Name the four voices or instruments for the following **OPEN** Scores.  (Do not use
   abbreviations.)

10

Modern Vocal Score: _____  _____  _____  _____

String Quartet:        _____  _____  _____  _____

b) Rewrite the excerpt in **OPEN** Score for each of the following:

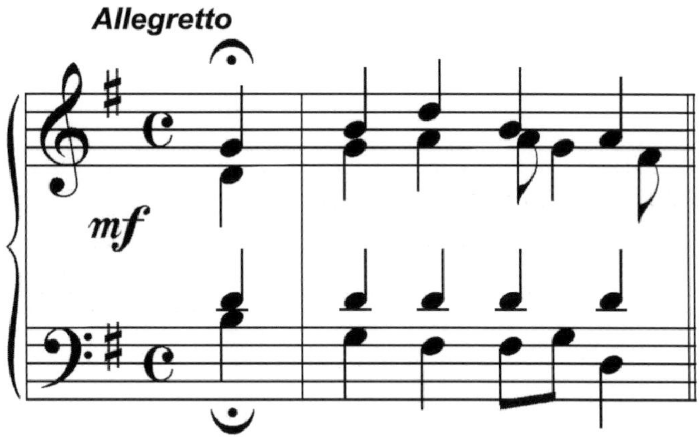

**Modern Vocal Score**                              **String Quartet**

**10.** Analyze the following piece of music by answering the questions below.

# Friday Night

Scherzando

G. St. Germain

a) Add the correct Time Signature directly on the music.

b) Name the key of this piece. _____

c) Name the composer. _____

d) Name the intervals at the letters: **A** _____ **B** _____ **C** _____

e) Explain the relationship between mm. 5 and 6 in the R.H. _____

f) For the chord at **D**, name:  Root: _____  Type/Quality: _____  Position: _____

g) For the chord at **E**, name:  Root: _____  Type/Quality: _____  Position: _____

h) Name the type of scale at the letter **F**. _____

i) Name the type of cadence at the letter **G**. _____

j) Explain the meaning of **Scherzando**. _____

# Lesson 12      Musical Terms, Definitions and Signs

**MUSICAL TERMS** and **SIGNS** (usually in Italian) indicate tempo, changes in tempo, pedal, articulation, dynamics and style in performance.  Terms may also be written in German or French.

## TEMPO, CHANGES in TEMPO and PEDAL

| Tempo | Definition |
|---|---|
| *adagio* | a slow tempo (slower than *andante* but not as slow as *largo*) |
| *allegretto* | fairly fast (a little slower than *allegro*) |
| *allegro* | fast |
| *andante* | moderately slow; at a walking pace |
| *andantino* | a little faster than *andante* |
| *comodo* | at a comfortable, easy tempo |
| *con moto* | with movement |
| *grave* | slow and solemn |
| *larghetto* | not as slow as *largo* |
| *largo* | very slow |
| *lento* | slow |
| *moderato* | at a moderate tempo |
| *presto* | very fast |
| *prestissimo* | as fast as possible |
| *stringendo* | pressing, becoming faster |
| *vivace* | lively, brisk |

| Changes in Tempo | Definition |
|---|---|
| *accelerando, accel.* | becoming quicker |
| *allargando, allarg.* | broadening, becoming slower |
| *a tempo* | return to the original tempo |
| *calando* | becoming slower and softer |
| *l'istesso tempo* | the same tempo |
| *meno mosso* | less movement, slower |
| *più mosso* | more movement, quicker |
| *rallentando, rall.* | slowing down |
| *ritardando, rit.* | slowing down gradually |
| *ritenuto, riten.* | suddenly slower, held back |
| *rubato* | with some freedom of tempo to enhance musical expression |
| *Tempo primo, Tempo I* | return to the original tempo |

| Pedal | Definition |
|---|---|
| *pedale, ped* | pedal |
| *con pedale,* 𝄚 | with pedal |
| *tre corde* | three strings; release the left (piano) pedal |
| *una corda* | one string;  depress the left (piano) pedal |
| L_____J | pedal marking |

1.  Give the Italian term for each of the following definitions:

_____     _____     _____

at a comfortable, easy tempo     becoming slower and softer     one string; depress the left pedal

247

# ARTICULATION, DYNAMICS and ITALIAN TERMS

| Articulation | Definition | Sign |
|---|---|---|
| *marcato, marc.* | marked or stressed | |
| *martellato* | strongly accented, hammered | |
| *accent* | a stressed note | |
| *pesante* | weighty, with emphasis | |
| *legato* | smooth | |
| *slur* | play the notes *legato* | |
| *leggiero* | light, nimble, quick | |
| *staccato* | detached | |
| *sostenuto* | sustained | |
| *tenuto* | held, sustained | |

| Dynamics | Definition |
|---|---|
| *crescendo, cresc.* | becoming louder |
| *decrescendo, decresc.* | becoming softer |
| *diminuendo, dim.* | becoming softer |
| *forte, f* | loud |
| *fortepiano, fp* | loud, then suddenly soft |
| *fortissimo, ff* | very loud |
| *mezzo forte, mf* | moderately loud |
| *mezzo piano, mp* | moderately soft |
| *piano, p* | soft |
| *pianissimo, pp* | very soft |
| *sforzando, sf, sfz* | a sudden strong accent of a single note or chord |

| Italian Terms | Definition |
|---|---|
| *arco* | for stringed instruments: resume bowing after a *pizzicato* passage |
| *attacca* | proceed without a break |
| *con sordino* | with mute |
| *fine* | the end |
| *loco* | return to normal register |
| *ottava, 8va* | the interval of an octave |
| *pizzicato* | for stringed instruments:  pluck the string instead of bowing |
| *primo, prima* | first; the upper part of a duet |
| *quindicesima alta (15ma)* | two octaves higher |
| *risoluto* | resolute |
| *secondo, seconda* | second; second or lower part of a duet |
| *simile* | continue in the same manner as has just been indicated |
| *tacet* | be silent |
| *tempo* | speed at which music is performed |
| *tutti* | a passage for the ensemble |
| *volta* | time (for example, *prima volta*, first time; *seconda volta*, second time) |
| *volti subito, v.s.* | turn the page quickly |

1. Give the Italian term for each of the following definitions:

| _____ | _____ | _____ |
|---|---|---|
| strongly accented, hammered | loud, then suddenly soft | proceed without a break |

# PREFIX and SIGNS

| Prefix | Definition |
|---|---|
| *alla, all'* | in the manner of |
| *assai* | much, very much (for example: *allegro assai,* very fast) |
| *ben, bene* | well (for example: *ben marcato,* well marked) |
| *col, coll', colla, colle* | with (for example: *coll'ottava,* with an added octave) |
| *con* | with |
| *e, ed* | and |
| *ma* | but (for example: *ma non troppo,* but not too much) |
| *meno* | less |
| *molto* | much, very |
| *non* | not |
| *non troppo* | not too much |
| *più* | more |
| *poco* | little |
| *poco a poco* | little by little |
| *quasi* | almost, as if |
| *sempre* | always, continuously |
| *senza* | without |
| *sopra* | above |
| *subito* | suddenly |
| *troppo* | too much |

| Signs | Definition |
|---|---|
| D.C. al *Fine* | repeat from the beginning and end at *Fine* |
| D.C. | *da capo,* from the beginning |
| 𝄋 | *dal segno, D.S.,* from the sign |
| 𝄐 | *fermata:* a pause; hold the note or rest longer than its written value |
| M.D. | *mano destra,* right hand |
| M.S. | *mano sinistra,* left hand |
| M.M. | Maelzel's metronome |
| *8ᵛᵃ- - -⌐ ottava, 8ᵛᵃ* | play one octave above the written pitch |
| *8ᵛᵃ- - -⌐ ottava, 8ᵛᵃ* | play one octave below the written pitch |
| repeat signs | *repeat signs:* repeat the music within the double bars |
| tie | *tie:* hold for the combined value of the tied notes |

1. Give the Italian term or sign for each of the following definitions:

_____    _____    _____    _____

      suddenly             above           from the beginning         left hand

# STYLE in PERFORMANCE, FRENCH TERMS and GERMAN TERMS

| Style in Performance | Definition |
| --- | --- |
| ad libitum, ad lib. | at the liberty of the performer |
| agitato | agitated |
| animato | lively, animated |
| brillante | brilliant |
| cantabile | in a singing style |
| con brio | with vigor, spirit |
| con espressione | with expression |
| con fuoco | with fire |
| con grazia | with grace |
| dolce | sweet, gentle |
| dolente | sad |
| espressivo, espress. | expressive, with expression |
| giocoso | humorous, jocose |
| grandioso | grand, grandiose |
| grazioso | graceful |
| largamente | broadly |
| maestoso | majestic |
| mesto | sad, mournful |
| morendo | dying, fading away |
| scherzando | playful |
| semplice | simple |
| sonore | sonorous |
| sotto voce | soft, subdued, under the breath |
| spiritoso | spirited |
| tranquillo | quiet, tranquil |
| vivo | lively |

| French Term | Definition |
| --- | --- |
| cédez | yield; hold the tempo back |
| léger | light; lightly |
| lentement | slowly |
| modéré | at a moderate tempo |
| mouvement | tempo; motion |
| vite | fast |

| German Term | Definition |
| --- | --- |
| bewegt | moving |
| langsam | slow, slowly |
| mässig | moderate, moderately |
| mit Ausdruck | with expression |
| sehr | very |
| schnell | fast |

1. Give the term in Italian, French and German for the following definition:

| _____ | _____ | _____ |
| --- | --- | --- |
| slow (Italian) | slowly (French) | slow, slowly (German) |

# Lesson 12    Final Complete Exam

Write the Circle of Fifths on a blank piece of paper. Use it as a reference when doing the review test.

**1.**    a)  Name the following intervals.

10

_____    _____    _____    _____    _____

     b)  Invert the above intervals in the Treble Clef. Name the inversions.

_____    _____    _____    _____    _____

**2.**    For each of the following seventh chords, name:
     a)  the key to which each chord belongs (Major or minor).
     b)  the type (Dominant seventh, $V^7$, or diminished seventh, vii$^{\circ 7}$).
     c)  the position (root, 1st inversion, 2nd inversion or 3rd inversion).

10

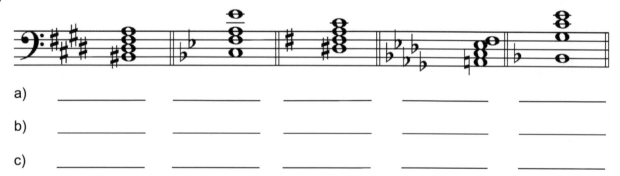

a)  _____    _____    _____    _____    _____

b)  _____    _____    _____    _____    _____

c)  _____    _____    _____    _____    _____

**3.**    Name the following for each of the triads below:
     a)  the Root.
     b)  the type/quality (Major, minor, Augmented or diminished).
10    c)  the position (root position, 1st inversion or 2nd inversion).

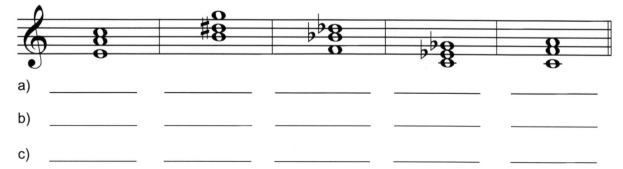

a)  _____    _____    _____    _____    _____

b)  _____    _____    _____    _____    _____

c)  _____    _____    _____    _____    _____

**4.** **a)** The following melody is written for Trumpet in B flat. Name the key in which it is written. Transpose it to concert pitch in the Bass Clef. Use the correct Key Signature. Name the new key.

Key: _____

Key: _____

**b)** Transpose the given melody **DOWN** a minor sixth in the Bass Clef. Use the correct Key Signature. Name the new key.

Key: _____

**5.** Write the Basic Beat and the pulse below each measure. Add rests below each bracket to complete the measure. Cross off the Basic Beat as each beat is completed.

Basic Beat: _____

Pulse:

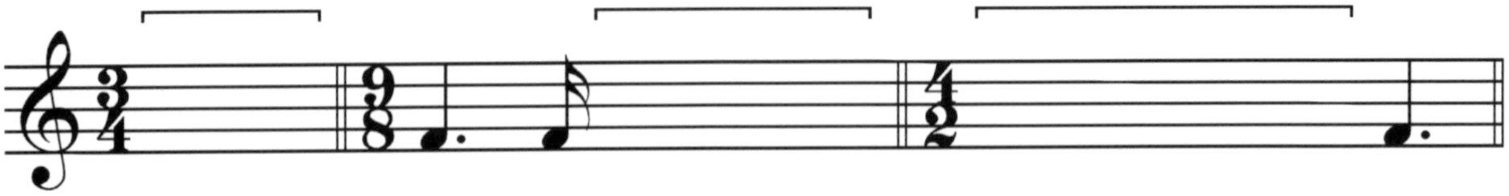

Basic Beat: _____

Pulse:

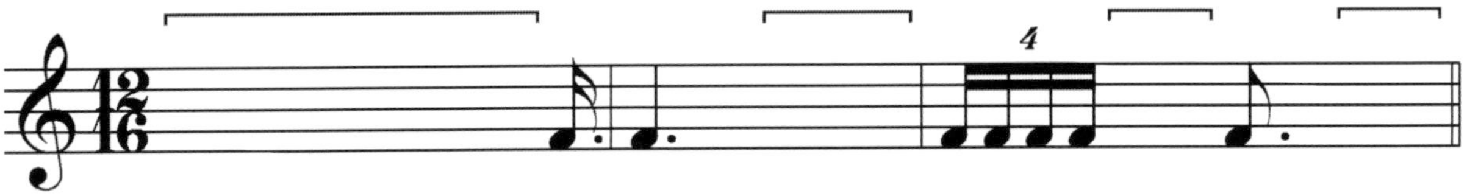

Basic Beat: _____

Pulse:

**6.** Write the following scales, ascending and descending, in the clefs indicated. Use whole notes.

a) B Major, from Supertonic to Supertonic, using the correct Key Signature
b) f minor melodic, from Leading note to Leading note, using the correct Key Signature
c) enharmonic Tonic minor, harmonic form, of g sharp minor using accidentals
d) Mixolydian mode starting on F using any standard notation

10

a)

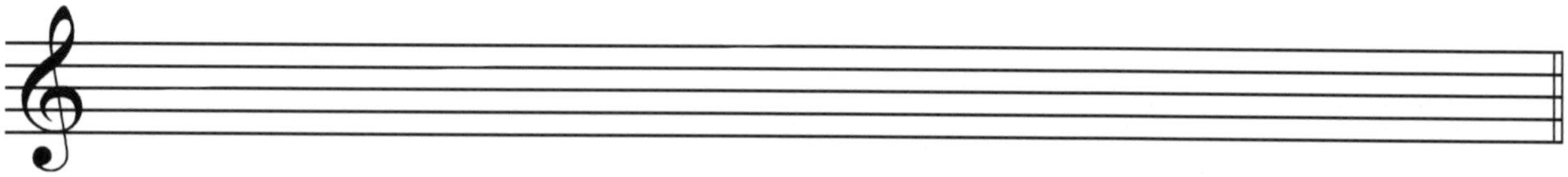

b)

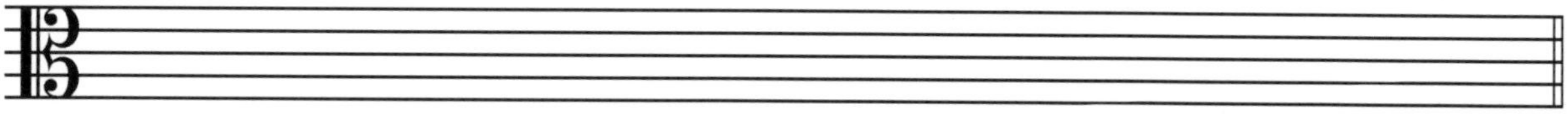

c)

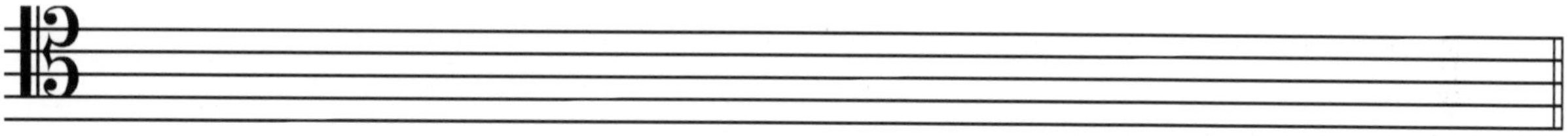

d)

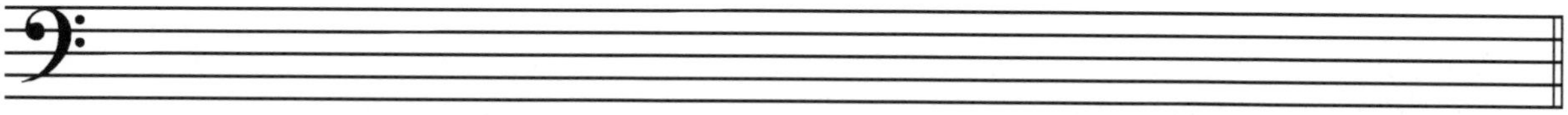

e) Identify the following scales as Major pentatonic, minor pentatonic, octatonic, blues, whole tone or chromatic.

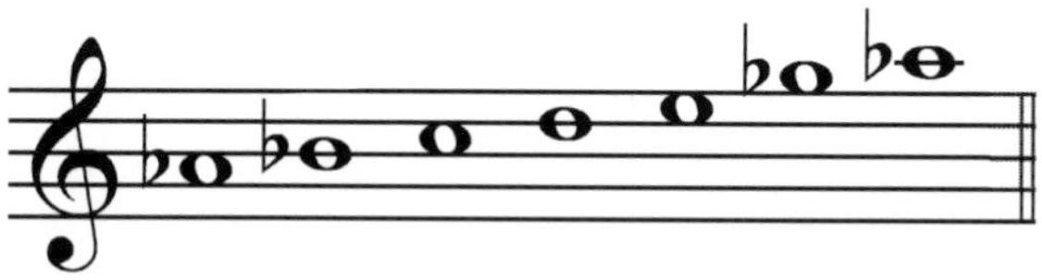

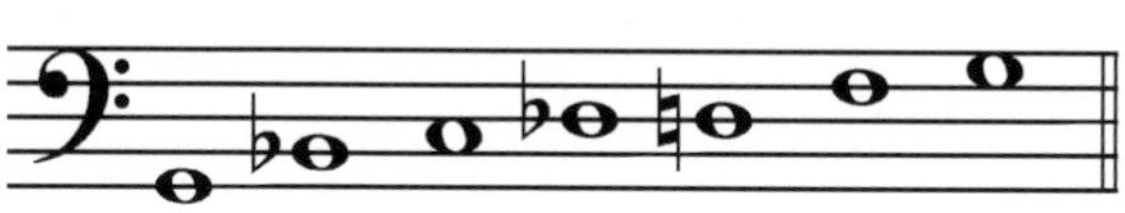

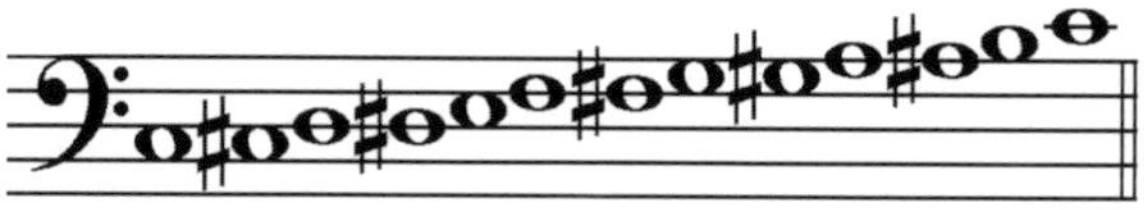

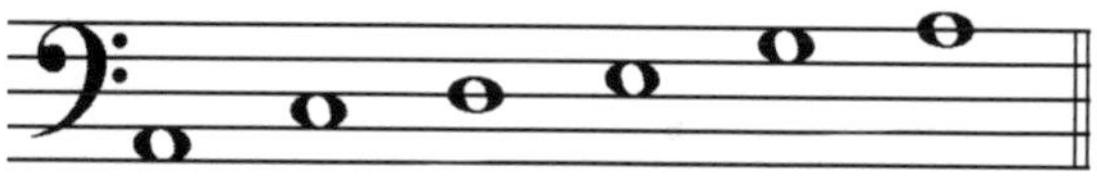

7. a) Name the key for the following melodic fragments. Use chord symbols to identify the cadence. Write a cadence (keyboard style) **BELOW** the bracketed notes. Name the type of cadence (Perfect, Plagal or Imperfect).

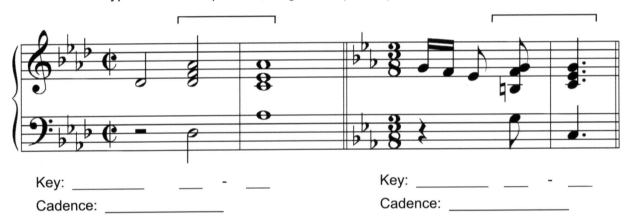

Key: _____ ___ - ___        Key: _____ ___ - ___

Cadence: _____        Cadence: _____

b) Name the key for each of the following cadences. Use chord symbols to identify the cadence. Name the type of cadence (Perfect, Plagal or Imperfect).

Key: _____ ___ - ___        Key: _____ ___ - ___

Cadence: _____        Cadence: _____

8. Match each musical term with its English definition. (Not all definitions will be used.)

| Term | | Definition |
|------|---|------------|
| a tempo | _____ | a) be silent |
| bewegt | _____ | b) slow, slowly |
| tacet | _____ | c) dying, fading away |
| mässig | _____ | d) always, continuously |
| langsam | _____ | e) fairly fast (a little slower than *allegro*) |
| morendo | _____ | f) return to the original tempo |
| sempre | _____ | g) moving |
| coll'ottava | _____ | h) becoming faster |
| allegretto | _____ | i) moderate, moderately |
| fine | _____ | j) with an added octave |
| | | k) the end |

**9.** Rewrite the following excerpt in Open Score for String Quartet. Name the four instruments.

10. Analyze the following piece by answering the questions below.

# Blue Melody

R. St. Germain
G. St. Germain

*Dolce, con espressione*

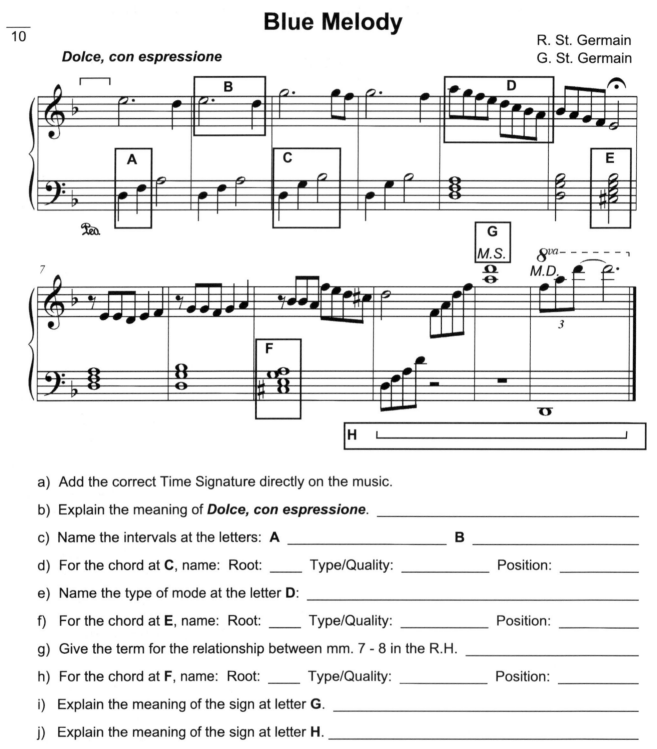

a) Add the correct Time Signature directly on the music.

b) Explain the meaning of **Dolce, con espressione**. _____

c) Name the intervals at the letters: **A** _____ **B** _____

d) For the chord at **C**, name: Root: _____ Type/Quality: _____ Position: _____

e) Name the type of mode at the letter **D**: _____

f) For the chord at **E**, name: Root: _____ Type/Quality: _____ Position: _____

g) Give the term for the relationship between mm. 7 - 8 in the R.H. _____

h) For the chord at **F**, name: Root: _____ Type/Quality: _____ Position: _____

i) Explain the meaning of the sign at letter **G**. _____

j) Explain the meaning of the sign at letter **H**. _____

UltimateMusicTheory.com

The Ultimate Music Theory™ Program and Supplemental Workbooks help students prepare for nationally recognized theory examinations including the Royal Conservatory of Music.

## UMT Workbooks plus UMT Supplemental Workbooks = RCM Theory Levels

Prep 1 Music Theory Workbook plus:

♪ PREP LEVEL Supplemental = Preparatory Theory (No Exam)

♪ LEVEL 1 Supplemental = Level 1 Theory (No Exam)

Prep 2 Music Theory Workbook plus:

♪ LEVEL 2 Supplemental = Level 2 Theory (No Exam)

♪ LEVEL 3 Supplemental = Level 3 Theory (No Exam)

Basic Music Theory Workbook plus:

♪ LEVEL 4 Supplemental = Level 4 Theory (No Exam)

♪ LEVEL 5 Supplemental = Level 5 Theory (Exam - 1 hour)

Intermediate Music Theory Workbook plus:

♪ LEVEL 6 Supplemental = Level 6 Theory (Exam - 2 hours)

♪ LEVEL 7 Supplemental = Level 7 Theory (Exam - 2 hours)

Advanced Music Theory Workbook plus:

♪ LEVEL 8 Supplemental = Level 8 Theory (Exam - 2 hours)

Complete Music Theory Workbook plus:

♪ COMPLETE Supplemental = Level 8 Theory (Exam - 2 hours)

# UltimateMusicTheory.com

# ULTIMATE MUSIC THEORY GUIDE - COMPLETE

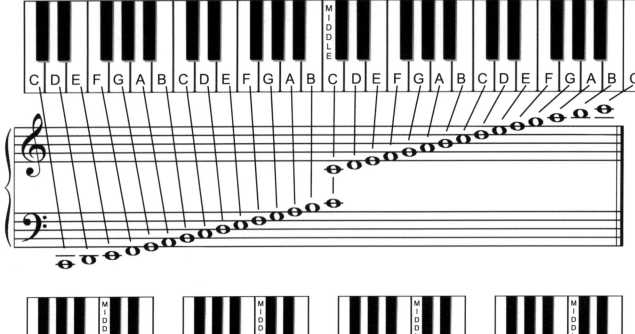

Treble Clef          Alto Clef          Tenor Clef          Bass Clef

**Chromatic** semitone (half step) uses the SAME letter name.  (A to A♯)
**Diatonic** semitone (half step) uses a DIFFERENT letter name.  (A to B♭)
**Enharmonic Equivalent** - SAME pitch with a DIFFERENT letter name.  (A♯, B♭)
**Whole tone** (whole step, tone) is equal to two semitones.
Chromatic whole tone (A to A✕)  Diatonic whole tone (A to B)

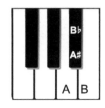

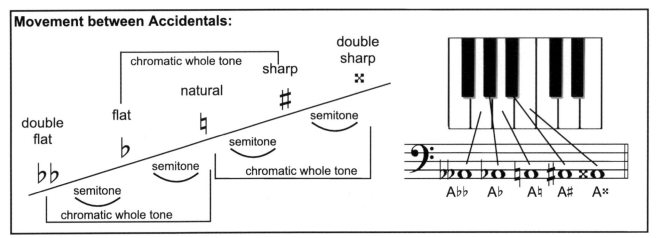

**Movement between Accidentals:**

# ULTIMATE MUSIC THEORY CHART - COMPLETE
## Circle of Fifths

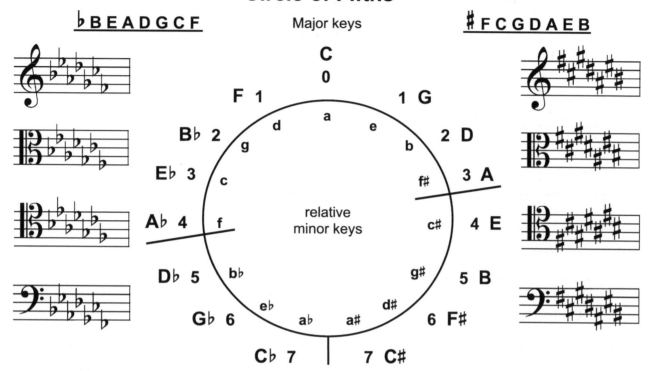

♭ B E A D G C F      Major keys      ♯ F C G D A E B

C 0

F 1      1 G

B♭ 2      2 D

E♭ 3      3 A

A♭ 4      4 E

D♭ 5      5 B

G♭ 6      6 F♯

C♭ 7      7 C♯

relative minor keys

d a e b g f# c c# bb g# eb d# ab a#

A **Major key** and its **relative minor key** have the SAME Key Signature. The distance between a Major key and its relative minor key is three semitones and three letter names (a minor 3rd).

 **Natural** minor scale - Nothing added.

 **Harmonic** minor scale - Raise the 7th note ascending and descending. (Find the 7 in the H)

**Melodic** minor scale - Raise the 6th and 7th notes ascending and lower the 6th and 7th notes descending. (Find the 6 and 7 in the M)

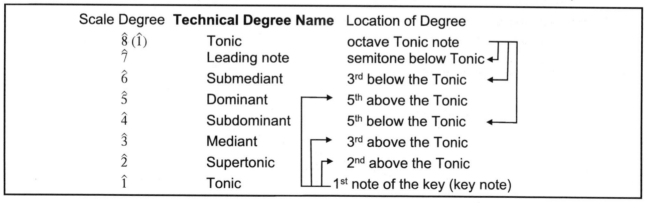

| Scale Degree | Technical Degree Name | Location of Degree |
|---|---|---|
| $\hat{8}$ ($\hat{1}$) | Tonic | octave Tonic note |
| $\hat{7}$ | Leading note | semitone below Tonic |
| $\hat{6}$ | Submediant | 3rd below the Tonic |
| $\hat{5}$ | Dominant | 5th above the Tonic |
| $\hat{4}$ | Subdominant | 5th below the Tonic |
| $\hat{3}$ | Mediant | 3rd above the Tonic |
| $\hat{2}$ | Supertonic | 2nd above the Tonic |
| $\hat{1}$ | Tonic | 1st note of the key (key note) |

Key: C Major

$\hat{1}$ Tonic   $\hat{2}$ Supertonic   $\hat{3}$ Mediant   $\hat{4}$ Subdominant   $\hat{5}$ Dominant   $\hat{6}$ Submediant   $\hat{7}$ Leading note   $\hat{8}$ ($\hat{1}$) Tonic

UltimateMusicTheory.com

# ULTIMATE MUSIC THEORY

*Enriching Lives Through Music Education*

## Workbooks, Exams, Answers, Online Courses & More!

**Beginner ABC Series** - Easy Music Theory Workbooks (ages 6 - 10)

♪ Innovative Teaching Techniques for *"young musicians"* to develop Sight Reading and Ear Training Skills with amazing accuracy!

Bonus - Music Theory Guide & Chart and Fun Activities!

**Ultimate Music Theory Workbooks** - A Proven Approach to the study of music theory. UMT Rudiments Workbooks include:

♪ 12 Lessons & accumulative comprehensive Review Tests! Music Theory Guide & Chart PLUS downloadable Flashcards!

Bonus - The ONLY Series with identical matching Answer Books!

**Ultimate Music Theory Exam Series** - *The Way to Score Success!* Set #1 and Set #2 with Four Exams in each. Workbooks include:

♪ UMT Tips on how to score 100% on Music Theory Exams!

Bonus - The ONLY Series with identical matching Answer Books!

**UMT Supplemental Series** - A Step-by-Step System with engaging lessons in Form & Analysis, Melody Writing, Music History & more, designed to be completed with the UMT Rudiments Workbooks.

♪ Free Resources - Videos & Listening Guide for Music History organized for each Supplemental Level. Easy online access!

Bonus - The ONLY Series with identical matching Answer Books!

**UMT Courses** - Exclusive Online Training Courses include:

♪ The Ultimate Music Theory Certification Course for Teachers, The Complete Music Theory Course for advanced learners and more!

Bonus - Learn at your own tempo. All downloadable materials included!

## UltimateMusicTheory.com

Printed in Great Britain
by Amazon